Entrepreneurship

Entrepreneurship

Alan S. Gutterman

BEP BUSINESS EXPERT PRESS

Entrepreneurship

First published in 2018 by
Business Expert Press, LLC
222 East 46th Street, New York, NY 10017
www.businessexpertpress.com

ISBN-13: 978-1-94897-653-4 (paperback)
ISBN-13: 978-1-94897-654-1 (e-book)

Business Expert Press Entrepreneurship and Small Business Management Collection

Collection ISSN: 1946-5653 (print)
Collection ISSN: 1946-5661 (electronic)

Cover and interior design by Exeter Premedia Services Private Ltd., Chennai, India

First edition: 2018

10 9 8 7 6 5 4 3 2 1

Printed in the United States of America.

Abstract

Entrepreneurship has become a popular career option in developed and developing countries, a phenomenon that has contributed to the intense interest in the subject shown by researchers and policymakers around the world. Several factors have come into play, including advances in technology that allowed smaller firms to take advantage of economies of scale that previously were available only to larger firms; the ability of smaller firms, because of their size, to be more flexible and responsive to market changes; implementation of government policies intended to encourage entrepreneurial activities and behavior; support from governments and other economic units that established procurement programs to assist small businesses; high unemployment rates in recent decades due to corporate restructuring and downsizing, which have caused some workers to choose an entrepreneurial path rather than retrain for placement in an unsteady job market as a means for dealing with their "midlife crisis"; and changes in typical career patterns away from expectations of long-term employment with large firms in a single occupation toward a "flexible" labor force, a phenomenon that has led to increased interest in entrepreneurship among those with post-secondary education and an established career record built over several decades in the workplace.

This book provides an introduction to a number of important topics relevant to the study and understanding of entrepreneurship and the process of creating, or giving birth to, a new business. The chapters cover definitions and types of entrepreneurship; the relationships among entrepreneurship, innovation and development; research on entrepreneurship, comparative research into entrepreneurship in multiple countries and research into cross-border entrepreneurship (i.e., international activity of small- and medium-sized enterprises and new ventures); factors influencing entrepreneurial activities; motivational traits of prospective entrepreneurs; the influence of societal culture on entrepreneurial activities and attitudes regarding entrepreneurship as a career path; the influence that the institutional environment has on entrepreneurship; and the role of entrepreneurs in launching new businesses. This book is an excellent introductory source of information on entrepreneurship research for use by academics and other professionals in their courses and for entrepreneurs looking to fit their dreams and aspirations in the broader context of entrepreneurship.

Keywords

definitions of entrepreneurship, entrepreneurship, roles of entrepreneurs, traits of entrepreneurship, types of entrepreneurship

Contents

CHAPTER 1

Definitions and Types of Entrepreneurship

Definitions of Entrepreneurship

Few topics in the business area have attracted more attention among academics and journalists than "entrepreneurship." From an economic perspective, *entrepreneurship* is generally conceptualized as the creation of a new business and the bearing of the risk associated with that business in exchange for profits to be derived from the exploitation of opportunities in the marketplace (e.g., demands of consumers that are not currently being satisfied). Defined in this manner, entrepreneurship can take a variety of forms. One of the most famous types of entrepreneurship, one that has also become closely aligned with conceptualizations of various forms of entrepreneurship, is Schumpeter's "creative destruction." In Schumpeter's view, the entrepreneur is driven by innovation, which can take the form of a totally new product or process or an innovative change to existing products or processes, which ultimately "destroy," or render obsolete, products and processes that have been used in the past. While entrepreneurship is often discussed in the context of policies for encouraging and supporting small businesses, Graham observed that entrepreneurship differs from small business in four critical ways: amount of wealth creation, speed of wealth accumulation, risk, and innovation.[1]

Entrepreneurship is widely celebrated as an engine for progress that brings growth to the economy, makes the marketplace more competitive, makes individual firms more productive through technological change and creates jobs, and added value and welfare for members of

---

[1] Graham, S. September 16, 2010. "What is Sustainable Entrepreneurship?" http://ezinearticles.com/?What-is-Sustainable-Entrepreneurship?&id=5045492

society. However, while entrepreneurship is generally lauded for the positive impacts and benefits it has provided to society, it is also true that entrepreneurial activities can have negative consequences such as environmental degradation or unequal distribution of wealth.[2] Recognizing this situation, researchers have made a call for entrepreneurial skills and processes to be applied to mitigate and resolve some of the problems that entrepreneurs may have created, an idea which provides the foundation for ecopreneurship, social entrepreneurship, and sustainable entrepreneurship.[3] For example, Hall et al. argued that "entrepreneurship may be a panacea for many social and environmental concerns" and Pacheco et al. asserted that entrepreneurs can be an important force for social and ecological sustainability.[4]

---

[2] See, for example, Cohen, B., and M. Winn. 2007. "Market Imperfections, Opportunity and Sustainable Entrepreneurship." *Journal of Business Venturing* 22, no. 1, p. 29; and Dean, T., and J. McMullen. 2007. "Toward a Theory of Sustainable Entrepreneurship: Reducing Environmental Degradation through Entrepreneurial Action." *Journal of Business Venturing* 22, no. 1, p. 50.

[3] Hall, J., G. Daneke. and M. Lenox. 2010. "Sustainable Development and Entrepreneurship: Past Contributions and Future Directions." *Journal of Business Venturing* 25, no. 5, p. 439; Hockerts, K., and R. Wüstenhagen. 2010. "Greening Goliaths Versus Emerging Davids: Theorizing about The Role of Incumbents and New Entrants in Sustainable Entrepreneurship." *Journal of Business Venturing* 25, no. 5, p. 481; O'Neil, I., and D. Ucbasaran. February 1–4, 2011. "Sustainable Entrepreneurship and Career Transitions: The Role of Individual Identity." *Conference Proceedings in 8th International AGSE Entrepreneurship Research Exchange Conference*, Swinburne University of Technology, Melbourne, Australia; Parrish, B. 2010. "Sustainability-Driven Entrepreneurship: Principles of Organization Design." *Journal of Business Venturing* 25, no. 5, p. 510; and Tilley, F., and W. Young. 2009. "Sustainability Entrepreneurs: Could They Be the True Wealth Generators of the Future?" *Green Management International* 55, p. 79.

[4] Majid, I., and W.L. Koe. June 2012. "Sustainable Entrepreneurship (SE): A Revised Model Based on Triple Bottom Line (TBL)." *International Journal of Academic Research in Business and Social Sciences* 2, no. 6, pp. 293, 96 (citing Hall, J., G. Daneke, and M. Lenox. 2010. "Sustainable Development and Entrepreneurship: Past Contributions and Future Directions." *Journal of Business Venturing* 25, no. 5, pp. 439, 440); and Pacheco, D., T. Dean, and D. Payne. 2010. "Escaping the Green Prison: Entrepreneurship and the Creation of Opportunities for Sustainable Development." *Journal of Business Venturing* 25, no. 5, p. 464.

Research regarding "entrepreneurship" has been made challenging by the absence of a consistent definition of the term across the universe of studies on the topic.[5] According to Stokes et al., the concept of entrepreneurship has existed for centuries and has been important to the development of modern economic and social life.[6] The term itself has been linked to the French word "entreprendre," which means "to undertake" or "to do something," and early definitions and descriptions of the concept can be found in works of economists going back as far as the eighteenth century (e.g., Cantillon, Adam Smith, Say, John Stuart Mill, and Hermann).[7] For example, one of the first uses of the term "entrepreneur" has been attributed to Cantillon, who wrote in the eighteenth century about individuals who bought materials and means of production at prices that enabled them to combine them into a new product.[8]

Many researchers have focused on the economic function served by the entrepreneur. For example, one of the earliest definitions of entrepreneurship focused on merchants who were willing to take the risks of purchasing items at certain prices while there was uncertainty about the prices at which those items could eventually be resold. Later definitions of entrepreneurship began to focus on the risks and challenges associated with combining various factors of production to generate outputs that would be made available for sale in constantly changing markets. Schumpeter was one of the first to include innovation in the definition of entrepreneurship and believed strongly that the essential role of the entrepreneur was creating and responding to economic discontinuities. Others involved in the study of entrepreneurship focus on the personality traits

---

[5] Shane, S., E. Locke, and C. Collins. 2003. "Entrepreneurial Motivation." *Human Resource Management Review* 13, no. 2, pp. 257–79, 274.

[6] Stokes, D., N. Wilson, and M. Mador. 2010. *Entrepreneurship*. Hampshire, UK: South-Western Cengage Learning.

[7] Veciana, J. 2007. "Entrepreneurship as a Scientific Research Program." In *Entrepreneurship: Concepts, Theory and Perspective*, 23, eds. A. Cuervo, D. Ribeiro and S. Roig. Berlin. Heidelberg: Springer-Verlag.

[8] Tilley, F., and W. Young. 2009. "Sustainability Entrepreneurs—Could they be the True Wealth Generators of the Future?" *Greener Management International* 55, p. 79 (citing Hisrich, P., and M. Peters. 1998. *Entrepreneurship*, International Edition. Boston, MA: Irwin McGraw-Hill).

and life experiences of the entrepreneur in an attempt to generate lists of common entrepreneurial characteristics—propensity for "risk taking," need for achievement, and childhood deprivation. While these studies are interesting they have generally been far from conclusive and often have generated conflicting results.

Gartner surveyed the landscape of the attempts to define entrepreneurship and concluded that finding a common definition of the entrepreneur remains "elusive."[9] Gartner quoted an observation made by Cole in 1969:

My own personal experience was that for 10 years we ran a research center in entrepreneurial history, for 10 years we tried to define the entrepreneur. We never succeeded. Each of us had some notion of it—what he thought was, for his purposes, a useful definition. And I don't think you're going to get farther than that.[10]

Gartner also pointed out that Borkchuas and Horwitz, who reviewed the literature on the psychology of the entrepreneur in the mid-1980s, struck a similar note when they reported:

The literature appears to support the argument that there is no generic definition of the entrepreneur, or if there is we do not have the psychological instruments to discover it at this time. Most of the attempts to distinguish between entrepreneurs and small

[9] Gartner, W. Spring 1988. "'Who Is an Entrepreneur?' Is the Wrong Question." *American Journal of Small Business* 12, no. 4, pp. 11–32, 11 (citing, among others, Carsrud, A., K. Olm, and G. Eddy. 1985. "Entrepreneurship: Research in Quest of a Paradigm." In *The Art and Science of Entrepreneurship*, eds. D. Sexton and R. Smilor. Cambridge. MA: Ballinger; and Sexton, D., and R. Smilor. 1985. "Introduction." In *The Art and Science of Entrepreneurship*, eds. D. Sexton and R. Smilor. Cambridge, MA: Ballinger).

[10] Id. quoting Cole, A. 1969. "Definition of Entrepreneurship." In *Karl A. Bostrom Seminar in the Study of Enterprise*, ed. J. Komives, 10–22, 17. Milwaukee, WI: Center for Venture Management.

business owners or managers have discovered no significant differentiating features.[11]

Gartner also counseled against the so-called *trait approach* that focuses on identifying "entrepreneurs"[12] and argued that the study of new venture creation must take into account the interaction among several variables or dimensions including not only the personal characteristics of the individual entrepreneur but also competitive entry strategies, "push" and "pull" factors and the actions taken by the entrepreneur during the new venture creation process.[13] Other researchers, including Schumpeter, have added the availability of prospective entrepreneurs with the requisite entrepreneurial orientation (e.g., self-reliance, self-confidence, and perseverance) as a prerequisite to effective new venture creation.[14]

Acknowledging the lack of a universally accepted definition of entrepreneurship, Hessels did comment that "[t]here seems to be agreement . . . that entrepreneurship involves the creation of something new."[15] For Gartner, that "something new" was a "new organization" and he suggested that the most fruitful path for studying entrepreneurship was to view it as a process that includes a series of behaviors and activities intended to

---

[11] Id. quoting Brockhaus, R., and P. Horwitz. 1985. "The Psychology of the Entrepreneur." In *The Art and Science of Entrepreneurship*, ed. D. Sexton and R. Smilor, 42–43. Cambridge, MA: Ballinger.

[12] Id. at p. 26.

[13] Gartner, W. 1985. "A Conceptual Framework for Describing the Phenomenon of New Venture Creation." *Academy of Management Review* 10, no. 4, pp. 696–706.

[14] Mueller, S., and A. Thomas. 2000. "Culture and Entrepreneurial Potential: A Nine Country Study of Locus of Control and Innovativeness." *Journal of Business Venturing* 16, pp. 51–75, 53–54, 62. citing Schumpeter, J. 1934. *The Theory of Economic Development*, 132. Cambridge, MA: Harvard University Press.

[15] Hessels, J. 2008. *International Entrepreneurship: An Introduction, Framework and Research Agenda*, 6. Zoetermeer, The Netherlands: Scientific Analysis of Entrepreneurship and SMEs. (citing Reynolds, P., N. Bosma, E. Autio, S. Hunt, N. De Bono, I. Servais, P. Lopez-Garcia, and N. Chin. 2005. "Global Entrepreneurship Monitor: Data Collection Design and Implementation 1998–2003." *Small Business Economics* 24, no. 3, pp. 205–31).

create organizations.[16] Davidsson et al. referred to entrepreneurship as "the creation of new economic activity" that occurs both through the creation of new ventures and new economic activity of established firms.[17] Use of the concept of "creation of new economic activity" includes not only the creation of new organizations championed by Gartner but also recognition and exploitation of opportunities, conversion of new ideas into innovations, and even imitative behavior that is new to a firm.[18] It is not necessary that the same person or entity that discovered an opportunity actually exploit that opportunity and entrepreneurship should be defined broadly enough to include the sale of opportunities to others. For that matter, discovery of a new technology should not be a prerequisite to entrepreneurship with respect to that opportunity and the concept of entrepreneurship should include actions taken to interpret the capabilities of the technology so as to identify applications of the technology that eventually become the foundation of opportunities.

All of the foregoing was taken into account by Shane and Venkataraman when they defined entrepreneurship as "the process by which 'opportunities to create future goods and services are discovered, evaluated and exploited.'"[19] A few years later, Shane, working with

---

[16] Gartner, W. Spring 1988. "'Who Is an Entrepreneur?' Is the Wrong Question." *American Journal of Small Business*, pp. 11–32, 26. Gartner argued that all of the different studies of entrepreneurship that can be identified in the field actually begin with the creation of new organizations including research on "psychological characteristics of entrepreneurs, sociological explanations of entrepreneurial cultures, economic and demographic explanations of entrepreneurial locations, and so on." Id.

[17] Davidsson, P., F. Delmar, and J. Wiklund. 2006. "Entrepreneurship as Growth; Growth as Entrepreneurship." In *Entrepreneurship and the Growth of Firms*, eds. P. Davidsson, F. Delmar and J. Wiklund, 21–38, 27. Cheltenham, UK: Edward Elgar Publisher.

[18] Hessels, J. 2008. *International Entrepreneurship: An Introduction, Framework and Research Agenda*, 6. Zoetermeer, The Netherlands: Scientific Analysis of Entrepreneurship and SMEs.

[19] Shane, S., and S. Venkataraman. 2000. "The Promise of Entrepreneurship as a Field of Research." *Academy of Management Review* 25, no. 1, pp. 217–26, 218 (as cited in Shane, S., E. Locke, and C. Collins. 2003. "Entrepreneurial Motivation." *Human Resource Management Review* 13, pp. 257–79, 259).

Eckhardt, elaborated on the previous definition by describing entrepreneurship as a business process that encompassed several stages and activities including the identification and appraisal of opportunities, the choice to whether to exploit or sell the opportunities, efforts to acquire resources needed to exploit the opportunities, the development of an appropriate strategy for exploiting the opportunity, and the design of the new project or business model relating to the exploitation of the opportunity.[20] Shane et al. highlighted several key points that followed from using these definitions.[21] For example, the definition does not require that the entrepreneur be a firm founder or business owner, a common assumption in the research relating to entrepreneurship, and allows for the fact that new and innovative ideas for goods and services can come from anywhere in the organizational hierarchy and not just from the top, such as sales managers who develop new ways to market products and services to target markets.[22] In addition, it calls for interpreting entrepreneurship as a "process" rather than a one-time event, action, or decision. For example, the decision to form and organize a new firm, while important, is just one of a series of actions that must be taken in order to effectively discover, evaluate, and exploit an opportunity. Finally, the definition recognizes that entrepreneurship is based on "creativity," which can include not only uncovering new ideas and knowledge but also arranging resources in ways that have not been done before. There is no minimum threshold of "creativity" that must be met in order for an activity to qualify as "entrepreneurship" and, as Shane et al. pointed out, "the degree of creativity involved in entrepreneurship varies across the types of resource recombination that occurs."[23]

---

[20] Eckhardt, J., and S. Shane. 2003. "Opportunities and Entrepreneurship." *Journal of Management* 29, p. 333.

[21] Shane, S., E. Locke, and C. Collins. 2003. "Entrepreneurial Motivation." *Human Resource Management Review* 13, pp. 257–79, 259.

[22] See, for example, McClelland, D. 1961. *The Achieving Society*. Princeton, NJ: Van Nostrand and Kirzner, I. 1973. *Competition and Entrepreneurship*. Chicago, IL: University of Chicago Press.

[23] Shane, S., E. Locke, and C. Collins. 2003. "Entrepreneurial Motivation." *Human Resource Management Review* 13, pp. 257–79, 259.

Later, Oviatt and McDougall acknowledged and added the definition offered by Shane and Venkataraman in the context of their effort to describe "international entrepreneurship" by referring to entrepreneurship as "the discovery, enactment, evaluation, and exploitation of opportunities . . . to create future goods and services."[24] According to Harper, the opportunities associated with entrepreneurship may call for development of new markets, new products, new methods of production and management, the discovery of new inputs, the establishment of new businesses and the creation and design of new organizational forms.[25]

Majid and Koe observed that Stokes et al. separated the various definitions of entrepreneurship into three categories: purposes, behaviors, and outcomes.[26] The first category included definitions that focused on "what entrepreneurs do"; in other words the activities and processes of entrepreneurship such as "creating something new,"[27] "pursuing opportunities,"[28] and "discovering, creating and exploiting opportunity for future goods and services."[29] The second category focused on "who are entrepreneurs" and included definitions that provided insights into the specific behaviors of individuals who engage in entrepreneurial activities such as

---

[24] Oviatt, B., and P. McDougall. 2005. "Defining International Entrepreneurship and Modeling the Speed of Internationalization." *Entrepreneurship Theory and Practice* 29, no. 5, pp. 537–53, 540.

[25] Harper, D. 2003. *Foundations of Entrepreneurship and Economic Development.* New York, NY: Routledge.

[26] Majid, I., and W.L. Koe. June 2012. "Sustainable Entrepreneurship (SE): A Revised Model Based on Triple Bottom Line (TBL)." *International Journal of Academic Research in Business and Social Sciences* 2, no. 6, pp. 293, 295 (citing Stokes, D., N. Wilson, and M. Mador. 2010. *Entrepreneurship.* Hampshire, UK: South-Western Cengage Learning).

[27] Hisrich, R., and M. Peters. 2002. *Entrepreneurship*, 5th ed. London: McGraw Hill.

[28] Stevenson, H., and J. Jarillo. 1990. "A Paradigm of Entrepreneurship: Entrepreneurial Management." *Strategic Management Journal: Special Edition Corporate Entrepreneurship* 11, no. 17.

[29] Venkataraman, S. 1996. "The Distinctive Domain of Entrepreneurship Research." In *Advances in Entrepreneurship, Firm Emergence and Growth*, eds. J. Katz and R. Brockhaus, 119. Greenwich, CT: JAI Press.

"competitive and drive market process"[30] and "creative and innovative."[31] The third category focused on "what entrepreneurs produced," such as creating new organizations.[32]

The Global Entrepreneurship Monitor (GEM), a partnership between London Business School and Babson College that has been administering a comprehensive research program since 1999 to produce annual assessments of national levels of entrepreneurial activity, broadly defines entrepreneurship to include "... any attempt at new business or new venture creation, such as self-employment, a new business organization, or the expansion of an existing business, by an individual, teams of individuals, or established businesses."[33] J. G. Burch, who has written extensively on the subject, has referred to entrepreneurship as the "initiation of change" and the "process of giving birth to a new business."[34] Burch has also developed a list of the following categories of innovations that tend to be the specific by-products of entrepreneurial activities: introduction of a new product or service that is an improvement in the quality of an existing product or service; introduction of a new process or method that increases productivity; the opening of a new market, particularly an export market in a new territory; the conquest of a new source of supply of raw materials, half-manufactured products, or alternative materials; and the creation of a new organization.

Finally, Acs and Szerb, who created the Global Entrepreneurship Development Index, argued that

---

[30] Kizner, I. 1973. *Competition and Entrepreneurship*. Chicago, IL: University of Chicago Press.

[31] Schumpeter, J. 1934. *The Theory of Economic Development*. Cambridge, MA: Harvard University Press.

[32] Gartner, W. 1988. "Who Is an Entrepreneur? Is the Wrong Question." *American Journal of Small Business* 12, no. 4, p. 11.

[33] For further discussion of the GEM, see "Research in Entrepreneurship" in "Entrepreneurship: A Library of Resources for Sustainable Entrepreneurs" prepared and distributed by the Sustainable Entrepreneurship Project (www.seproject.org).

[34] Burch, J.G. 1986. *Entrepreneurship*. New York, NY: John Wiley & Sons.

> [w]hile a generally accepted definition of entrepreneurship is lacking there is agreement that the concept comprises numerous dimensions . . . [t]he most common features of the various definitions involve unique traits, risk taking, opportunity recognition, motivation and exploitation, and innovation. (citations omitted)[35]

They believed that it was important to distinguish entrepreneurship from small businesses, self-employment, craftsmanship, and "usual businesses" and defined entrepreneurship as "a dynamic interaction or entrepreneurial attitudes, entrepreneurial activity, and entrepreneurial aspiration that vary across stages of economic development."[36] They also emphasized that entrepreneurship included not only individual variables but institutional and environmental variables as well and that consideration must be given to the quality of entrepreneurial activity as reflected in the aspirations and skills of entrepreneurs with respect to commercializing innovative products and technologies, building a global business and creating organizations that significantly contribute to higher employment.

Theoretical Underpinnings of Entrepreneurship

Lawai et al. summarized some of the various theories that have been advanced by researchers to explain the field of entrepreneurship, noting that the theories had drawn on principles for a wide array of academic fields including economics, psychology, sociology, anthropology, and management[37]:

---

[35] Acs, Z., and L. Szerb. June 2010. "The Global Entrepreneurship and Development Index (GEDI)" Paper Presented at Summer Conference 2010 on "Opening Up Innovation: Strategy, Organization and Technology." Imperial College London Business School. For further discussion of the GEDI, see "Research in Entrepreneurship" in "Entrepreneurship: A Library of Resources for Sustainable Entrepreneurs" prepared and distributed by the Sustainable Entrepreneurship Project (www.seproject.org).

[36] Id.

[37] Lawai, F., R. Worlu, and O. Ayoade. May 2016. "Critical Success Factors for Sustainable Entrepreneurship in SMEs: Nigerian Perspective." *Mediterranean*

- *Economic entrepreneurship theories:* Economic theories of entrepreneurship highlight the economic factors that enhance entrepreneurial behavior. For example, classical theory is based on the benefits of free trade, specialization, and competition, and sees the entrepreneur as the essential director of the production and distribution of goods in a competitive marketplace. Classical theory has been criticized as failing to take into account the role that entrepreneurs have played in disrupting existing markets and economists such as Schumpeter have argued that the role of the entrepreneur was to drive market-based systems by creating something new, which resulted in processes that transformed the market economy.
- *Psychological entrepreneurship theories:* Psychological theories emphasize personal characteristics of individuals who seek to engage in entrepreneurial activities including personality traits, need for achievement and locus of control, ability to take risk, innovativeness, and tolerance for ambiguity. For example, Coon identified the following characteristics or behaviors associated with entrepreneurs: tendency toward being more opportunity driven, demonstration of high level of creativity and innovation, display of high level of management skills and business know-how, optimism, emotional resilience and mental energy, hard-working spirit, intense commitment and perseverance, competitive desire to excel and win, tendency to be dissatisfied with the status quo and desire for improvement, transformational in nature, lifelong learners, and able to use failure as a tool and springboard.[38]
- *Sociological entrepreneurship theories:* Sociological entrepreneurship theories focus on the social context

---

Journal of Social Sciences 7, no. 3, pp. 340–42, 338. See also Simpeh, K.N. 2011. "Entrepreneurship Theories and Empirical Research: A Summary Review of the Literature." *European Journal of Business and Management* 3, no. 6, pp. 1–8.

[38] Id. at p. 341 (citing Coon, D. 2004. *Introduction to Psychology*, 9th ed. Minneapolis, MN: West Publishing Company).

for entrepreneurship. For example, Reynolds claimed to have identified four social contexts that relate to entrepreneurial opportunity such as building social relationships and bonds that fosters trust instead of opportunism; ethnic identification where individual's sociological background serve as decisive factor in propelling entrepreneurial affinity; population ecology (in which case environmental factors) determining the survival of new ventures; and life course stage context, which involves analyzing life situations and characteristics of individuals who have decided to become entrepreneurs.[39]

- *Anthropological entrepreneurship theories:* Related to sociological entrepreneurship theories, anthropological entrepreneurship theories focus on the importance of both social and cultural context as determinants of successful entrepreneurship. Specific issues include cultural attitudes toward entrepreneurship and integration of cultural values and norms into the processes used to launch new ventures.

- *Opportunity-based entrepreneurship theories:* Opportunity-based entrepreneurship theories are based on the premise that entrepreneurs do not necessarily being about change directly but scan the environment for changes and then seize and exploit the opportunities that change create (e.g., opportunities related to change in technology and/or consumer preferences).

- *Resource-based entrepreneurship theories:* Resource-based entrepreneurship theories are focused on the importance of access to resources (e.g., financial, social, and human resources) as a facilitator and predictor of identifying opportunities suitable for entrepreneurial activities.[40]

---

[39] Id. at pp. 341–42 (citing Reynolds, P. 1991. "Sociology and Entrepreneurship: Concepts and Contributions." *Entrepreneurship: Theory & Practice* 16, no. 2, p. 47).

[40] Alvarez, S., and L. Busenitz. 2001. "The Entrepreneurship of Resource based Theory." *Journal of Management* 27, no. 6, pp. 755–75; and Davidson, P., and B. Honing. 2003. "The Role of Social and Human Capital among Nascent Entrepreneurs." *Journal of Business Venturing* 18, no. 3, pp. 301–31, 20, 121.

The Entrepreneur in Economic Theory

Acs and Virgill, while writing about the relationship between entrepreneurship and economic development, commented that "[t]he entrepreneur has been ignored in economic theory."[41] Others have voiced similar critiques: Cole took economists of the 1800s to task for "overlooking the entrepreneur as a source of economic change" and failing to give proper notice and weight to the "disruptive, innovating energy" associated with entrepreneurial activities.[42] Schumpeter referred to entrepreneurs as "sadly neglected"[43]; Soltow claimed that economic historians were more concerned with "businessmen and firms" than entrepreneurs[44]; Kirzner argued that neoclassical microeconomics, with its focus on "perfect" information and competition and general equilibrium, failed to explain how "real markets" worked and the role that entrepreneurs played in identifying and rectifying market imperfections.[45]

Acs and Virgill described the views of several well-known economic historians and theorists regarding entrepreneurs. They explained that Say saw entrepreneurs as "perform[ing] a specific role in the economy by coordinating other factors of production (i.e., labor, capital etc.) with his knowledge" in order to "meet the demands of the final consumers" and that Say recognized that entrepreneurs "assumed risks and employed judgment in [their] entrepreneurial activities."[46] Schumpeter's interest in entrepreneurship is well known and focused on entrepreneurial activity

---

[41] Acs, Z., and N. Virgill. March 2009. "Entrepreneurship in Developing Countries." Jena Economic Research Papers, No. 2009–023, 27.

[42] Cole, A. 1946. "An Approach to the Study of Entrepreneurship: A Tribute to Edwin F. Gay." *The Journal of Economic History* 6, no. S1, pp. 1–15, 3.

[43] Schumpeter, J. 1947. "The Creative Response in Economic History." *The Journal of Economic History* 7, no. 2, pp. 149–59, 149.

[44] Soltow, J. 1968. "The Entrepreneur in Economic History." *The American Economic Review* 58, no. 2, pp. 84–92, 84.

[45] Acs, Z., and N. Virgill. March 27, 2009. "Entrepreneurship in Developing Countries." Jena Economic Research Papers No. 2009–023. (citing and quoting Kirzner, I. 1997. "Entrepreneurial Discovery and the Competitive Market Process: An Austrian Approach." *Journal of Economic Literature* 35, no. 1, pp. 60–85).

[46] Id. at pp. 28–29 citing Koolman, G. 1971. "Say's Conception of the Role of the Entrepreneur." *Economica* 38, pp. 269–86, 151.

that was "innovative" (i.e., discovery and exploitation of new products, processes, and/or markets). For Schumpeter, the entrepreneur thrived on risk-taking while responding to "exogenous shocks of new information" and also was a primary driver of development through his or her attempts to instigate change and "disturb" the status quo.[47] The "Kirznerian entrepreneur" was important because he or she "restored a market to equilibrium" after it had been disrupted by previous errors made by entrepreneurs.[48] As described by Acs and Virgill:

> . . . disequilibrium generated new "profit opportunities" . . . [and] "alert, imaginative entrepreneurs," imbued with superior knowledge, were able to exploit these "profit opportunities" by recognizing or "discovering" these errors and by taking action to correct the market.[49]

The theories of both Schumpeter and Kirzner assumed, to some extent, that new information is not always communicated to everyone in the market and/or used correctly by all recipients and that these "mistakes and misallocations" provide opportunities for entrepreneurs.[50]

---

[47] Id. at p. 29 citing Schumpeter, J. 1947. "The Creative Response in Economic History." *The Journal of Economic History* 7, no. 2, pp. 149–59; Shane, S., and J. Eckhardt. Springer, 2005. "The Individual–Opportunity Nexus." In *Handbook of Entrepreneurship Research: An Interdisciplinary Survey and Introduction*, 161–91, 171, eds. Z. Acs and D. Audretsch, New York, NY: Heidelberg; and Schumpeter, J. 2002. "The Economy as a Whole: Seventh Chapter of the Theory of Economic Development." *Industry and Innovation* 9, nos. 1/2, pp. 93–145, 97.

[48] Id. (citing and quoting Kirzner, I. 1997. "Entrepreneurial Discovery and the Competitive Market Process: An Austrian Approach." *Journal of Economic Literature* 35, no. 1, pp. 60–85, 68).

[49] Id. at p. 29–30 (citing and quoting Kirzner, I. 1997. "Entrepreneurial Discovery and the Competitive Market Process: An Austrian Approach." *Journal of Economic Literature* 35, no. 1, pp. 60–85, 71–72).

[50] See also Kirzner, I. 1999. "Creativity and/or Alertness: A Reconsideration of the Schumpeterian Entrepreneur." *The Review of Austrian Economics* 11, no. 1, pp. 5–17.

Types of Entrepreneurship

Entrepreneurship can take a variety of forms and a number of researchers have suggested that it is important to recognize different "types" of entrepreneurship when analyzing issues such as the characteristics of entrepreneurs, their motives for choosing entrepreneurship, and the contributions of their entrepreneurial activities to economic development.[51] The GEM researchers acknowledged that entrepreneurship is a process that extends over multiple phases, thus allowing opportunities for assessing the state of entrepreneurship in a particular society at different phases. Four of the phases are readily identifiable stages of the new venture formation process and each stage has its own "type" of entrepreneur[52]:

- *Potential entrepreneurs*: These are persons who see opportunities in their areas, believe they have the abilities and resources to start businesses to pursue those opportunities, and who are not deterred by fear of failure in pursuing those opportunities. The level of broader societal support for entrepreneurship is also important at this phase. The GEM survey uses a variety of measures of entrepreneurial perceptions, intentions, and societal attitudes including perceived opportunities, perceived capabilities, fear of failure, entrepreneurial intentions, entrepreneurship as a "good career choice" high status to successful entrepreneurs, and media attention for entrepreneurship.

---

[51] See, for example, Baumol, W. 1990. "Entrepreneurship—Productive, Unproductive and Destructive." *Journal of Political Economy* 98, no. 5, pp. 893–921.

[52] Kelley, D., S. Singer, and M. Herrington. 2012. *Global Entrepreneurship Monitor: 2011 Global Report*. Babson Park, MA: Global Entrepreneurship Research Association. The GEM researchers actually identified six phases; the four mentioned in the text and two more: "established businesses" (i.e., businesses that have been operating for more than three and one-half years, thus moving beyond "new business owner" status) and "discontinued businesses," which were factored into the analysis regardless of how long they were operating because they are a source of experienced entrepreneurs who may start new businesses and/or use their expertise and experience to support other entrepreneurs (e.g., by providing financing and/or business advice).

- *Expected entrepreneurs*: Expected entrepreneurs are those persons who have not yet started a business but who have expressed an expectation that they would start a business within the next three years.
- *Nascent entrepreneurs*: This phase covers the first three months after the entrepreneur establishes a new business to pursue the identified opportunities.
- *New business owners*: These are persons who have successfully emerged from the nascent phase and have been in business more than three months but less than three and one-half years.

Two other popular methods for classifying entrepreneurs are the distinctions that have been made between "push" and "pull" entrepreneurs[53] and the distinctions between "necessity-based" and "opportunity-based" entrepreneurs. Others, when analyzing conditions in transition economies, have distinguished between "proprietorship," which includes situations where individuals start their own businesses to generate income to sustain their families when no other options are available, and "genuine entrepreneurship," which is a term that describes situations where individuals start businesses with the goal of generating sufficient income so that a portion of it can be reinvested in order to underwrite business growth and development.[54]

A number of researchers have focused on the existence and influence of "push/pull situational factors" in motivating individuals to engage in entrepreneurial activities and the factors identified have included the frustration of the entrepreneur with his or her current lifestyle, childhood

---

[53] See, for example, Amit. R., and E. Muller. 1995. "'Push' and 'Pull' Entrepreneurship." *Journal of Small Business and Entrepreneurship* 12, no. 4, pp. 64–80.

[54] Scase, R. 1997. "The Role of Small Businesses in the Economic Transformation of Eastern Europe: Real but Relatively Unimportant." *International Small Business Journal* 16, pp. 113–21; Scase, R. 2003. "Entrepreneurship and Proprietorship in Transition: Policy Implications for the SME Sector." In *Small and Medium Enterprises in Transitional Economies*, eds. R. McIntyre, R. Dallago and B. Houndsmill, 64–77. Basingstoke: Palgrave Macmillan.

influences, family environment, age, education, work history, role models, and support networks.[55] In many instances, entrepreneurs may be literally "pushed" into entrepreneurship, often against their wishes, by unanticipated and unwelcome lifecycle developments such as loss of employment, extreme dissatisfaction with a current job, and other career setbacks. Unfortunately, these entrepreneurs are frequently viewed in a somewhat negative fashion by society—"misfits" or "rejects."[56] On the other hand, entrepreneurs may be "pulled" into creating a new venture by factors viewed more positively in most societies including training and exposure to business that creates interest and confidence in looking for new opportunities to exploit.[57] Some researchers have viewed either a

---

[55] Mueller, S., and A. Thomas. 2000. "Culture and Entrepreneurial Potential: A Nine Country Study of Locus of Control and Innovativeness." *Journal of Business Venturing* 16, pp. 51–75, 54 (citing Hisrich, R. 1990. "Entrepreneurship/Intrapreneurship." *American Psychologist* 45, no. 2, pp. 209–22; Martin, M. 1984. *Managing Technological Innovation and Entrepreneurship*. Reston, VA: Prentice-Hall); Moore, C. 1986. "Understanding Entrepreneurial Behavior: A Definition and Model." *Proceedings of the National Academy of Management*, pp. 66–70; Krueger, N. 1993. "The Impact of Prior Entrepreneurial Exposure on Perceptions of New Venture Feasibility and Desirability." *Entrepreneurship Theory and Practice* 18, no. 1, pp. 5–21; Scheinberg, S., and I. MacMillan. 1988. "An 11 Country Study of the Motivations to Start a Business." In *Frontiers of Entrepreneurship Research*, eds. B. Kirchhoff, W. Long, W. McMullan, K.H. Vesper, and W. Wetzel. Wellesley, MA: Babson College.

[56] Brockhaus, R. 1980. "The Effect of Job Dissatisfaction on the Decision to Start a Business." *Journal of Small Business Management* 18, no. 1, pp. 37–43; Shapero, A. 1975. "The Displaced, Uncomfortable Entrepreneur." *Psychology Today* 9, no. 6, pp. 83–88; Kets de Vries, M. 1977. "The Entrepreneurial Personality: A Person at the Crossroads." *Journal of Management Studies* 14, no. 1, pp. 34–57; Gilad, B., and P. Levine. 1986. "A Behavioral Model of Entrepreneurial Supply." *Journal of Small Business Management* 24, no. 4, pp. 44–53.

[57] Krueger, N. 1993. "The Impact of Prior Entrepreneurial Exposure on Perceptions of New Venture Feasibility and Desirability." *Entrepreneurship Theory and Practice* 18, no. 1, pp. 5–21; Mancuso, J. 1973. *Fun and Guts: The Entrepreneur's Philosophy*. Reading, MA: Addison-Wesley; Gilad, B., and P. Levine. 1986. "A Behavioral Model of Entrepreneurial Supply." *Journal of Small Business Management* 24, no. 4, pp. 44–53; Scheinberg, S., and I. MacMillan. 1988. "An Eleven Country Study of the Motivations to Start a Business." In *Frontiers*

"push" or a "pull" as a prerequisite to new venture formation since it triggers a state of general readiness to take action once a suitable opportunity and the necessary resources can be identified.[58]

The terms "opportunity-based" and "necessity-based" entrepreneurship have been popularized by their use in the GEM.[59] The questions asked of entrepreneurs included seeking information about why they decided to start and grow their businesses. Respondents who indicated that they chose entrepreneurship to "take advantage of a business opportunity" or "seek better opportunities" were practicing opportunity-based entrepreneurship while respondents starting businesses "because [they had] no better choices for work" were identified as necessity-based entrepreneurs.[60] The key characteristic among opportunity-based entrepreneurs is their acknowledgment that they made a voluntary career choice to pursue an entrepreneurial path. The GEM also recognizes another type of entrepreneurship, referred to as "improvement-driven," that includes persons interested in pursuing an opportunity and who do so in order to improve their incomes and/or independence in their work, as opposed to "necessity."

In contrast, necessity-based entrepreneurs choose entrepreneurship only because other options were not available or were considered to be unsatisfactory. The term "reluctant entrepreneurship" is sometimes used to describe these persons and it is common to find that they have been pushed to start their own businesses because they have either lost the jobs they had with their employers or had been placed in the path of what appears to be an inevitable elimination of their positions. In either

---

of Entrepreneurship Research, eds. B. Kirchhoff, W. Long, W. McMullan, K.H. Vesper and W. Wetzel. Wellesley, MA: Babson College.

[58] See also Shapero, A. 1975. "The Displaced, Uncomfortable Entrepreneur." *Psychology Today* 9, no. 6, pp. 83–88.

[59] For a further discussion of the GEM surveys, see "Research on Entrepreneurship" in "Entrepreneurship: A Library of Resources for Sustainable Entrepreneurs," prepared and distributed by the Sustainable Entrepreneurship Project (www.seproject.org).

[60] For further discussion, see Reynolds, P., W. Bygrave, E. Autio, L. Cox, and M. Hay. 2002. "Global Entrepreneurship Monitor: 2002." *Executive Report*, 12. London: Global Entrepreneurship Monitor.

instance, entrepreneurship was, at least initially, a means of survival. It should be noted, however, that there appears to be some debate about whether problems in the overall economy that lead to increased unemployment will lead to higher levels of necessity-based entrepreneurship and one researcher has summarized the findings of various researchers as follows: "It does seem then that there is some disagreement in the literature on whether high unemployment acts to discourage self-employment because of the lack of available opportunities or encourage it because of the lack of viable alternatives."[61]

The GEM research confirms that it is more likely than not that persons start a new business in order to take advantage of a perceived business opportunity, the so-called *opportunity entrepreneurship*; however, the existence of "necessity entrepreneurship" must be acknowledged and considered when researching entrepreneurship. It is not surprising to find that there are differences among countries, particularly groups of countries with similar cultural characteristics, with regard to the prevalence of specific types of entrepreneurs. For example, differences between countries with respect to the incidence of entrepreneurial activity have been attributed to differences in "risk tolerance" since there are significant variations among countries with respect to the level of risk (and possibility of failure) that persons are willing to assume before they start a new business. Even within countries, however, variations in the incidence of entrepreneurial activity can be seen when one looks at different characteristics such as age, education, industry, and location. Several studies have confirmed what would appear to be fairly obvious: necessity-based entrepreneurship in a country tends to decline as the level of economic development in that country increases and the overall business environment in the country stabilizes.[62] In addition, one sees lower levels of necessity-based entrepreneurship in "innovation-driven countries."[63]

---

[61] Blanchflower, D. 2004. *Self-Employment: More May Not Be Better*. Cambridge MA: National Bureau of Economic Research.

[62] See, for example, Bosma, N., and J. Levie. 2010. *Global Entrepreneurship Monitor: 2009 Global Executive Report*. London: Global Entrepreneurship Monitor.

[63] Bosma, N., and J. Levie. 2010. *Global Entrepreneurship Monitor: 2009 Global Executive Report*. London: Global Entrepreneurship Monitor.

There has been a good deal of research on the relationship between the motives and reasons of the entrepreneur for embarking on a business activity and the subsequent performance (i.e., "success") of the entrepreneur's business venture.[64] Predictably, the findings appear to be mixed. In some instances, researchers have claimed that there is a positive relationship between the intentions of the entrepreneur and the growth realized by the entrepreneurial activity, at least when the relevant measure is employment growth; however, when reporting their results the researchers have also cautioned that the entrepreneur's intention to grow, while relevant, is not the only factor that influences the performance of the entrepreneurial activities and that one needs to take into account other factors such as the availability of resources.[65] A number of researchers using data from the GEM have found that while necessity-based entrepreneurs create jobs for themselves, they generally do not contribute to economic growth,[66] and, in fact, one scholar looking at the research work in the area has concluded that "[i]n general, studies based on GEM data (citations omitted) tend to view so-called necessity entrepreneurship as

---

[64] Dahlqvist, J., P. Davidsson, and J. Wiklund. 2000. "Initial Conditions as Predictors of New Venture Performance: A Replication and Extension of the Cooper et al. Study." *Enterprise and Innovation Management Studies* 1, no. 1; Delmar, F., and J. Wiklund. 2008. "The Effect of Small Business Manager's Growth Motivation on Firm Growth: A Longitudinal Study." *Entrepreneurship Theory and Practice* 32, no. 3, pp. 437–57; and Wiklund, J., and D. Shepherd. 2003. "Aspiring for, and Achieving Growth: The Moderating Role of Resources and Opportunities." *Journal of Management Studies* 40, no. 8, pp. 19–41. Motives and goals have not been the only factor considered in these studies and researchers have also looked at other characteristics of entrepreneurs to see whether they might be accurate predictors of distinctive entrepreneurial behavior, including an orientation toward pursuing and achieving growth for their entrepreneurial businesses. See, for example, Cooper, A., and W. Dunkelberg. 1986. "Entrepreneurship and Paths to Business Ownership." *Strategic Management Journal* 7, no. 1, pp. 53–68; and Stanworth, M., and J. Curran. 1976. "Growth and Small Firm—Alternative View." *Journal of Management Studies* 13, no. 2, pp. 95–110.

[65] Delmar, F., and J. Wiklund. 2008. "The Effect of Small Business Manager's Growth Motivation on Firm Growth: A Longitudinal Study." *Entrepreneurship Theory and Practice* 32, no. 3, pp. 437–57.

[66] Van Stel, A., and D. Storey. 2004. "The Link Between Firm Births and Job Creation: Is There a Upas Tree Effect?" *Regional Studies* 38, no. 8, pp. 893–909.

a more negative factor as far as national growth and development are concerned."[67] On the other hand, different studies have concluded that the initial reasons for launching a new business are not reliable indicators of whether the business will survive and, if it does, the size and/or rate of growth of the business.[68] Those studies emphasize that the likelihood of success for an entrepreneur will be impacted by a number of other factors apart from the reasons for launching a new business such as the availability of capital and skilled personnel, governmental policies, and the communications and transportation infrastructure.

Welter acknowledged the utility of a dichotomy of concepts pertaining to the motivations for entrepreneurship such as "push/pull" and "opportunity" versus "necessity" entrepreneurship and the concepts of "productive" and "unproductive" entrepreneurship; however, he argued that one should avoid categorizing or otherwise describing ventures once and for all into a single category into order to assess their contribution to economic development at the macro level.[69] According to Welter, entrepreneurship must be seen as a "dynamic phenomenon," which is

---

[67] Welter, F. 2010. "Entrepreneurship and Development—Do We Really Know Which Entrepreneurship Types Contribute (Most)?" *Strategic Entrepreneurship— The Promise for Future Entrepreneurship, Family Business and SME Research*. Papers presented to the Beitrage zu den Rencontres de St-Gall 2010 (St. Gallen: KMU-Verlag HSG) (citing Acs, Z., and A. Varga. 2005. "Entrepreneurship, Agglomeration and Technological Change." *Small Business Economics* 24, no. 3, pp. 323–34; Wennekers, S., A. van Stel, R. Thurik, and P. Reynolds. 2005. "Nascent Entrepreneurship and the Level of Economic Development." *Small Business Economics* 24, no. 3, pp. 293–309; and Wong, P., Y. Ho, and E. Autio. 2005. "Entrepreneurship, Innovation and Economic Growth: Evidence from GEM Data." *Small Business Economics* 24, no.3, pp. 335–50).

[68] Dahlqvist, J., P. Davidsson, and J. Wiklund. 2000. "Initial Conditions as Predictors of New Venture Performance: A Replication and Extension of the Cooper et al. Study." *Enterprise and Innovation Management Studies* 1, no. 1; and Solymossy, E. 1997. "Push/Pull Motivation: Does It Matter in Venture Performance?" In *Frontiers of Entrepreneurship Research 1997*, 204–17, eds. P. Reynolds, W. Bygrave, N. Carter, P. Davidsson, W. Gartner, C. Mason and P. McDougall. Wellesley: Babson College.

[69] Welter, F. 2010. *Entrepreneurship and Development—Do We Really Know Which Entrepreneurship Types Contribute (Most)?* In *Rencontre de St-Gall 2010*. KMU-Verlag HSG.

fluid and individual entrepreneurs bring their own previous experience and other antecedent influences to the process of launching a new business. As such, it can be expected that the motivations, behaviors, and contributions of an entrepreneur may change over time. For example, a person may begin down the path of entrepreneurship driven primarily by the desire to simply "survive," even though he or she may harbor personal ambitions and strategies to pursue "genuine" entrepreneurship at some point in the future once the immediate basic needs for self and family have been meant. In the same vein, temporary "unproductive" behavior, such as acting informally for a time to evade legal and tax requirements that would make it too difficult to launch the business at all, may eventually give way to a "productive" venture that makes a substantial contribution to job creation and tax revenues for the state. Welter pressed for recognition that a multitude of motivations and entrepreneurial behaviors may exist over the life of a particular venture and that the productivity of a particular venture should be measured by taking into account both output and behavior.[70]

Wagner was especially interested in gaining a better understanding of persons falling within the definition of "nascent entrepreneurs,"[71] which Wagner explained by referencing a suggested model for the process of creating a new venture that included four stages (conception, gestation, infancy, and adolescence) and the three transitions between those stages.[72] In Wagner's words:

---

[70] See Sauka, A., and F. Welter. 2007. "Productive, Unproductive and Destructive Entrepreneurship in an Advanced Transition Setting: The Example of Latvian Small Enterprises." *Empirical Entrepreneur in Europe*, 9. Cheltenham: Edward Elgar.

[71] The Panel Study of Entrepreneurial Dynamics (PSED) and the Global Entrepreneurship Monitor (GEM) both referred to a "nascent entrepreneur," a term that was defined as "a person who is now trying to start a new business, who expects to be the owner or part owner of the new firm, who has been active in trying to start the new firm in the past 12 months, and whose start-up did not have a positive monthly cash flow that covers expenses and the owner-manager salaries for more than three months" [quoted from Wagner paper referred to in following note (citations omitted)].

[72] Wagner, J. September 2004. *Nascent Entrepreneurs*. Institute for the Study of Labor, Bonn, Discussion Paper No. 1293. See Reynolds, P., and S. White. 1997.

The first transition begins when one or more persons start to commit time and resources to founding a new firm. If they do so on their own, and if the new venture can be considered as an independent start-up, they are called nasce*nt entrepreneurs. The* second transition occurs when the gestation process is complete, and when the new venture either starts as an operating business, or when the nascent entrepreneurs abandon their effort and a stillborn happens. The third transition is the passage from infancy to adolescence—the fledgling new firm's successful shift to an established new firm.

Wagner's view was that nascent entrepreneurs were important due to their roles as the main actors in the first two stages and transitions of the new venture creation process and that he was not, at least for purposes of that particular analysis, interested in what happened to businesses that were formed after the second transition or in persons who had gone through the first two stages and transitions because they preferred being self-employed over being an employee but were not that interested in trying to start and own a whole new business (i.e., persons commonly referred to as "latent entrepreneurs").

Wagner's paper covered several fundamental questions about nascent entrepreneurship, collecting and analyzing data from various sources on each of the questions: how many nascent entrepreneurs are there, around the world; what do nascent entrepreneurs do; who are the nascent entrepreneurs; what makes a nascent entrepreneur; and what happens to nascent entrepreneurs and why. He noted that information on these questions had improved substantially with the launch and development of the GEM, which incorporates reliable information on the prevalence of nascent entrepreneurship in a large number of countries; however, he felt that much work still needed to be done in order to understand the

The Entrepreneurial Process: Economic Growth, Men, Women, and Minorities, 6. Westport, CT and London: Quorum Books; and. Reynolds, P. 2000. "National Panel Study of U.S. Business Startups: Background and Methodology." In *Data Bases for the Study of Entrepreneurship* (*Advances in Entrepreneurship, Firm Emergence, and Growth*), ed. J. Katz, 153, 158ff. 4 vols. Amsterdam: JAI.

substantial differences between countries with respect to the percentage of adults engaged in nascent entrepreneurship and understand why people decide to become nascent entrepreneurs, what activities they engage in once they do, and what factors are most important in helping them push forward into the later stages of the new venture creation process.

Wagner bemoaned the fact that there was no "comprehensive and comparable evidence on the set of activities nascent entrepreneurs are involved in, and on the timing of these events, for a large number of countries." A few studies were conducted in the United States, Norway, and Canada in the 1990s and early 2000s and the most common responses by survey participants regarding their activities included "spending a lot of time thinking about starting a business," taking classes or workshops on starting a new business, saving money to invest in a new business, and/ or investing personal funds in a new business and developing a model or prototype for the first product or service.[73] Other actions included writing

---

[73] Wisconsin Entrepreneurial Climate Study conducted in Spring 1993 in a national pilot study for the United States done in October/November 1993 (Reynolds, P. 1997. "Who Starts New Firms?—Preliminary Explorations of Firms-in-Gestation." *Small Business Economics* 9, p. 449); Reynolds, P., and S. White. 1997. *The Entrepreneurial Process: Economic Growth, Men, Women, and Minorities*. Westport, CT and London: Quorum Books, and in the Panel Study of Entrepreneurial Dynamics (PSED) that started in 1998 (Reynolds, P. 2000. "National Panel Study of U.S. Business Startups: Background and Methodology." In *Data Bases for the Study of Entrepreneurship Advances in Entrepreneurship, Firm Emergence, and Growth*, eds. J. Katz, 153. 4 vols. Amsterdam etc.: JAI); Reynolds, P., N. Carter, W. Gartner, P. Greene, and L. Cox. 2002. *The Entrepreneur Next Door: Characteristics of Individuals Starting Companies in America. An Executive Summary of the Panel Study of Entrepreneurial Dynamics*. Kansas City, MI: Ewing Marion Kauffman Foundation; Gartner, W., and N. Carter. 2003. "Entrepreneurial Behavior and Firm Organizing Processes." In *Handbook of Entrepreneurship Research*, eds. Z. Acs and D. Audret, 195–221. 1 vols. International Handbook Series on Entrepreneurship. Boston, MA: Kluwer Academic Publishers; Reynolds, P., N. Carter, W. Gartner, and P. Greene. 2004. "The Prevalence of Nascent Entrepreneurs in the United States: Evidence from the Panel Study of Entrepreneurial Dynamics." *Small Business Economics* 23, p. 263. Wagner also noted additional evidence from surveys conducted in Norway Alsos, G., and E. Ljunggren. 1998. *Does the Business Start-Up Process Differ by Gender?: A Longitudinal Study of Nascent Entrepreneurs*. Frontiers of Entrepreneurship Research,

an initial business plan, purchasing facilities and/or equipment, seeking financial support, applying for permits and/or patents, and organizing a startup management team. Almost all of the nascent entrepreneurs canvassed in these surveys engaged in two or more activities and the medium number of actions taken was 7.

Wagner reported that a study of nascent entrepreneurship in the United States conducted by Kim, Aldrich, and Keister found that while financial resources were not significantly associated with becoming a nascent entrepreneur, there were positive relationships between the probability of becoming a nascent entrepreneur and several human capital variables such as level of education, full-time work experience, previous startup experience, current self-employment, and the percentage of relatives who are entrepreneurs.[74] Information collected in 2001 from 29 countries that participated in the GEM survey for that year indicated that higher prevalence of nascent entrepreneurship among people with certain personal characteristics and attitudes including being male and younger, knowing an entrepreneur, perceiving a good opportunity for business, having business skills, not being overly fearful of business failure, having

---

Wellesley, MA: Babson College, and in Canada (Diochon, M., Y. Gasse, T. Menzies, and D. Garand. May 26–29, 2001. "From Conception to Inception: Initial Findings from the Canadian Study on Entrepreneurial Emergence." *Proceedings of the Administrative Science Association of Canada, Entrepreneurship Division, London, Ontario* 21, pp. 41–51).

[74] Kim, P., H. Aldrich, and L. Keister. January 2003. *If I Where Rich? The Impact of Financial and Human Capital on Becoming a Nascent Entrepreneur.* University of North Carolina at Chapel Hill and Ohio State University (draft mimeo). See also Delmar, F., and P. Davidsson. 2000. "Where Do They Come from? Prevalence and Characteristics of Nascent Entrepreneurs." *Entrepreneurship and Regional Development* 12, no. 1 (analyzing data from Sweden using an approach similar to that adopted by Reynolds, P., and S. White. 1997. *The Entrepreneurial Process: Economic Growth, Men, Women, and Minorities.* Westport, CT and London: Quorum Books, and Reynolds, P. 1997. "Who Starts New Firms?—Preliminary Explorations of Firms-in-Gestation." *Small Business Economics* 9, p. 449 and finding a negative impact of age, and positive effects of being male, having self-employed parents, education, being self-employed, and having experience in management).

higher household income, and feeling good about the future security of the family.[75]

For example, Wagner found relatively meager assessment of how nascent entrepreneurs fared in their efforts—did they move forward or did they stop and, if so, why—and expressed particular concerns about fundamental methodology issues such as the time frame for follow-up and the specification for empirical models of new venture creation process. The studies available at the time that Wagner wrote his paper were primarily from the United States[76] and among the persons evaluated in those studies one-third to one-half of them move forward to become "infant entrepreneurs" within a year following the point where they were first surveyed. A number of the nascent entrepreneurs concluded that their ideas were not viable and among those who had identified a viable business opportunity the responses indicated that the ones who "were more aggressive in making their business real, acting with a greater level of intensity, and undertaking more activities" were the nascent entrepreneurs most like to actually launch a business. In general, however, it was difficult to find a significant and consistent relationship between personal characteristics of the nascent entrepreneurs and the ultimate outcome with respect to the creation of new businesses.

Categories of Entrepreneurship

The development of thought on the consequences and purposes and goals of entrepreneurship have led to an expansion of the field based on new and different ideas about the processes, behaviors, and outcomes associated with entrepreneurship. Among other things, the recent growing recognition of social and environmental issues, and the accompanying

---

[75] Reynolds, P., S. Camp, W. Bygrave, E. Autio, and M. Hay. 2001. *Global Entrepreneurship Monitor 2001 Summary Report*, 32. London Business School and Babson College.

[76] See, for example, Carter, N., W. Gartner, and P. Reynolds. 1996 ."Exploring Start-up Event Sequences." *Journal of Business Venturing* 11, p. 151 and Reynolds, P., and S. White. 1997. *The Entrepreneurial Process: Economic Growth, Men, Women, and Minorities*. Westport, CT and London: Quorum Books, Chapter 4.

opportunities to develop innovation solutions to problems in each of those areas, has led to the emergence of several new types or categories of entrepreneurs in addition to traditional commercial entrepreneurs: environmental entrepreneurs, or ecopreneurs; social entrepreneurs; and sustainable entrepreneurs.[77]

Majid and Koe explained that the study of entrepreneurship has been broken out into several subfields or categories that simultaneously overlap (e.g., each category of entrepreneurship includes a need to survive economically at some level in order to remain viable) yet also have their own distinctive characteristics or primacies[78]:

- Regular/economic/commercial: Being economically orientated by discovering and exploiting opportunities to make profit, through processes of venture startup, risk assumption, product or process innovation, and resources management. The primary focus is on economic performance, although activities may also general environmental and/or social benefits.

---

[77] Crals, E., and L. Vereeck. February 2004. "Sustainable entrepreneurship in SMEs. Theory and Practice." *Copenhagen: 3rd Global Conference in Environmental Justice and Global Citizenship*; Dees, G. 2001. *The Meaning of Social Entrepreneurship*. Stanford, CA: Stanford University—Graduate School of Business; Schaper, M. 2002. "The Essence of Ecopreneurship." *Greener Management International* 38, p. 26; Young, W., and F. Tilley. 2006. "Can Businesses Move Beyond Efficiency? The Shift toward Effectiveness and Equity in the Corporate Sustainability Debate." *Business Strategy and the Environment*; and Isaak, R. 1998. *Green Logic: Ecopreneurship, Theory and Ethics*. Sheffield, UK: Greenleaf Publishing.

[78] Majid, I., and W.L. Koe. June 2012. "Sustainable Entrepreneurship (SE): A Revised Model Based on Triple Bottom Line (TBL)." *International Journal of Academic Research in Business and Social Sciences* 2, no. 6, pp. 296–97, 293 (citing Richomme-Huet, K., and J. Freyman. 2009. "What Sustainable Entrepreneurship Looks Like: An Exploratory Study from a Student Perspective." *Conference Proceedings in 56th Annual International Council for Small Business (ICSB) World Conference*, June 15–18, 2011. Stockholm, Sweden; and Tilley, F., and W. Young. 2009. "Sustainability Entrepreneurs: Could They Be the True Wealth Generators of the Future?" *Green Management International* 55, p. 79).

- Green/environmental/ecopreneurship: Being environmentally or ecologically embedded by preserving natural resources and creating economic development. The focus is on addressing environmental or ecological problems and issues.[79]
- Social: Being socially embedded by complementing social and profit goals. The focus is on contributing to social or public welfare and creating social values.[80]
- Sustainable: Being future orientated by balancing the efforts in making contributions to produce economic prosperity; social justice and social cohesion; as well as environmental protection. Focus is "holistic" and includes and attempts to equally balance economic, environmental, and social contributions.[81]

Majid and Koe noted that the emergence of the subfields described above and the expanded focus of entrepreneurs beyond economic considerations represents a significant transition in entrepreneurship from the early 1970s when Friedman, one of the leading economists of his day, went on record as saying that "the social responsibility of business is to increase its profits."[82]

---

[79] Chick, A. 2009. "Green Entrepreneurship: A Sustainable Development Challenge." In *Entrepreneurship for Everyone: A Student Textbook*, eds. R. Mellor, G. Coulton, A. Chick, A. Bifulco, N. Mellor, and A. Fisher, 139. London: SAGE Publications; and Dean, T., and J. McMullen. 2007. "Toward a Theory of Sustainable Entrepreneurship: Reducing Environmental Degradation through Entrepreneurial Action." *Journal of Business Venturing* 22, no. 1, p. 50.

[80] Austin, J., H. Stevenson, and J. Wei-Skillern. January 2006. "Social and Commercial Entrepreneurship: Same, Different or Both?" *Entrepreneurship Theory and Practice* 30, no. 1, pp. 1–22.

[81] O'Neill, G., J. Hershauer, and J. Golden. 2009. "The Cultural Context of Sustainability Entrepreneurship." *Green Management International* 55, p. 33; and Tilley, F., and W. Young. 2009. "Sustainability Entrepreneurs: Could They Be the True Wealth Generators of the Future?" *Green Management International* 55, p. 79.

[82] Majid, I., and W.L. Koe. June 2012. "Sustainable Entrepreneurship (SE): A Revised Model Based on Triple Bottom Line (TBL)." *International Journal of Academic Research in Business and Social Sciences* 2, no. 6, pp. 293–97 (citing

Lam created a classification scheme for different types of nontraditional entrepreneurs based on comparing their core motivations, main goals, and the role of nonmarket goals in the activities of the entrepreneur.[83] The first type was ecopreneurship, which was described as having the core motivation of contributing to solving environmental problems and creating economic value. The main goal of ecopreneurship was to earn money by solving environmental problems and environmental issues were an integrated core element of the activities. The next type was social entrepreneurship, which was described as having a core motivation of contributing to solving societal problems and creating value for society. The main purpose of social entrepreneurship was to achieve societal goals and securing funding to achieve this and the societal goals were the ends for the activities. Finally, sustainable entrepreneurship was described as having a core motivation of contributing to solving environmental and social problems through the realization of a successful business. The main goal of the sustainable entrepreneur was to create sustainable development through entrepreneurial business activities and contributing to sustainable development was a core and integrated element.

Tilley and Young noted that entrepreneurs who place a primacy on environment protection or social equity are sometimes, incorrectly in their view, collectively labeled as social entrepreneurs.[84] They argued that while this conflation probably occurs as a way to make a simple distinction from economic entrepreneurs, placing social and environmental entrepreneurs together under the heading of social enterprise often leads

---

Friedman, M. September 13, 1970. "The Social Responsibility of Business is to Increase its Profits." *The New York Times Magazine*).

[83] *What Is Sustainable Entrepreneurship?* (Amsterdam: Sustainable Entrepreneurship Research Platform, 2015) (citing Lam, T. Spring 2014. Bachelor Thesis for International Business School. AUAS).

[84] Tilley, F., and W. Young. 2009. "Sustainability Entrepreneurs—Could they be the True Wealth Generators of the Future?" *Greener Management International* 55, p. 79 (citing *Social Enterprise: A Strategy for Success*. London: Department of Trade and Industry, 2002); and Drayton, W. 2002. "The Citizen Sector: Becoming as Competitive and Entrepreneurial as Business." *California Management Review* 44, no. 3, p. 120.

to misunderstanding about the ways in which these entrepreneurs and their organizations contribute to sustainable development.

Growth-Oriented Entrepreneurship

Entrepreneurship is a popular topic for researchers and policymakers around the world and much of the work in the area does not distinguish new businesses by size or strategy. However, it is now widely acknowledged that a subclass of entrepreneurs, often referred to as "growth-oriented entrepreneurs" or "high-growth entrepreneurs," can be identified and distinguished by their aspirations relating to job creation, innovation, and internationalization, all of which have been positively related to the economic development, which is important to so many governments.[85] Acs and Szerb, the creators of the Global Entrepreneurship and Development Index (GEDI), argued that international rankings of entrepreneurial activities in various countries should place more weight and importance on the amount of entrepreneurial activity directed toward innovation, high-impact entrepreneurship, and globalization focused their research on international entrepreneurship and "the efforts of the early-stage entrepreneur to introduce new products and services, develop new production processes, penetrate foreign markets, substantially increase the number of firm employees, and finance the business with either formal or informal venture capital, or both."[86]

As to what constitutes a "high-growth firm," Audretsch offered several definitions.[87] For example, the 2007 OECD-Eurostat Manual on Business Demography Statistics defined the term to include: "All enterprises with average annualized growth greater than 20 percent per annum, over a three-year period, and with ten or more employees at the beginning

---

[85] Amoros, J., and N. Bosma. 2014. *Global Entrepreneurship Monitor 2013 Global Report: Fifteen Years of Assessing Entrepreneurship Across the Globe*, 37–41.

[86] Acs, Z., and L. Szerb. June 2010. "The Global Entrepreneurship and Development Index (GEDI)" Paper Presented at Summer Conference 2010 on "Opening Up Innovation: Strategy, Organization and Technology." Imperial College London Business School.

[87] Audretsch, D. March 2012. "High-Growth Entrepreneurship." *OECD*.

of the observation period. Growth is thus measured by the number of employees and by turnover." The same source explained "gazelle firms" to be "[a]ll enterprises up to five years old with average annualized growth greater than 20 percent per annum over a three-year period, and with ten or more employees at the beginning of the observation period." When Delta Economics surveyed "growth-oriented" entrepreneurs in BRICS (Brazil, India, China, and South Africa) countries, the United States and Europe, it limited its survey to entrepreneurs running relatively young businesses (between 2 and 10 years old) that had turned over a minimum of $300,000 after the second year of trading and found that "growth-oriented" businesses shared several common features: high growth rate in turnover; average employment of around 25 people and expectations of doubling the size of the workforce within three years; high likelihood that initial financing came from self-investment, usually from savings; some level of innovation in the way in which they approached their markets, product differentiation or research, and development; and international orientation.[88] For Llisterri and Garcia-Alba, "new, dynamic ventures" in Latin America, Asia, and Europe were "firms between three and 10 years old that had grown to employ at least 15 workers, and no more than 100, during the study" and which were likely to engage in export activities and compete on innovation (i.e., offering differentiated products or services) rather than price.[89]

As for characteristics of growth-oriented entrepreneurs, Delta noted that there did not appear to be significant differences in the educational background of the founders of the dynamic and less dynamic companies. In most cases, they had attained high education levels and their college degrees had provided them with important technical knowledge, especially

---

[88] The Association of Chartered Certified Accountants, High-growth SMEs: Understanding the Leaders of the Recovery (July 2012) (based on data and analysis provided by Delta Economics in "Challenges and Opportunities for Growth and Sustainability").

[89] Llisterri, J., and J. Garcia-Alba. 2008. "HGSMEs in Latin American Emerging Economies." The Paper Was Prepared for "The OECD Kansas City Workshop," Session III. "From Invention to the Market Place: Acquiring Knowledge and Intellectual Assets: The Interaction between Large Firms and Small Business in the Fast Growth Process."

for the dynamic entrepreneurs; however, the educational system did little to transfer other skills necessary for successful entrepreneurship. Dynamic entrepreneurs appeared to have distinctly different learning processes for entrepreneurship than their counterparts among the less dynamic companies. For example, the previous work experiences of dynamic entrepreneurs provided significant advantages in terms of gathering information on business ideas and learning the skills necessary to commercialize those ideas. In addition, dynamic entrepreneurs were better able to establish and mine networks of relationships that provided them with valuable support on such things as identifying business opportunities, accessing funds, forging relationships with executives at larger companies, and obtaining access to information and nonfinancial resources such as raw materials or facilities. Delta found that the top four drivers in motivating growth-oriented entrepreneurs worldwide were in order: following a dream; taking advantage of a market opportunity; getting autonomy over the entrepreneur's time; and "making a lot of money."[90] While growth is an important facet of growth-oriented entrepreneurship, recognition has also been given to smaller firms that had opportunities to grow, and grow quickly, yet decided that while growth was a sign of health it was better to focus on "other, nonfinancial priorities as well, such as being great at what they do, creating great places to work, providing great service to customers, making great contributions to their communities and finding great ways to lead lives."[91]

Growth-Oriented Entrepreneurship
A number of different methods have been used to describe "growth-oriented entrepreneurship"; however, there is a consensus that there is a particularly desirable form of entrepreneurship that seeks to create and scale up businesses that will drive productivity growth, create new employment, increase innovation, promote business internationalization, and achieve sustainable economic growth.

---

[90] The Association of Chartered Certified Accountants, High-growth SMEs: Understanding the Leaders of the Recovery (July 2012) (based on data and analysis provided by Delta Economics in "Challenges and Opportunities for Growth and Sustainability").

[91] Burlingham, B. February 8, 2016. "Best Small Companies." *Forbes*, 86.

Criterion for growth-oriented entrepreneurship can be understood from the following descriptions:

- "Knowledge-based entrepreneurship" is entrepreneurship in the context of medium- and high-technology industries, both in the manufacturing and service sectors as well. Distinguishing factors include the sophistication or intensity of technology involved, level of education, and product/service uniqueness.

- "Innovation" is a condition of growth-oriented entrepreneurship that includes both the development and commercialization of new products and services and the development and implementation of new or improved processes that enhance productivity or reduce costs associated with manufacturing or distributing existing products. Innovation involves firms pursuing distinctive business strategies and doing new things in new ways to increase productivity, product development, sales, and profitability, including finding and developing new ways of identifying the needs of new and existing customers and making and marketing products that satisfy those needs.

- "Opportunity-based entrepreneurship" focuses on the motives of the entrepreneur and includes entrepreneurship undertaken to take advantage of a business opportunity. The key characteristic among opportunity-based entrepreneurs is their acknowledgment that they made a voluntary career choice to pursue an entrepreneurial path.

- "Genuine entrepreneurship" describes situations where individuals start businesses with the goal of generating sufficient income so that a portion of it can be reinvested in order to underwrite business growth and development.

- "High-impact entrepreneurship" combines various characteristics and goals of entrepreneurial activity including innovation (i.e., development of new technologies, products and/or services and/or development of new production processes), penetration of foreign markets and globalization of overall business activities, an objective of substantially increasing the number of firm employees and financing the business with risk capital.

Relevant metrics for growth-oriented entrepreneurship include changes in sales, assets, employment, productivity, profits, and profit margins.

The goal of the launch phase for growth-oriented entrepreneurial ventures is to reach the point of "scale up" and common goals and activities associated with the launch phase include market disruption and penetration; gaining access to capital and markets and mentorship opportunities; organizational growth through management capacity, systems, resources (i.e., people, product and assets) management; embedding organizational culture; development of stakeholder relationships; monitoring and evaluation; and governance and reporting.

Finally, framework conditions for growth-oriented entrepreneurship to flourish and sustain include financial support, government policies, government programs, education and training, research and development transfer, commercial and professional infrastructure, internal market openness, access to physical infrastructure, cultural and social norms, and protection of intellectual property rights.

Knowledge-Based Entrepreneurship

A topic closely related to "entrepreneurship and innovation" is "knowledge-based entrepreneurship," which has been defined by Mani as "entrepreneurship in the context of medium and high technology industries, both in the manufacturing and service sectors as well."[92] According to Aidis, "[k]nowledge based entrepreneurship focuses on the development of innovation in sectors that necessitate high levels of human capital, technology and research."[93] The China Association for Management of Technology has provided support for the publication of the *Journal of Knowledge-based Innovation in China*, which is focusing on knowledge, innovation, and development; the development of global, national, regional, and sectoral innovation systems for knowledge creation and sharing; the role of governments, universities, and public institutions in the "knowledge economy"; venture capital in knowledge-based innovation and entrepreneurship; regional economic and social development strategy; knowledge management and learning networks; managing intellectual property rights and international technology transfer; and culture and innovation.

With respect to India, Mani noted that the specific industries considered to meet the criteria for "knowledge-based" status include chemical and chemical products, metal products and machinery, electrical machinery, transport equipment, communication services, computer-related services, and research and development services. Scholars and policymakers have shown a strong interest in promoting knowledge-based entrepreneurship, particularly in developing countries, and the GEM has identified the following facilitating factors or framework conditions for

---

[92] Mani, S. 2009. "The Growth of Knowledge-intensive Entrepreneurship in India, 1991–2007." *Analysis of its Evidence and the Facilitating Factors*, 7. The Netherlands: United Nations University-MERIT Working Paper Series No. 2009-051. For further discussion of knowledge-intensive entrepreneurship, see "Managing Knowledge-Intensive Firms" in "Entrepreneurship: A Library of Resources for Sustainable Entrepreneurs" prepared and distributed by the Sustainable Entrepreneurship Project (www.seproject.org).

[93] Aidis, R. 2005. *Entrepreneurship in Transition Countries: A Review*, 26–27, London: SSEES, University College London.

"knowledge-intensive entrepreneurship" to flourish and sustain: financial support; government policies; government programs; education and training; research and development transfer; commercial and professional infrastructure; internal market openness; access to physical infrastructure; cultural and social norms; and intellectual property rights protection.[94]

Gupta, focusing specifically on facilitating and supporting "technology-based" entrepreneurship in India, suggested similar types of supporting activities, including creating the right environment for success (i.e., entrepreneurs should find it easy to start a business); ensuring that entrepreneurs have access to the right skills, both entrepreneurial (i.e., how to manage, finance, and grow businesses) and functional (i.e., technical, product development, marketing, human resources, etc.); ensuring that entrepreneurs have access to "risk capital" and enabling networking and exchange so that entrepreneurs can learn quickly from the experiences of others.[95] Gupta is one of many researchers who have used "technology-based" entrepreneurship as the point of reference and Mani has cautioned that knowledge-based entrepreneurship is a narrower concept focusing on medium- and high-technology industries.

Successes in larger developing countries such as India and China have triggered interest in the potential of knowledge-based entrepreneurship in other developing countries; however, researchers have identified some of

---

[94] Global Entrepreneurship Monitor. 2007 (as cited and quoted in Mani, S. 2009. *The Growth of Knowledge-intensive Entrepreneurship in India 1991–2007*, 21. Maastricht, The Netherlands: United Nations University-MERIT Working Paper Series No. 2009—051).

[95] Gupta, R. February 12, 2001. "Creating Indian Entrepreneurs." *India Today*, (as cited and summarized in S. Mani, *The Growth of Knowledge-intensive Entrepreneurship in India, 1991–2007*. Maastricht, The Netherlands: United Nations University-MERIT Working Paper Series No. 2009—051, 2009, 21). For further discussion of technology entrepreneurship in India, see Taube, F. 2009. "Diversity and the Geography of Technology Entrepreneurship: Evidence from the Indian IT Industry." In *Sustaining Entrepreneurship and Economic Growth—Lessons in, Policy and Industry Innovations from Germany and India.* eds. M. Keilback, J. Tamvada and D. Audretsch. New York, NY: Springer (testing whether the pattern of knowledge-intensive industries such as software is influenced by education, venture capital, and social and culture factors such as ethnic and gender diversity).

the specific challenges to knowledge-based entrepreneurship in developing countries, such as understanding and overcoming contextual factors (e.g., reliance on agrarian activities, low literacy rates, low exposure and mobility and cultural/religious beliefs that are not conducive to entrepreneurial activities), lack of technical knowledge and practice experience, and lack of industrial and social infrastructure and access to financing. Even in those developing countries where a private sector has emerged firms still have difficulties with knowledge-based activities because of their lack of familiarity with knowledge management systems, a reluctance of employees to share information and ideas and a lack of experience in managing the development and commercialization of knowledge-based products and services.[96]

Entrepreneurship in Large Companies: "Intrapreneurship"

The term "entrepreneurial" has become synonymous with the innovative and adaptive qualities associated with smaller firms and larger companies have taken affirmative steps to integrate entrepreneurial features into their organizational structures and cultures in an effort to compete successfully with emerging companies launched with much fewer people and resources. Some companies implemented the practice of "intrapreneurship," which was first formally defined in the *American Heritage Dictionary* as "a person within a large corporation who takes direct responsibility for turning an idea into a profitable finished product through assertive risk-taking and innovation." The core of intrapreneurship is creating opportunities for employees to be more self-directed in order to enable them to be more creative and innovative. For example, companies might adopt programs that allow groups of employees to propose their own team projects focusing on new products or technologies and obtain funding and other resources for those projects. Other companies have formal policies that allow employees to spend a specified percentage of the working time on developing their own business ideas. Intrapreneurship has required large

---

[96] Liang, T.W. ed. 2003. *Entrepreneurship and Innovation in the Knowledge-based Economy: Challenges and Strategies.* Tokyo: Asian Productivity Organization.

companies to modify their organizational structures to accommodate teams that work separately on new ideas as a de facto "startup" business within the company. In order for intrapreneurship to be successful, companies must identify and empower the right people, separate them from the regular bureaucracy that generally emerges as companies grow and mature so that they are free to develop new ideas that sometimes displace the company's traditional products and technologies, and develop tangible and intangible rewards for intrapreneurial behavior.

Team-Based Venturing and Entrepreneurship

While a good deal of the research on entrepreneurship and entrepreneurial personalities assumes, at least implicitly, that there is a single actor (i.e., one "entrepreneur"), there is a growing interest in studying the dynamics of "team venturing," which assumes that the pursuit of an entrepreneurial activity such as the creation of a new venture is done by a team of two or more persons acting in concert. Researchers have observed that "[t]eam-based entrepreneurship reduces the scarcity of resources by bringing founders with diverse profiles together, who also contribute a broader portfolio of technical and managerial knowledge and resources."[97] In fact, several studies have concluded that team-based entrepreneurship is more successful when compared to the activities overseen by

---

[97] Bouncken, R., J. Zagvozdina, and A. Golze. 2009. "A Comparative Study of Cultural Influences on Intentions to Found a New Venture in Germany and Poland." *International Journal of Business and Globalisation* 3, no. 1, pp. 47–65, 61. See also the work of the following researchers who concluded that team venturing provides opportunities for gaining the advantages of diverse resources and competencies of several individuals: Garcia-Prieto, P., E. Bellard, and S. Schneider. 2000. *A Dynamic Model of Diversity, Emotions, and Conflict in Teams.* Geneva: University of Geneva; Harrison, D., A. Kenneth, J. Gavin, and A. Florey. 2002. "Time, Teams, and Task Performance: Changing Effects of Surface- and Deep-level Diversity on Group Functioning." *Academy of Management Journal* 45, pp. 1029–45; and Kilduff, M., R. Angemar, and A. Mehra. 2000. "Top Management Team Diversity and Firm Performance: Examining the Role of Cognitions." *Organization Science* 11, no. 1, pp. 11–34.

single entrepreneurs.[98] Additional research is required on the dynamics of team-based entrepreneurship, particularly given the high likelihood of conflicts among individuals with strong streaks of individualism and internal locus of control. The situation becomes even more interesting when venturing teams include members from different countries with diverse cultural backgrounds. A multicultural team is certainly advantageous when embarking on international entrepreneurship activities since it is presumably useful to have team members with experience and knowledge about the economic, cultural, social, and political environment of the countries in which the venture will be operating; however, cultural diversity increases the possibility of conflicts beyond that which has already been alluded to above.[99]

Definitions and Types of Entrepreneurship in Developing Countries

Acs and Virgill observed that the term "entrepreneurship" is often used in several different ways when discussed in connection with developing countries.[100] For example, studies of entrepreneurship in developing countries often focus explicitly and primarily on *small- and medium-sized enterprises* (SMEs). In other cases, discussions of entrepreneurial activities in developing countries include persons and firms found in the "informal sector" as well as those engaged in "petty capitalism."[101] In many cases,

---

[98] See, for example, Keeley, R., and R. Knapp. 1994. "Founding Conditions and Business Performance: 'High Performers' vs. Small vs. Venture Capital Start-ups." *Frontiers of Entrepreneurship Research*. Boston, MA: Babson College; and Mellewigt, T., and J. Späth. 2002. "Entrepreneurial Teams—A Survey of German and US Empirical Studies." *Zeitschrift für Betriebswirtschaft* 5, pp. 107–25.

[99] Bouncken, R., J. Zagvozdina, and A. Golze. 2009. "A Comparative Study of Cultural Influences on Intentions to Found a New Venture in Germany and Poland." *International Journal of Business and Globalisation* 3, no. 1, pp. 47—65, 61.

[100] Acs, Z., and N. Virgill. March 31, 2009 "Entrepreneurship in Developing Countries." Jena Economic Research Papers, No. 2009–023.

[101] Id. at p. 31 (citing Smart, A., and J. Smart. 2005. *Petty Capitalists and Globalization: Flexibility, Entrepreneurship, and Economic Development*. Albany, NY: State University of New York Press).

combining firms in the informal sector with SMEs in developing regions such as Africa results in a large group of small traders, which is collectively responsible for 65–70 percent of total GDP[102] and this means that efforts to study and incentivize entrepreneurial activities in developing countries must take into account firms operating both inside and outside the formal institutional framework. Petty capitalism can be found in many forms and has been described as including "small businesses which employ relatively few employees and rely heavily on their owner's and owner's family's labor."[103] Acs and Virgill cited several examples of petty capitalism including the numerous export enterprises of Hong Kong, the maquila workshops in Mexico, and furniture manufacturers in Italy.[104] The terminology landscape in developing countries clearly contrasts with the approach taken by scholars of entrepreneurship in the United States and other developed countries—they make a strong distinction between entrepreneurship and SMEs based on their intentions with respect to growth[105]; however, in developing countries it is generally advisable to adopt a broader definition of entrepreneurship that includes SMEs, the informal sector, petty capitalists, and the relatively rare dynamic entrepreneur given that each of these actors is capable of generating something that is "new" in what Schumpeter probably meant when he referred to "the humblest levels of the business world."[106]

---

[102] Id. at p. 31 (citing Ayyagari, M., T. Beck, and A. Demirgüc-Kunt. 2003. *Small and Medium Enterprises across the Globe.* Washington, DC: World Bank Policy Research Working Paper No. 3127). With regard to the "entrepreneurial landscape in Africa," which includes informal and formal sector businesses, traditional and modern, indigenous, and foreign-owned enterprises geographically dispersed in rural and urban areas, see McDade, B., and A. Spring. January 2005. "The 'New Generation of African Entrepreneurs': Networking to Change the Climate for Business and Private Sector-Led Development." *Entrepreneurship and Regional Development* 17, pp. 17–42.

[103] Id.

[104] Id.

[105] Id. (citing Carland, J.W., F. Hoy, W. Boulton, and J.C. Carland. 1984. "Differentiating Entrepreneurs from Small Business Owners: A Conceptualization." *The Academy of Management Review* 9, no. 2, pp. 354–59, 357).

[106] Id. (citing Schumpeter, J. 1947. "The Creative Response in Economic History." *The Journal of Economic History* 7, no. 2, pp. 149–59, 151). Notice

Studies of entrepreneurship in developing countries have often focused extensively on distinctions between "necessity-based" and "opportunity-based" entrepreneurs, which is often viewed as a distinction between proprietors who start their own businesses when no other options are available in order to find a way to sustain their families and persons who start businesses with the intent of not only bringing in sufficient income to support themselves and their families but also to generate excess capital that can be reinvested in order to underwrite business growth and development.[107] For example, Mani noted that it is often assumed that economic growth in developing countries will necessarily follow efforts to increase measured levels of entrepreneurship in those countries; however, he observed that

> ... the reality is more complicated. It is important to distinguish between "necessity entrepreneurship" and "opportunity entrepreneurship." In necessity entrepreneurship, one has to become an entrepreneur because there is no better option for the person involved, whereas opportunity entrepreneurship is an active choice to start a new enterprise based on the perception that an unexploited or underexploited business opportunity exists. Necessity entrepreneurship has little or no effect on economic growth while opportunity entrepreneurship has a positive and significant effect.

---

should be taken that there is also debate as to which firms in developing countries are most effective at driving innovation. Amsden, for example, has argued that large privately owned enterprises are the innovative firms in developing countries since they are more flexible and innovative then subsidiaries of foreign multinationals or state-owned enterprises. See Amsden, A. 2011. "Firm Ownership and Entrepreneurship." In *Entrepreneurship, Innovation and Economic Development*, eds. A. Szirmai, W. Naude, and M. Goedhuys, 65–77. Oxford: Oxford University Press.

[107] Scase, R. 1997. "The Role of Small Businesses in the Economic Transformation of Eastern Europe: Real but Relatively Unimportant." *International Small Business Journal* 16, pp. 113–21; Scase, R. 2003. "Entrepreneurship and Proprietorship in Transition: Policy Implications for the SME Sector." In *Small and Medium Enterprises in Transitional Economies*, eds. R. McIntyre, R. Dallago, and B. Houndsmill, 64–77. Basingstoke: Palgrave Macmillan.

Acs and Szerb, like others,[108] observed that an understanding of entrepreneurship requires going beyond the traits and characteristics of the individual entrepreneur to also consider institutional variables and they noted that "[t]he dynamics of the [entrepreneurial] process can be vastly different depending on the institutional context and level of development within an economy."[109] They explained that entrepreneurship occurs within an environment that is influenced by economic development and that development directly impacts and strengthens institutions that eventually affect characteristics that are considered to be vitally important to the phenomenon of entrepreneurship such as quality of governance, access to capital and other resources, the perceptions of entrepreneurs, and incentive structures for prospective entrepreneurs. Researchers have found evidence that the strengthening of institutions causes more entrepreneurial activity to be shifted toward "productive entrepreneurship," which, in turn, strengthens economic development.[110] Entrepreneurial activity reaches its highest level of intensity as countries go through the innovation-driven stage and eventually levels off as institutions are fully developed and the country has achieved a high level of innovation.[111]

The lack of institutions in many developing countries often results in a shortage of formal employment opportunities in those countries and leaves substantial portions of the population with little choice but to set out on own. The so-called reluctant entrepreneurship of this type also follows loss of employment, which may be caused by one of the frequent economic shocks that developing countries are prone to suffer. Several extensive studies of global entrepreneurship, including the Global Entrepreneurship Monitor, commonly referred to as the "GEM," and the

---

[108] See, for example, Busenitz, L., and J. Spencer. 2000. "Country Institutional Profiles: Unlocking Entrepreneurial Phenomena." *Academy of Management Journal* 43, no. 5, pp. 994–1003.

[109] Acs. Z., and L. Szerb. June 2010. "The Global Entrepreneurship and Development Index (GEDI)." Paper presented at Summer Conference 2010 on "Opening Up Innovation: Strategy, Organization and Technology." Imperial College London Business School.

[110] Acemoglu, D., and S. Johnson. 2005. "Unbundling Institutions." *Journal of Political Economy* 113, no. 5, pp. 949–95.

[111] Fukuyama, F. 1989. "The End of History?" *The National Interest* 16, pp. 3–18.

Global Entrepreneurship and Development Index, have provided additional information on entrepreneurial types in developing countries, the factors that have motivated them to choose and pursue entrepreneurship and the impact that economic development is likely to have on the face of entrepreneurship in those countries.[112]

Lingelbach et al. explored some of the factors that they perceived as making entrepreneurs in developing countries "different."[113] They first noted that researchers had identified several categories of entrepreneurial firms in developing countries including "newly established," "established but not growing," "established but growing slowly," "graduates of a larger size," and, a somewhat recent phenomenon, "new and growth-oriented firms" (similar to "opportunity-based entrepreneurs" mentioned above).[114] Turning their attention to the specifics of building successful growth-oriented firms in developing countries, Lingelbach et al. mentioned the following "distinctive attributes of entrepreneurship in developing countries":

- Since developing countries lack a "stable of mature markets," entrepreneurs in those countries have a broader range of opportunities available to them than their counterparts in developed countries. In other words, while entrepreneurs in developed countries generally operate on the fringes of the economy, developing country entrepreneurs can, if they wish, place themselves in the core of their economies pursuing solutions for needs and opportunities that are more widespread.

---

[112] For further discussion of both the GEM and the Global Entrepreneurship and Development Index, see "Entrepreneurship: A Library of Resources for Sustainable Entrepreneurs." Prepared and distributed by the Sustainable Entrepreneurship Project (www.seproject.org).

[113] Lingelbach, D., L. De La Vina, and P. Asel. March 2005. *What's Distinctive about Growth-Oriented Entrepreneurship in Developing Countries?* San Antonio, TX: UTSA College of Business Center for Global Entrepreneurship Working Paper No. 1.

[114] Id. at p. 3 (citing Liedholm, C., and D. Mead. 1999. *Small Enterprises and Economic Development: The Dynamic Role of Micro and Small Enterprises.* London: Routledge).

- The fragmented and immature markets in developing countries reduce the threat of well-established incumbents; however, entrepreneurs must contend with the much higher levels of risk associated with the economic, political, and regulatory uncertainties that generally exist in developing countries. Lingelbach et al. suggested that entrepreneurs in developing countries cope with these risks by operating a portfolio of businesses to manage risks through diversification. Capital raised in one business can be used to providing financing for other businesses and Lingelbach et al. suggested that "interlocking businesses provide a source of informal information flow, access to a broader pool of skills and resources and, when well implemented, a brand name that can be leveraged across all businesses."[115]

- Entrepreneurs in developing countries face significant challenges with obtaining the necessary financial resources and use several strategies to overcome those problems. They typically start downstream businesses to reduce initial capital requirements and gain access to customers and information flow. They also rely on informal funding provided through well-developed family networks rooted in both urban and rural areas—Lingelbach et al. noted that there are "greater pools of private saving in the countryside."[116]

- Family-owned and -operated businesses remain more common in emerging markets than in developed countries since entrepreneurs in developing countries still lack mentorship and apprenticeship opportunities that can expose them to the skills and experiences needed to launch and expand businesses in challenging environments. Developing country entrepreneurs must have different skills including the ability to "see through the fog of politics and economics in crisis-prone developing countries" and to be perceived as "trustworthy"

---

[115] Id. at p. 4.
[116] Id. at p. 5.

in a situation where transactions are most often based on trust rather than formal contracting rules.[117]

Environmental Entrepreneurship (Ecopreneurship)

Interest in sustainable development has arisen from concerns about the impact that economic growth would have on the Earth's finite natural resources and some of the parties involved in that debate argued that while overuse was an issue it would eventually be addressed through market forces. According the York and Venkataraman, there are several different ways that environmental degradation can be addressed[118]:

- Government regulation and control, the so-called *visible hand*; however, while the government has promulgated an expansive portfolio of regulations over the last several decades environmental degradation has continued to occur;
- Stakeholder activism, such as lobbying action by nongovernmental organizations focusing on perseveration of natural resources;
- Corporate social responsibility initiatives launched by individual corporations on their own initiative as ethics-based programs to address environmental problems they are responsible for or have association with—initiatives that have been critiqued as being more about doing "less bad" than doing good; and
- Other forms of corporate action that include cost savings and differentiation with an important goal of gain a competitive advantage by implementing environmentally friendly practices (e.g., creating a positive public image by being perceived as a "green business").

---

[117] Id. at p. 7.
[118] York, J., and S. Venkataraman. 2010. "The Entrepreneur-Environment Nexus: Uncertainty, Innovation, and Allocation." *Journal of Business Venturing* 25, no. 5, p. 449.

Going down a path on which market forces would eventually address the environmental problems that the market itself created, Gibbs explained the concept of "ecological modernization," which he described as a process of the progressive transformation and modernization of the institutions of modern society in order to avoid ecological crisis.[119] In this view, it was not just market forces that would "save the Earth," but also the inert drive of capitalism for innovation that would be harnessed to realize environmental improvements, thus allowing the world to continue forward with "modernization" undeterred by environmental crises.[120] According to Roberts and Colwell, "ecological modernization suggests that it is possible to integrate the goals of economic development, social welfare and environmental protection, and that through this reconciliation synergies will be generated which can be harnessed and put to good use."[121]

While appealing, there is no sufficient evidence to conclude that ecological modernization is inevitable and it would certainly require cooperation and participation by various actors. Incumbent businesses in the private sector would presumably consider acting in order to gain various advantages: through greater business efficiency due to reduced pollution and waste production; avoiding future financial liabilities, such as the potential cost of contaminated land cleanup; through improved recruitment and retention of the workforce due to the creation of a better work environment; from the potential for increased sales of more "environmentally friendly" products and services; and through the sale of pollution prevention and abatement technologies.[122] As for political

---

[119] Gibbs, D. September 2006. "Sustainability Entrepreneurs, Ecopreneurs and the Development of a Sustainable Economy," *Greener Management International* 55, pp. 63–66.

[120] Beveridge, R., and S. Guy. 2005. "The Rise of the Eco-preneur and the Messy World of Environmental Innovation." *Local Environment* 10, no. 6, pp. 665–66.

[121] Roberts, P., and A. Colwell. 2001. "Moving the Environment to Centre Stage: A New Approach to Planning and Development at European and Regional Levels." *Local Environment* 6, no. 4, pp. 421–24.

[122] Drysek, J. 1997. *The Politics of the Earth: Environmental Discourses.* Oxford, UK: Oxford University Press, (as cited in Gibbs, D. September 2006. "Sustainability Entrepreneurs, Ecopreneurs and the Development of a Sustainable Economy." *Greener Management International* 55, pp. 63–67).

institutions, several measures would seem to be appropriate: restructuring of production and consumption toward ecological goals, including the development and diffusion of clean production technologies; decoupling economic development from the relevant resource inputs, resource use and emissions; exploring alternative and innovative approaches to environmental policy, such as "economizing ecology" by placing an economic value on nature and introducing structural tax reform; and integrating environmental policy goals into other policy areas; and the invention, adoption, and diffusion of new technologies and production processes.[123]

In 1987 the World Commission on Environment and Development of the United Nations (generally referred to simply as the Brundtland Commission) issued a report that described sustainable development as "a process in which the exploitation of natural resources, the allocation of investments and the process of technological development and organizational change are in harmony with each other for both current and future generations."[124] The publication of the report fueled what quickly became a comprehensive dialogue on the impact that economic growth was having on the global environment and biodiversity. The early 1990s saw the adoption of extensive new environmental regulations and the emergence of what was referred to as the "green agenda."[125] Corporate social responsibility was also becoming more important and businesses were beginning to see that integrating ecological concerns into their business models could not only be popular with consumers but also help them reduce costs and the risks associated with operations that might be harmful to surrounding communities and the world generally. Given these changes

---

[123] Gouldson, A., and J. Murphy. 1997. "Ecological Modernisation: Restructuring Industrial Economies." In *Greening the Millennium? The New Politics of the Environment*, ed. M. Jacobs, 74. Oxford, UK: Blackwell. (as cited in Gibbs, D. September 2006. "Sustainability Entrepreneurs, Ecopreneurs and the Development of a Sustainable Economy." *Greener Management International* 55, pp. 63–66).

[124] United Nations World Commission on Environment and Development. 1987. *Our Common Future*. New York, NY: Oxford University Press.

[125] Holt, D. 2010. "Where Are They Now? Tracking the Longitudinal Evolution of Environmental Businesses from the 1990s." *Business Strategy and the Environment* 20, no. 4, p. 238.

in behavioral patterns and the rise of social institutions concerned with protecting the environment, the scene was set for the emergence of environmental entrepreneurship, or "ecopreneurship," which often took the form of startups based on more sustainable business models and deploying processes reflecting greater concern for environmental and, later, more social issues.[126] Like traditional entrepreneurs, ecopreneurs sought to satisfy unmet needs or identify an unresolved problem in the marketplace; however, while traditional entrepreneurs focused on generating economic value, the creation of social value being ancillary, an ecopreneur is a mission-driven individual "who starts up a business with 'green' initiatives from day one, with strong commitment to transforming a sector of the economy toward becoming more sustainable and environmentally responsible."[127] Ecopreneurship offered another path to addressing issues of environmental degradation and ecopreneurs did not just run a "green business" but incorporated innovation into a mission that focused on creating value for sustainable development with products and services that not only generated economic growth but also created societal benefits.

Researchers noted that ecological modernization was arguably an area particularly well suited to entrepreneurial action by ecopreneurs.[128] While ecopreneurs have been described as "social activists, who aspire to restructure the corporate culture and social relations of their business sectors through proactive, ecologically oriented business strategies,"[129] they are

---

[126] See Holt, D. 2010. "Where Are They Now? Tracking the Longitudinal Evolution of Environmental Businesses from the 1990s." *Business Strategy and the Environment*, 20, no. 4, p. 238; and Randjelovic, J., A. O'Rourke, and R. Orsato. 2003. "The Emergence of Green Venture Capital." *Business Strategy and the Environment* 12, no. 4, pp. 240–41.

[127] Bell, J., and J. Stellingwerf. 2012. *Sustainable Entrepreneurship: The Motivations & Challenges of Sustainable Entrepreneurs in the Renewable Energy Industry* 7, Jonkoping, Sweden: Jonkoping International Business School Master Thesis in Business Administration 7, (citing Isaak, R.R. 2002. "The Making of the Ecopreneur." *Greener Management International*, pp. 38—81).

[128] Schaper, M. 2005. *Making Ecopreneurs: Developing Sustainable Entrepreneurship*. Aldershot, UK: Ashgate.

[129] Isaak, R. 1998. *Green Logic: Ecopreneurship, Theory and Ethics*, 88. Sheffield, UK: Greenleaf Publishing.

also able to attack and address environmental issues using the Schumpeterian "process of creative destruction" that includes creating new products, services, processes, and "ways of doing work" that challenge, and eventually overturn, conventional methods.[130] As explained by Schaltegger, "ecopreneurs destroy existing conventional production methods, products, market structures and consumption patterns and replace them with superior environmental products and services ... [and] ... create the market dynamics of environmental progress."[131] The businesses that they form have been referred to by Isaak as "green-green businesses," firms that have been founded from the outset on an environmentally friendly basis and with a focused mission on achieving social and ethical transformation of their specific business sectors.[132]

It has been argued that the emergence and success of ecopreneurship has turned on the ability of ecopreneurs to exploit sources of opportunity such as uncertainty and market failure. There is significant uncertainty with respect to the environment and multiple stakeholders continuously struggle to find solutions for problems such as environmental degradation, pollution, waste and contamination, and resource depletion. While incumbent companies recognize these problems, they are often reluctant to invest in the development of innovative solutions due to the opportunity costs of their current investments. In contrast, ecoentrepreneurs are willing and eager to accept uncertainty in exchange for the possibility of being rewarded with a premium and also do not have to worry about diminishing the value of their previous investments. Environmental degradation is also a form of market failure: government regulations, subsidies, and incentives have proven to be inappropriate and ineffective interventions in many cases and traditional commercial entrepreneurs have struggled to appropriate the gains emanating from their investments

---

[130] Schumpeter, J. 1934. *The Theory of Economic Development*. Cambridge, MA: Harvard University Press.

[131] Schaltegger, S. 2002 "A Framework for Ecopreneurship: Leading Bioneers and Environmental Managers to Ecopreneurship." *Greener Management International* 38, pp. 45–46.

[132] Isaak, R. 1998. *Green Logic: Ecopreneurship, Theory and Ethics*, 87. Sheffield, UK: Greenleaf Publishing.

in new environmental technology and convince consumers to pay for the related products and services. Ecopreneurs have been successful where the government and commercial entrepreneurs have struggled by engaging customer-focused entrepreneurship that emphasizes identifying specific customer needs for environmental products and services and then addressing another form of market failure, imperfect information, by informing customers about the environmental attributes of products and services and the health and environment effect of methods of production, product contents, product use, and postconsumption disposal.[133]

Bell and Stellingwerf noted that a variety of terms have been used to describe "entrepreneurship behavior conducted through an environmental lens" including eco-entrepreneurship, environmental entrepreneurship, enviropreneurship, green entrepreneurship, and green–green businesses.[134] They preferred "ecopreneurship" and included the following examples of definitions and conceptualizations of that term[135]:

- "A person who seeks to transform a sector of the economy toward sustainability by starting up a business in that sector with a green design, with green processes and with a life-long commitment to sustainability."[136]

---

[133] van Eijck, P. January 2012. *Sustainable Entrepreneurship: Institutional Profile and Cross-country Comparison Denmark & US and Its Viability*, 10. Rotterdam: Bachelor Thesis in Entrepreneurship, Strategy and Organizations Economics from Erasmus School of Economics.

[134] Bell, J., and J. Stellingwerf. 2012. *Sustainable Entrepreneurship: The Motivations & Challenges of Sustainable Entrepreneurs in the Renewable Energy Industry*, 7. Jonkoping, Sweden: Jonkoping International Business School Master Thesis in Business Administration (citing Schaltegger, S. 2005. "Chapter 4: A Framework and Typology of Ecopreneurship: Leading Bioneers and Environmental Managers to Ecopreneurship." In *Making Ecopreneurs: Developing Sustainable Entrepreneurship*, ed. M. Shaper, 43, Burlington: Ashgate Publishing Company. For a brief summary and critique of research on ecopreneurship, see Gibbs, D. 2009. "Sustainability Entrepreneurs, Ecopreneurs and the Development of a Sustainable Economy." *Greener Management International* 55, no. 63, pp. 73–74).

[135] Id. at pp. 7–8.

[136] Isaak, R. 2002. "The Making of the Ecopreneur." *Greener Management International* 38, p. 81.

- "Entrepreneurs who found new businesses based on the principle of sustainability. Ecopreneurs are those entrepreneurs who start for-profit businesses with strong underlying green values and who sell green products or services."[137]
- "Individuals or institutions that attempt to popularise eco-friendly ideas and innovations either through the market or non-market routes may be referred to as Ecopreneurs."[138]
- "Usually the Ecopreneur has a 'raison d'ˆetre' that exceeds their desire for profits and often this is associated with making the world a better place to live."[139]
- "Ecopreneurs can be classified according to two criteria: (1) their desire to change the world and improve the quality of the environment and life; and (2) their desire to make money and grow as a business venture."[140]
- Ecopreneurs are visionaries, with the ability to foresee a "demand for fundamental innovations in traditional markets. The challenge is to be economically successful with the supply of products and services that change—on a purely voluntary basis—consumption patterns and market structures, leading to an absolute reduction of environmental impacts."[141]
- Ecopreneurs are effectively decisive change agents, enabling the world to change its path, are highly motivated in making

[137] Kirkwood, J., and S. Walkton. 2010. "What Motivates Ecopreneurs to Start a Business?" *International Journal of Entrepreneurial Behaviour & Research* 16, no. 3, p. 204.

[138] Pastakia, A. 1998. "Grassroots Ecopreneurs." *Journal of Organisational Change Management* 11, no. 2, p. 157.

[139] Linnanen, L. 2002. "An Insider's Experiences with Environmental Entrepreneurship." *Greener Management International* 38, p. 71.

[140] Id. (cited in Rogers, C. 2010. "Sustainable Entrepreneurship in SMEs: A Case Study Analysis." *Corporate Social Responsibility and Environmental Management* 17, p. 125).

[141] Schaltegger, S., and M. Wagner. 2011. "Sustainable Entrepreneurship and Sustainability Innovation: Categories and Interactions." *Business Strategy and the Environment* 20, p. 222.

a difference and displacing unsustainable means, an important transitional role in sustainability.[142]

Bell and Stellingwerf argued that ecopreneurs filled gaps in the marketplace that could not be effectively addressed by a large number of incumbent firms or traditional entrepreneurs. While many established companies appreciate the importance of taking steps to operate in a more environmentally friendly manner, many feel that the sustainability strategies of these companies are "push" strategies driven by their need to comply with the demands of external regulatory bodies and other stakeholders. In contrast, ecopreneurs act to implement "pull" strategies based on actively taking a stance toward becoming "greener" and building a competitive advantage over less "green" firms.[143] As for distinctions between traditional entrepreneurship and ecopreneurship, the following words of Bell and Stellingwerf are instructive: "Entrepreneurs may effectively bring new combinations to the economy—that is, new products, methods and markets. However, it is the Ecopreneur who plays a critical role in the development process, constructing environmentally friendly products, processes, and services toward the sustainable development objective—'development that meets the needs of the present generation without compromising the ability of future generations to meet their own needs.'"[144]

While their small size and relative lack of resources appeared to make ecopreneurial startups unlikely candidates for transforming business sectors, many researchers believed that these startups were actually well positioned to identify and exploit innovative technological strategic niches that can not only bring about technological change but also challenge and

---

[142] Cohen, B., and M. Winn. 2007. "Market Imperfections, Opportunity and Sustainable Entrepreneurship." *Journal of Business Venturing* 22, no. 1, p. 29.

[143] Bell, J., and J. Stellingwerf. 2012. *Sustainable Entrepreneurship: The Motivations & Challenges of Sustainable Entrepreneurs in the Renewable Energy Industry*, 8. Jonkoping, Sweden: Jonkoping International Business School Master Thesis in Business Administration.

[144] Id. at pp. 8–9.

pressure existing institutions, rules, and norms.[145] As explained by Smith, ecopreneurs are

> the "idealists (producers and supportive users) who initiate a sustainable niche [and] are later joined by entrepreneurial 'system builders' who open the niche out to a wider set of users) and, eventually, by serious amounts of capital seeking to profit from the proto-regime."[146]

Social Entrepreneurship

According to Daft and Marcic, "social entrepreneurship" seeks to launch and build companies that are entirely focused on combining good business with good citizen and the leaders of these companies, the "social entrepreneurs," are primarily interested in improving society rather than maximizing profits while nonetheless demanding high performance standards and accountability for results.[147] Examples of "for profit" social entrepreneurship run the gambit of commercial activities from partnering with traditional banks to offer microloans to small businesses in developing countries to launching manufacturing facilities in poor areas to provide jobs and produce products that can be distributed at no cost to the community members to improve their lives. While many of these businesses are not started with the intent to generate significant profits, a number of them have achieved impressive profits margins and market shares. In addition, Tilley and Young observed that

---

[145] Gibbs, D. September 2006. "Sustainability Entrepreneurs, Ecopreneurs and the Development of a Sustainable Economy." *Greener Management International* 55, pp. 63–68.

[146] Smith, A. 2003. "Transforming Technological Regimes for Sustainable Development: A Role for Alternative Technology Niches?" *Science and Public Policy* 30, no. 2, pp. 127–30. For further discussion of environmental entrepreneurship, see the Part on "Sustainable Entrepreneurship" in "Entrepreneurship: A Library of Resources for Sustainable Entrepreneurs." Prepared and distributed by the Sustainable Entrepreneurship Project (www.seproject.org).

[147] Daft, R., and D. Marcic. 2006. *Understanding Management*, 5th ed. 147–48, Mason, OH: South-Western Publishing Co.

the concept of social entrepreneur is very broadly interpreted to mean any organization that is operating in a not-for-profit capacity ... [including] ... community based organizations tackling education, poverty, health, welfare and well-being issues as well as organizations attempting to address environmental concerns relating to renewable energy, waste minimization, pollution abatement and water quality (to name a few).[148]

Austin et al. defined social entrepreneurship as an "innovative, social value creating business activity that can occur within or across the nonprofit, business, or government sectors"[149] and van Eijck observed that the "organizational form is usually based on the most attractive form to gain resources for the social mission."[150] Dees described social entrepreneurs as companies who play the role of change agents in the social sector by adopting a mission to create and sustain value (not just private value); recognizing and relentlessly pursuing new opportunities to serve that mission; engaging in a process of continuous innovation, adaptation, and learning; acting boldly without being limited by resources currently in hand, and exhibiting a heightened sense of accountability to the constituencies served and for the outcomes created.[151]

When writing about social entrepreneurship, some researchers have largely ignored the economic outcomes associated with the entrepreneurial activities while other researchers do acknowledge that economic performance is relevant but cannot be more important than the social

---

[148] Tilley, F., and W. Young. 2009. "Sustainability Entrepreneurs—Could they be the True Wealth Generators of the Future?" *Greener Management International* 55, p. 79.

[149] Austin, J., H. Stevenson, and J. Wei-Skillern. 2006. "Social and Commercial Entrepreneurship: Same, Different, or Both?" *Entrepreneurship Theory and Practice* 30, no. 1, pp. 1–2.

[150] van Eijck, P. January 2012. *Sustainable Entrepreneurship: Institutional Profile and Cross-country Comparison Denmark & US and Its Viability*, 7. Rotterdam: Bachelor Thesis in Entrepreneurship, Strategy and Organizations Economics from Erasmus School of Economics.

[151] Dees, J. 1998. *The Meaning of Social Entrepreneurship*. Stanford, CA: Stanford University Graduate School of Business.

goals and objectives.[152] When social entrepreneurship was first recognized it was typically associated with nonprofit organizations; however, as time has gone by the conceptualization has broadened and even nonprofits have participated in commercial activities to access financial resources for the social activities that would have otherwise been difficult to obtain.[153] Social entrepreneurship can also create competitive advantages similar to those sought by traditional entrepreneurs (e.g., developing and offering innovation solutions to environmental degradation or a social justice problem) that allow social entrepreneurs to enjoy economic returns without impairing or interfering with their social objectives. As such, it is no longer taboo to profit from satisfying humanitarian and ecological needs so long as the profits are reinvested in activities that further the social objectives (e.g., distribute and add value to employment, investments in machines, infrastructure, sponsoring and labor participation).[154] These elements appear in the definition of sustainable, not social, entrepreneurship offered by Crais and Vereeck: "the continuing commitment by business to behave ethically and contribute to economic development while improving the quality of life of the workforce."[155]

Social entrepreneurship drew research interest first in the 1990s and emerged naturally with the popularization of ecopreneurship, which was no surprise given that it was impossible for ecopreneurs to achieve their goal of "changing the world" and improving the overall quality of life

---

[152] Dacin, P., M. Dacin, and M. Matear. 2010. "Social Entrepreneurship: Why We Don't Need a New Theory and How We Move Forward from Here." *Academy of Management Perspectives* 24, no. 2, p. 36.

[153] Dees, J. 1998. "Enterprising Nonprofits." *Harvard Business Review* 76, no. 1, p. 54.

[154] van Eijck, P. January 2012. *Sustainable Entrepreneurship: Institutional Profile and Cross-country Comparison Denmark & US and Its Viability,* 7–8. Rotterdam: Bachelor Thesis in Entrepreneurship, Strategy and Organizations Economics from Erasmus School of Economics.

[155] Crals, E., and L. Vereeck. 2005. "The Affordability of Sustainable Entrepreneurship Certification for SMEs." *International Journal of Sustainable Development & World Ecology* 12, no. 2, p. 173.

without also acting in a socially responsible fashion.[156] In fact, several of the definitions of ecopreneurship presented elsewhere in this chapter explicitly incorporate a social dimension.[157] However, as opposed to the ecological and environmental issues and problems that ecopreneurs were focusing on, social entrepreneurship gathered speed on the heels of four trends: global wealth disparity; the growth of the corporate social responsibility movement; market, institutional, and state failures; technological advances and shared responsibility.[158]

Lumpkin et al. suggested that both "traditional" and social entrepreneurs have a lot in common and that many entrepreneurial processes used by the two groups remained the same or are affected only slightly.[159] However, while a traditional entrepreneur measures his or her performance primarily through profits and return on investment, social entrepreneurs generally measure success by creating social capital, social change, and addressing social needs.[160] These distinctions are important because they influence the opportunities that social entrepreneurs pursue and their behaviors while operating their businesses (i.e., as opposed to traditional entrepreneurs who are comfortable with and must engage in high-risk/high-reward behaviors, social entrepreneurs, who are not focused on quick economic profits, are more risk averse but no less committed to their goals of social improvement). As is the case with ecopreneurs, social

---

[156] Bell, J., and J. Stellingwerf. 2012. *Sustainable Entrepreneurship: The Motivations & Challenges of Sustainable Entrepreneurs in the Renewable Energy Industry*, 9. Jonkoping, Sweden: Jonkoping International Business School Master Thesis in Business Administration.

[157] Dixon, S., and A. Clifford. 2007. "Managing Ecopreneurship: A New Approach the Triple Bottom Line." *Journal of Organisational Change Management* 20, no. 3, p. 326.

[158] Zahra, S., H. Rawhouser, N. Bhaw, D. Neubaum, and J. Hayton. 2008. "Globalisation of Social Entrepreneurship Opportunities." *Strategic Entrepreneurship Journal* 2, p. 117.

[159] Lumpkin, G., T. Moss, D. Gras, S. Kato, and A. Amezua. 2011. "Entrepreneurial Processes in Social Contexts: How Are They Different, If at All?" *Small Business Economics* 1.

[160] Bornstein, D. 2004. *How to Change the World: Social Entrepreneurs and the Power of New Ideas*, 15. New York, NY: Oxford University Press.

entrepreneurs are not totally indifferent to profits, or at least "breaking even," since capital is necessary in order for their businesses to survive over the often lengthy journeys to the desired social impact. This is no small challenge for social entrepreneurs since they often are involved in activities that address a social-market failure caused by a lack of interest of traditional entrepreneurs due to the belief that there is no viable commercial market that will generate an acceptable level of revenues to justify the investment of capital.[161]

Bell and Stellingwerf provided a variety of different definitions and conceptualizations of social entrepreneurship[162]:

- Profit making is not the primary goal of a social entrepreneur and generated profits from market activities should be used for the benefit of a specific disadvantaged group.[163]
- Profit is less important, and the social aspect should be balanced at least equally to profit, a challenge that has been conceptualized as the "double bottom line" that balances both social (people) and economic (profit) returns on investment.[164]

---

[161] See Austin, J., H. Stevenson, and J. Wei-Skillern. 2006. "Social and Commercial Entrepreneurship: Same, Different, or Both?" *Entrepreneurship: Theory and Practice* 30, no. 1, pp. 1–2 (stating that the existence of social-purpose organizations emerge when there is a social-market failure, that is, commercial market forces do not meet a social need).

[162] Bell, J., and J. Stellingwerf. 2012. *Sustainable Entrepreneurship: The Motivations & Challenges of Sustainable Entrepreneurs in the Renewable Energy Industry*, 10. Jonkoping, Sweden: Jonkoping International Business School Master Thesis in Business Administration. For further discussion of social entrepreneurship, see "Social Entrepreneurship" in "Entrepreneurship: A Library of Resources for Sustainable Entrepreneurs." Prepared and distributed by the Sustainable Entrepreneurship Project (www.seproject.org).

[163] Leadbeater, C. 1997. *The Rise of the Social Entrepreneur*. London: Demos.

[164] Zahra, S., H. Rawhouser, N. Bhaw, D. Neubaum, and J. Hayton. 2008. "Globalisation of Social Entrepreneurship Opportunities." *Strategic Entrepreneurship Journal* 2, p. 117.

- Social entrepreneurs "play the role of change agents in the social sector, by adopting a mission to create and sustain social value (not just private value), recognizing and relentlessly pursuing new opportunities to serve that mission, engaging in a process of continuous innovation, adaptation, and learning, acting boldly without being limited by resources currently in hand, and exhibiting heightened accountability to the constituencies served and for the outcomes created."[165]
- Social entrepreneurship "emphasizes innovation and impact, not income, in dealing with social problems" and social entrepreneurs are focused on introducing a novel, innovative technology or approach aimed at creating social impact.[166]
- Social entrepreneurship is "the innovative use and combination of resources to pursue opportunities to catalyze social change and/or address social needs."[167]
- "Social entrepreneurship encompasses the activities and processes undertaken to discover, define, and exploit opportunities in order to enhance social wealth by creating new ventures or managing existing organizations in an innovative manner."[168]

Like traditional entrepreneurs, social entrepreneurs need to identify and exploit opportunities, create and manage their organizations in innovative ways, and, as emphasized by Bell and Stellingwerf, "acquire substantial resources including, human, social and financial capital to not only accomplish their mission, but also to ensure such resources are

---

[165] Dees, G. 1998. *The Meaning of Social Entrepreneurship.*

[166] Dees, G. 2003. *New Definitions of Social Entrepreneurship: Free Eye Exams and Wheelchair Drivers.*

[167] Mair, J., and I. Martı´. 2006. "Social Entrepreneurship Research: A Source of Explanation, Prediction, and Delight." *Journal of World Business* 41, no. 1, p. 36.

[168] Zahra, S., E. Gedajlovic, D. Neubaum, and J. Shulman. 2009. "A Typology of Social Entrepreneurs: Motives, Search Processes and Ethical Challenges." *Journal of Business Venturing* 24, no. 5, p. 519.

sustaining the organization's longevity."[169] This is often quite challenging to social entrepreneurs who often are surprised to find competition that is as intense as it is commonplace in the commercial sector. For example, social entrepreneurs must be able to differentiate themselves from other worthy causes and forge and maintain relationships with a number of stakeholder groups including donors, professional employees, volunteers, and the intended beneficiaries of the entrepreneurial initiatives.[170]

Bell and Stellingwerf observed that the obvious similarity between ecopreneurship and social entrepreneurship is that they both incorporate a "double bottom line" within the company's mission: balancing economic returns with other considerations (i.e., environmental or social impact).[171] This observation is consistent with the views of Schaltegger and Wagner, who wrote: "Even though the historic trajectories of these types (Eco-and Social Entrepreneurship) differ, it seems that the underlying motivations for the activities are very similar and this seems to make likely a convergence of these currently rather independent literatures."[172] As discussed below, the anticipated convergence is often defined and described as "sustainable entrepreneurship" or "sustainability entrepreneurship" and is based on the conceptualization the deployment of entrepreneurial tools and practices to solve either an environmental or societal problem (i.e., recognize market imperfections and/or unmet needs in the realms of ecology or society and address them through the introduction of innovative

---

[169] Bell, J., and J. Stellingwerf. 2012. *Sustainable Entrepreneurship: The Motivations & Challenges of Sustainable Entrepreneurs in the Renewable Energy Industry*, 11. Jonkoping, Sweden: Jonkoping International Business School Master Thesis in Business Administration.

[170] Zahra, S., E. Gedajlovic, D. Neubaum, and J. Shulman. 2009. "A Typology of Social Entrepreneurs: Motives, Search Processes and Ethical Challenges." *Journal of Business Venturing* 24, no. 5, p. 526.

[171] Bell, J., and J. Stellingwerf. 2012. *Sustainable Entrepreneurship: The Motivations & Challenges of Sustainable Entrepreneurs in the Renewable Energy Industry*, 12. Jonkoping, Sweden: Jonkoping International Business School Master Thesis in Business Administration.

[172] Schaltegger, S., and M. Wagner. 2011. "Sustainable Entrepreneurship and Sustainability Innovation: Categories and Interactions." *Business Strategy and the Environment* 20, pp. 222–26.

products, services, and processes) while maintaining a focus on creating economic value—in other words, businesses that use the "triple bottom line" as their guide.[173]

Sustainable Entrepreneurship

By the 1990s it was becoming clear that sustainability had "become a multidimensional concept that extends beyond environmental protection to economic development and social equity"—in other words, entrepreneurship guided and measured by the three pillars of the "triple bottom line."[174] Crals and Vereeck reasoned that "sustainable entrepreneurship" could be interpreted as a spin-off concept from sustainable development and that sustainable entrepreneurs were those persons and companies that contributed to sustainable development by "doing business in a sustainable way."[175] According to the Brundtland Commission, sustainable entrepreneurship is the continuing commitment by businesses to behave ethically and contribute to economic development while improving the quality of life of the workforce, their families, the local and global community as well as future generations.[176] This definition recognizes that several stakeholder groups, not just shareholders, must be taken into account when managerial decisions are made and operational activities in furtherance of the organizational purposes are carried out. Crals and Vereeck argued that in order for entrepreneurial activity to be "sustainable" it must recognize, address, and satisfy certain standards for each of the 3 P's

---

[173] See Cohen, B., B. Smith, and R. Mitchell. 2008. "Toward a Sustainable Conceptualisation of Dependent Variables in Entrepreneurship Research." *Business Strategy and the Environment* 17, no. 2, p.107; and Cohen, B., and M. Winn. 2007. "Market Imperfections, Opportunity and Sustainable Entrepreneurship." *Journal of Business Venturing* 22, no. 1, p. 29.

[174] Gladwin, T., J. Kennelly, and T. Krause.1995. "Shifting Paradigms for Sustainable Development." *Academy of Management Review* 20, no. 4, p. 874.

[175] Crals, E., and L. Vereeck. July 18, 2016. *Sustainable Entrepreneurship in SMEs—Theory and Practice*, 2. http://inter-disciplinary.net/ptb/ejgc/ejgc3/cralsvereeck%20paper.pdf (accessed July 18, 2016).

[176] Id.

of the triple bottom-line described above.[177] Crals and Vereeck observed that the definition of sustainable entrepreneurship was not static given the dynamism of new ideas and standards with respect to the social and natural environment.[178]

Bell and Stellingwerf compiled what they considered to be a representative list of definitions of "sustainable entrepreneurship" that were suggested from 2003 through 2011, all of which are presented below in chronological order[179]:

- "Innovative behavior of single or organizations operating in the private business sector who are seeing environmental or social issues as a core objective and competitive advantage."[180]
- "The continuing commitment by business to behave ethically and contribute to economic development, while improving the quality of life of the workforce, their families, local communities, the society and the world at large, as well as future generations. Sustainable entrepreneurs are for-profit entrepreneurs that commit business operations toward the objective goal of achieving sustainability."[181]

---

[177] Crals, E., and L. Vereeck. July 18, 2016. *Sustainable Entrepreneurship in SMEs—Theory and Practice*, 3–4. http://inter-disciplinary.net/ptb/ejgc/ejgc3/cralsvereeck%20paper.pdf (accessed July 18, 2016).

[178] For a further discussion of sustainable entrepreneurship, see "Sustainable Entrepreneurship" in "Entrepreneurship: A Library of Resources for Sustainable Entrepreneurs." Prepared and distributed by the Sustainable Entrepreneurship Project (www.seproject.org).

[179] Bell, J., and J. Stellingwerf. 2012. *Sustainable Entrepreneurship: The Motivations & Challenges of Sustainable Entrepreneurs in the Renewable Energy Industry*, 13–14. Jonkoping, Sweden: Jonkoping International Business School Master Thesis in Business Administration.

[180] Gerlach, A. 2003. "Sustainable Entrepreneurship and Innovation." In *University of Leeds: The 2003 Corporate Social Responsibility and Environmental Management Conference Leeds*, 101–03. UK: University of Leeds.

[181] Crals, E., and L. Vereeck. 2005. "The Affordability of Sustainable Entrepreneurship Certification for SMEs." *International Journal of Sustainable Development and World Ecology* 12, p. 173.

- "The process of discovering, evaluating, and exploiting economic opportunities that are present in market failures which detract from sustainability, including those that are environmentally relevant."[182]
- "The examination of how opportunities to bring into existence future goods and services are discovered, created, and exploited, by whom, and with what economic, psychological, social, and environmental consequences."[183]
- "Create profitable enterprises and achieve certain environmental and/or social objectives, pursue and achieve what is often referred to as the double bottom-line or triple bottom line."[184]
- "The discovery and exploitation of economic opportunities through the generation of market disequilibria that initiate the transformation of a sector toward an environmentally and socially more sustainable state."[185]
- "An innovative, market-oriented and personality driven form of creating economic and societal value by means of breakthrough environmentally or socially beneficial market or institutional innovations."[186]
- "Sustainable entrepreneurship is focused on the preservation of nature, life support, and community in the pursuit of perceived opportunities to bring into existence future

[182] Dean, T., and J. McMullen. 2007. "Towards a theory of Sustainable Entrepreneurship: Reducing Environmental Degradation through Entrepreneurial Action." *Journal of Business Venturing* 22, pp. 50–58.

[183] Cohen, B., and M. Winn. 2007. "Market Imperfections, Opportunity and Sustainable Entrepreneurship." *Journal of Business Venturing* 22, no. 1, pp. 29–35.

[184] Choi, D., and E. Gray. 2008. "The Venture Development Process of 'Sustainable' Entrepreneurs." *Management Research News* 31, no. 8, pp. 558–59.

[185] Hockerts, K., and R. Wüstenhagen. 2010. "Greening Goliaths versus Emerging Davids—Theorizing about the Role of Incumbents and New Entrants in Sustainable Entrepreneurship." *Journal of Business Venturing* 25, pp. 481–82.

[186] Schaltegger, S., and M. Wagner. 2011. "Sustainable Entrepreneurship and Sustainability Innovation: Categories and Interactions." *Business Strategy and the Environment* 20, pp. 222–24.

products, processes, and services for gain, where gain is broadly construed to include economic and non-economic gains to individuals, the economy, and society."[187]

From their perspective, Bell and Stellingwerf believed that the definitions collectively identified four defining attributes of sustainable entrepreneurship[188]:

- *Balancing environmental and social concerns:* Bell and Stellingwerf observed that sustainable entrepreneurship was "a balancing act of strategically managing and orienting environmental and social objectives and considerations, with entity specific financial goals steering the business objective" and that sustainable entrepreneurship required finding the right balance with the disparate economic, social, cultural, and ecological environments in which businesses must operate. They also noted that in the course of their efforts to limit and minimize the environmental and social impact of their activities sustainable entrepreneurs focused on improving the quality of their processes.[189]
- *Economic gains:* Entrepreneurship, sustainable or otherwise, has making a profit as an essential characteristic and objective and the concept of "gain" can be found throughout the definitions reproduced above. However, sustainable entrepreneurship is a based on a broad construction of gain that includes economic and noneconomic gains to

---

[187] Shepherd, D., and H. Patzelt. 2011. "The New Field of Sustainable Entrepreneurship: Studying Entrepreneurial Action Linking 'What is to be Sustained' with 'What is to be Developed.'" *Entrepreneurship Theory and Practice* 35, no. 1, pp. 137–42.

[188] Bell, J., and J. Stellingwerf. 2012. *Sustainable Entrepreneurship: The Motivations & Challenges of Sustainable Entrepreneurs in the Renewable Energy Industry,* 14–17. Jonkoping, Sweden: Jonkoping International Business School Master Thesis in Business Administration.

[189] Choi, D., and E. Gray. 2008. "The Venture Development Process of 'Sustainable' Entrepreneurs." *Management Research News* 31, no. 8, p. 558.

individuals, the economy, and society. Profits are recognized as being essential to sustaining the livelihood of businesses and providing entrepreneurs with the resources that are needed for reinvestment in the sustainable goals of their companies. Bell and Stellingwerf argued that entrepreneurial activities can only be labeled sustainable, and therefore satisfy sustainable development, if there is an equal blending of, and equal consideration for, each of the 3 P's of the triple bottom line described above.[190]

- *Market failures and disequilibria:* Half of the definitions reproduced above explicitly mentioned recognition and exploitation of opportunities caused by environmental and/or social imperfections and identification of opportunities has been a long-standing tenant of disruptive entrepreneurship. Cohen and Winn argued that there are four types of market imperfections (i.e., inefficient firms, externalities, flawed pricing mechanisms, and information asymmetries) that contribute to environmental degradation and provide opportunities for sustainable entrepreneurs to create radical technologies and innovative business models that can achieve profitability while simultaneously improving local and global social and environmental conditions.[191]

- *Transforming sectors toward sustainability:* A number of theorists have argued that startups launched by sustainable entrepreneurs can solve sustainability-related problems

---

[190] Bell, J., and J. Stellingwerf. 2012. *Sustainable Entrepreneurship: The Motivations & Challenges of Sustainable Entrepreneurs in the Renewable Energy Industry,* 15. Jonkoping, Sweden: Jonkoping International Business School Master Thesis in Business Administration.

[191] Cohen, B., and M. Winn. 2007. "Market Imperfections, Opportunity and Sustainable Entrepreneurship." *Journal of Business Venturing* 22, no. 1, p. 29. See also Dean, T., and J. McMullen. 2007. "Towards a Theory of Sustainable Entrepreneurship: Reducing Environmental Degradation through Entrepreneurial Action." *Journal of Business Venturing* 22, pp. 50–58. ("Environmentally Relevant Market Failures Represent Opportunities for Simultaneously Achieving Profitability While Reducing Environmentally Degrading Economic Behaviors.")

through the introduction of innovative products, processes, and services and that the commercial success of these solutions, and accompanying support of professional investors and other influential stakeholders, can and will eventually influence incumbents to adopt similar solutions and otherwise take steps that will lead to the transformation of the entire industry toward sustainability.[192] Under these theories, sustainable entrepreneurs make their impact by targeting market niches defined by a particular sustainability-related problem, generally introducing the radical changes that are outside the comfort zone of incumbents that prefer change to be incremental; however, Bell and Stellingwerf cautioned that research "in the field" lacked support.[193]

From all of this, Bell and Stellingwerf proposed their own definition of sustainable entrepreneurship as "startups that introduce an innovation, with the aim to solve a sustainability-related market failure, which initiates the transformation of an industry toward sustainability."[194] The "innovation" could take the form of a product, process, or service and the sustainability objectives behind these innovations were equally important as the economic objectives associated with them. The use of the term "startups" is intentional and significant as it explicitly differentiates sustainable entrepreneurship from the activities of established organizations, such as corporations, to address sustainable development issues in their environment (i.e., corporate-sustainability or CSR initiatives).

Rey synthesized the results of his review of various definitions of sustainable entrepreneurship as follows: "conducting business which commits

---

[192] See, for example, Hockerts, K., and R. Wüstenhagen. 2010. "Greening Goliaths versus Emerging Davids—Theorizing about the Role of Incumbents and New Entrants in Sustainable Entrepreneurship." *Journal of Business Venturing* 25, pp. 481–82.

[193] Bell, J., and J. Stellingwerf. 2012. *Sustainable Entrepreneurship: The Motivations & Challenges of Sustainable Entrepreneurs in the Renewable Energy Industry*, 17. Jonkoping, Sweden: Jonkoping International Business School Master Thesis in Business Administration.

[194] Id.

to ethical standards and behavior, contributing to economic development, all the while maintaining a progressive upkeep of the well-being of society—including the labor-force and their families, their communities and the world on a whole, for the present and future inhabitants."[195] According to Rey, a sustainable company is one that operates in accord with the philosophy of the Brundtland Report while recognizing and balancing the economic, social, and environmental aspects and impacts of their businesses.[196] Rey noted that "sustainable entrepreneurship may seem odd as entrepreneurship is principally associated with accomplishing certain goals while maximizing profits in the most efficient way possible" and entrepreneurs who are focused on projecting a sustainable outlook for their business will likely stray from profit maximization due to the added costs of sustainable goods and practices that traditional entrepreneurs are able to avoid by simply going for the cheapest alternative.[197]

Rey noted that while CSR is often compared to sustainable entrepreneurship, he believed that there are significant differences between the two concepts. Most importantly, according to Rey, CSR is primarily concerned with the actions of corporations that have been operating for a significant period of time and which have reached a certain size and determined that they have a responsibility, beyond the traditional profit-making objectives, to be more aware of their *external* environment and stakeholders and find ways to give back to their local communities beyond their mandatory legal obligations. While these initiatives are generally welcomed, they typically lack certain core characteristics of sustainable entrepreneurship such as offering environmentally friendly products and services and making changes to *internal* operations of the company to bring sustainability practices to personnel matters and production processes.[198]

---

[195] Rey, L. December 2011. *Sustainable Entrepreneurship and Its Viability*, 12. Rotterdam: Master Thesis for MS in Entrepreneurship, Strategy and Organizations Economics from Erasmus School of Economics.

[196] Id.

[197] Id. at p. 9.

[198] Id.

Muñoz observed that the specific form of entrepreneurship engaged in by sustainability-driven enterprises is about simultaneously achieving three objectives (i.e., social, environmental, and economic), while committing to securing the economic welfare and social well-being of future generations and ensuring a long-term sustainability of the environment.[199] He then went on to propose that sustainable entrepreneurship should be defined and conceptualized as being "focused on pursuing business opportunities to bring into existence future products, processes and services, while contributing to sustain the development of society, the economy and the environment and consequently to enhance the well-being of future generations."[200] From this definition it is possible to identify certain central factors that sustainable entrepreneurs need to consider in developing and executing their business models: integrating environmental best practices and protection into all business activities; social justice; economic prosperity for investors, entrepreneurs, and economies; improving the well-being of communities; and intra- and intergenerational equity.[201] Muñoz pointed out that his definition acknowledged and integrated constructs from both sustainable development and entrepreneurship literature, a path also taken by Shepherd and Patzelt's opinion that the practice of sustainable entrepreneurship called for sustaining and developing three constructs informed by sustainable development literature (i.e., sustain nature, life support systems, and communities) and three constructs informed by entrepreneurship literature (i.e., develop

---

[199] Muñoz, P. November 2013. "The Distinctive Importance of Sustainable Entrepreneurship." *Creativity, Innovation and Entrepreneurship* 2, no. 1, (citing Young, W., and F. Tilley. 2006. "Can Businesses Move beyond Efficiency? The Shift towards Effectiveness and Equity in the Corporate Sustainability Debate." *Business Strategy and the Environment* 15, no. 6, p. 402).

[200] Id.

[201] Id. (citing Dresner, S. 2008. *The Principles of Sustainability*, 2nd ed. London: Earthscan); and Beckerman, W. 1999 "Sustainable Development and Our Obligations to Future Generations." In *Fairness and Futurity: Essays on Environmental Sustainability and Social Justice*, ed. A. Dobson, 71. Oxford: Oxford University Press.

economic gains, noneconomic gains to individuals, and noneconomic gains to society).[202]

Racelis used the term "authentic sustainable entrepreneurship" to describe the situation "when the economic, environmental, and social motives come together in the business action of the entrepreneur, along with the internalization of the fiduciary, stewardship, and moral responsibilities to future generations."[203] Racelis went on to suggest that the specific normative elements that should be found in the activities of the authentic sustainable entrepreneur should include "production of socially desirable products in a socially desirable manner, and advancement of the health and well-being of those affected by such, all within a values-driven framework."[204] Racelis pointed out that sustainable entrepreneurship is a model of entrepreneurship that enables founders to seize opportunities relating to environmental and social degradation, which are created by market imperfections (e.g., inefficient firms, externalities, flawed pricing mechanisms, and information asymmetries) to obtain entrepreneurial rents while simultaneously improving social and environmental conditions both locally and globally.[205] Racelis argued that the core motivation for sustainable entrepreneurs is to "contribute to solving societal and environmental problems through the realization of a successful business," while their main goal "is to create sustainable development through entrepreneurial corporate activities."[206]

---

[202] Shepherd, D., and H. Patzelt. 2011. "The New Field of Sustainable Entrepreneurship: Studying Entrepreneurial Action Linking 'What Is to Be Sustained' with 'What Is to Be Developed.'" *Entrepreneurship Theory and Practice* 35, no. 1, p. 137.

[203] Racelis, A. 2014. "Sustainable Entrepreneurship in Asia: A Proposed Theoretical Framework Based on Literature Review." *Journal of Management for Global Sustainability* 2, no. 1, pp. 49–72.

[204] Id. (citing Hodgkin, S. 2002. *Business Social Entrepreneurs: Working Towards Sustainable Communities through Socially Responsible Business Practices*. Master's thesis, University of Calgary, Calgary, Alberta, Canada).

[205] Id. (citing Dean, T., and J. McMullen. 2007. "Toward a Theory of Sustainable Entrepreneurship: Reducing Environmental Degradation through Entrepreneurial Action." *Journal of Business Venturing* 22, p. 50).

[206] Id.

Another important implicit condition for sustainable entrepreneurship is the capacity of the venture to survive, develop, and grow. Rey referred to this condition as "viability" and emphasized that a sustainable entrepreneurial company must, at a minimum, cover all costs, enjoy continuous growth in size and output, make a positive return on turnover and, fundamentally, "remain out of financial danger for years."[207] In other words, the company must seek and achieve long-term sustainability in order to successfully pursue and achieve its goals and purposes and provide prospective stakeholders, including employees, with security that their contributions to the enterprise will produce value over an extended period.

Entrepreneurship and Innovation

Any attempt at starting a new business, regardless of the size of the firm or the sophistication of its products or services, falls squarely within the definition of entrepreneurship and generally carries the same levels of risk and stress for the persons involved in the process. Entrepreneurship programs launched and administered by governmental agencies and non-profit organizations are primarily geared toward "small businesses" that often rely on readily available technologies and their goal is to ensure that interested persons have access to basic information about starting a business, complying with applicable laws, and locating financing sources. Proprietorships and small firms with less than 20 employees have always been an important part of the economic landscape and this should continue in the future as technology, such as the Internet, makes it easier for entrepreneurs to put their business ideas into practice and quickly and efficiently reach prospective customers and other business partners.

An important niche within the entrepreneurial community, which has been readily filled by universities, focuses on new business formation for the purpose of identifying, developing, and commercializing relatively risky and unproven technologies and business processes. The study of entrepreneurs and their firms that are involved in these sorts of activities

---

[207] Rey, L. December 2011. *Sustainable Entrepreneurship and Its Viability*, 14. Rotterdam: Master Thesis for MS in Entrepreneurship, Strategy and Organizations Economics from Erasmus School of Economics.

is referred to as "entrepreneurship and innovation." A number of different definitions and explanations of "innovation" have been offered by academicians and commentators. For our purposes, it is useful to think of innovation as the process of successfully acquiring and implementing new ideas within a business organization. As suggested by this formulation, new ideas can be developed and created internally, or can be borrowed or purchased from other organizations. New ideas are not confined to new products and services, but also include new or improved processes that enhance productivity or reduce costs associated with manufacturing or distributing existing products. Put another way, innovation involves firms doing new things in new ways to increase productivity, product development, sales, and profitability, including finding new ways of identifying the needs of new and existing clients and making and marketing products that satisfy those needs.

Drucker forcefully promoted the interrelatedness of entrepreneurship and innovation and the need for entrepreneurs to recognize and learn the disciplines and principles of innovation and practice them in the planning for their ventures:

> Innovation is the specific tool of entrepreneurs, the means by which they exploit change as an opportunity for a different business or a different service. It is capable of being presented as a discipline, capable of being learned, capable of being practiced. Entrepreneurs need to search purposefully for the sources of innovation, the changes and their symptoms that indicate opportunities for successful innovation. And they need to know and apply the principles of successful innovation.

Drucker believed that entrepreneurship could be understood as a systematic process and that opportunities for successful entrepreneurship could be uncovered through purposeful innovation and exploration of identified sources of innovation including incongruities, process needs, industry and market structures, demographics, changes in perception, new knowledge, and unforeseen events.[208]

---

[208] Drucker, P. 1993. *Innovation and Entrepreneurship*. New York, NY: Collins.

Certainly there are important and obvious differences between launching a small shoe repair shop and developing and commercializing a cutting-edge pharmaceutical product to fend off cancer; however, those who link entrepreneurship and innovation believe that any new venture, be it a separate startup business or a product development project within a large company, can increase its chances for success by understanding and applying the principles that have been gleaned from studies of what has been referred to as the "innovation process." Of course, while opinions vary on exactly what that process might be it has traditionally flowed sequentially through the following phases: idea generation, concept development, resource acquisition, ramp-up, and launch. Studies have shown that many of the elements required for successful innovation are constant across industries and business activities and include an emphasis on product innovation, a strong customer orientation, and a firm commitment to high-quality reliable service. Presumably these findings can be effectively deployed by all entrepreneurial ventures; however, it is should be understood that additional innovation strategies may be required in response to specific competitive factors in particular industries.

Carland et al. set out to determine whether it was possible to differentiate "entrepreneurs" from small business owners. They concluded that merely conceiving a new business was not sufficient to qualify as entrepreneurship and that the term was appropriate only for those persons who identified and created combinations of resources for the purpose of seeking profit and growth and then pursued those goals through innovative behavior and the implementation of creative management practices.[209] This position is consistent with the perspective taken by those who believe that strategy, rather than the personal characteristics of the founders and senior managers, is the most important and accurate predictor of whether or not a new firm will be successful in achieving its goals with respect to profits and growth. For persons in that camp the entrepreneurial event is

---

[209] Carland, J., F. Hoy, W. Boulton, and J.A. Carland. 1984. "Differentiating Entrepreneurs from Small Business Owners: A Conceptualization." *Academy of Management Review* 9, no. 2 pp. 354–59.

a moving target composed of parts that are in constant motion.[210] While certain personal characteristics of the founders and other members of the senior management team are important, particularly their leadership skills, it is their ability to develop and execute the appropriate strategy that is the most crucial success factor.

Entrepreneurship and Economic Development

Many commentators, beginning with Schumpeter, have argued that entrepreneurship is crucial for understanding economic development.[211] Acs and Virgill noted that "[t]he empirical evidence is . . . strong in support of a link between entrepreneurship and economic growth" and that "[s]tudies have found that regional differences in economic growth are correlated to levels of entrepreneurship."[212] They explained that entrepreneurs in developing countries play a key role in "fill[ing] in important gaps left by incomplete and underdeveloped markets" and referred also to Leff's explanation that

> a key function of entrepreneurship in developing countries is . . . to mobilize factors such as capital and specialized labor which, being imperfectly marketed, might otherwise not be supplied or allocated to the activities where there productivity is the greatest.[213]

---

[210] Timmons, J. 1986. "Growing Up Big: Entrepreneurship and the Creation of High-Potential Ventures." In *The Art and Science of Entrepreneurship*, 223–39. eds. D.L. Sexton and R.W. Smilor. Cambridge, MA: Ballinger Publishing Company.

[211] Acs, Z., and L. Szerb. June 2010. "The Global Entrepreneurship and Development Index (GEDI)." Paper Presented at Summer Conference 2010 on "Opening Up Innovation: Strategy, Organization and Technology." Imperial College London Business School. A review of the literature regarding the relationship of entrepreneurship to economic development appeared in Acs, Z., and N. Virgill. 2009. *Entrepreneurship in Developing Countries*. Foundations and Trends in Entrepreneurship.

[212] Acs, Z., and N. Virgill. March 2009. "Entrepreneurship in Developing Countries." Jena Economic Research Papers, No. 2009–023, p. 26.

[213] Id. (citing Leff, N. 1979. "Entrepreneurship and Economic Development: The Problem Revisited." *Journal of Economic Literature* 17, no. 1, pp. 46–64, 48).

According to Acs and Virgill, recognition of the unique value of entrepreneurship in developing countries has led policymakers in those countries to "begin to work on perfecting their markets by eliminating barriers to entrepreneurship and other market failures,"[214] a trend that can be seen in the increased interest of policymakers and researchers in the role that institutions play in promoting entrepreneurship that can lead to economic development.

While focusing on and describing the "economics of innovation," Porter suggested that countries go through three stages of economic development: a factor-driven stage, an efficiency-driven stage, and, finally, an innovation-driven stage.[215] Acs and Szerb provided the following brief description of each of these stages[216]:

- The factor-driven stage is marked by high rates of agricultural self-employment and countries in this stage generally compete based on low-cost efficiencies in the production of commodities or low value-added products. Countries in this stage do not create knowledge that can be used for innovation nor do they use knowledge to engage in exporting activities.
- The efficiency-driven stage requires that countries engage in efficient productive practices in large markets so that firms are able to achieve and exploit economies of scale. Industries in this stage are generally manufacturing-based and focused on the production and distribution of basic goods and services. Self-employment declines during this stage and capital, labor, and technology become the key drivers of productivity.
- In the innovation-driven stage, the key input is "knowledge" and decisions about embarking on new projects are based

---

[214] Id.

[215] Porter, M. 2002. *Global Competitiveness Report*. Geneva: World Economic Forum.

[216] Acs, Z., and L. Szerb. June 2010. "The Global Entrepreneurship and Development Index (GEDI)." Paper Presented at Summer Conference 2010 on "Opening Up Innovation: Strategy, Organization and Technology." Imperial College London Business School.

on primarily on expected net returns and the likelihood that economic activities can generate high value-added products and services.

Acs and Szerb discussed the relative importance of institutions and innovation as countries moved through the various stages and noted that while "[i]nstitutions dominate the first two stages of development," innovation spurred by entrepreneurship plays an increasingly important role in economic activity "in the innovation-driven stage when opportunities have been exhausted in factors and efficiency."[217] The institutional emphasis as the beginning of the continuum is illustrated by the need to increase production efficiency and the education level of the workforce in order to transition from the first stage to the second stage and its increased emphasis on technology. In contrast, the activity of individual agents in possession of new technology (i.e., "entrepreneurs") plays a bigger role in traveling the road from the second to third stage.[218]

The notion of "stages" of economic development has also been embraced and explained by other scholars. For Brinkman, economic development is "a process of structural transformations" that ultimately leads to an overall higher growth trajectory.[219] Liebenstein explained that

per capita income growth requires shifts from less productive to more productive techniques per worker, the creation or adoption of new commodities, new materials, new markets, new organizational forms, the creation of new skill, and the accumulation of new knowledge.[220]

---

[217] Id.

[218] Acs, Z., and S. Laszlo. 2009. "The Global Entrepreneurship Index (GEINDEX)." *Foundations and Trends in Entrepreneurship* 5, no. 5, pp. 341–435.

[219] Brinkman, R. 1995. "Economic Growth versus Economic Development: Towards a Conceptual Clarification." *Journal of Economic Issues* 29, no. 4, pp. 1171–88, 1183.

[220] Leibenstein, H. 1968. "Entrepreneurship and Development." *The American Economic Review* 58, no. 2, pp. 72–83, 77.

As noted elsewhere in this publication, the role of the entrepreneur has often been neglected in economic theory, including various "stages of development" models; however, Liebenstein explicitly and celebrated the entrepreneur as "gap filler and input-completer . . . [and] . . . probably the prime mover of the capacity creation part of [the] elements in the growth process" that occurs during the aforementioned processes of change as economies shift to higher productivity.[221]

Taken together, entrepreneurship plays a big role throughout the process of economic development, not just at the innovation-driven stage, and entrepreneurship makes a continuing contribution in various forms such as employment, innovation, and welfare. Acs and Szerb argued that relationship between entrepreneurship and economic development was "S-shaped": during the first transition—factor-driven stage to efficiency-driven stage—entrepreneurship plays a minimum role in productive entrepreneurship; however, entrepreneurship become increasingly important during the efficiency-driven stage and throughout the transition to the innovation-driven stage. Acs and Szerb also made the interesting observation that "economic activity" can be characterized as a societal "resource" that is capable of increasing and expanding over time as institutional support strengthens and the society learns how to use entrepreneurship in productive, rather than unproductive and destructive, ways.[222]

---

[221] Id.

[222] Acs, Z., and L. Szerb. June 2010. "The Global Entrepreneurship and Development Index (GEDI)." Paper Presented at Summer Conference 2010 on "Opening Up Innovation: Strategy, Organization and Technology." Imperial College London Business School) (citing Baumol, W. 1990. "Entrepreneurship: Productive, Unproductive and Destructive." *Journal of Political Economy* 98, pp. 893–921; and Acemoglu, D., S. Johnson, and J. Robinson. 2001. "The Colonial Origins of Comparative Development: An Empirical Investigation." *American Economic Review* 91, no. 5, pp. 1369–401). For further discussion of the Global Entrepreneurship and Development Index, see "Research on Entrepreneurship" in "Entrepreneurship: A Library of Resources for Sustainable Entrepreneurs." Prepared and distributed by the Sustainable Entrepreneurship Project (www.seproject.org).

Naude et al. acknowledged the utility of the model created by Acs and Szerb but also argued that it tends to "understate the importance of innovation by entrepreneurial innovation in the early stage of [economic] development."[223] Naude et al. believed that it was important to distinguish between "incremental" and "radical" innovations and focus on the impact that a particular type of innovation has on the local economy. Using this criterion, innovations that might not be that important in developed countries can, in fact, be quite significant in developing countries that are embarking on "catch-up change." For example, entrepreneurs in developing countries engage in innovation when they imitate products or processes originally developed in other parts of the world and adapt them for use in their local economies. This type of "innovation" serves an essential function with respect to technology upgrading and increasing production efficiency. Developing countries can also benefit from another type of "innovation": development of the capacity to "absorb and creatively adapt international technological knowledge . . . [to] . . . achieve accelerated growth,"[224] skills that served countries such as Chile, China, Korea, and Taiwan well. Finally, the "mere" exploitation of new markets and development of new ways to organize businesses, each somewhat commonplace in developed countries, is a key method of innovation in developing countries. Naude et al. concisely described the important role of "innovation" at the earlier stages of development as follows:

> Entrepreneurs in low-income developing countries provide innovations that are important for firm and country growth, even if they are incremental in nature. Innovation in developing countries involves the process by which firms master and implement the design and production of goods and services that are new to them. Many small improvements in product design and quality,

---

[223] Naude, W., A. Szirmai, and M. Goedhuys. November 1, 2011. *Policy Brief: Innovation and Entrepreneurship in Developing Countries*, 3. Helsinki, Finland: United Nations University-World Institute for Development Economics Research.
[224] Id.

changes in the way production is organized, creativity in marketing and modifications in production processes and techniques reduce costs, increase efficiency and flexibility to respond to changes in competitive conditions and enhance productivity and employment growth. In emerging economies innovation involves upgrading and shifting to higher levels of technological sophistication . . . Innovation plays an important role in catch-up and growth in a globalized economy.[225]

While on the face of it one might assume that entrepreneurship would have a positive impact on economic and social development, there are those that have questioned this proposition. Baumol, for example, has observed that "entrepreneurship can take various forms, and not everything labeled as 'entrepreneurial' might be desirable from a macroeconomic and societal perspective."[226] If this is true, policymakers developing tools to encourage and support "entrepreneurism" need to have a better understanding of just what types of entrepreneurial activities are likely to have the most positive impact on economic development. Baumol distinguished between "productive" and "unproductive" entrepreneurship while commenting that

. . . there are a variety of roles among which the entrepreneur's efforts can be allocated, and some of those roles do not following the constructive and innovative script that is conventionally attributed to that person. Indeed, at times the entrepreneur may even lead a parasitical existence that is actually damaging to the economy. How the entrepreneur acts at a given time and place

---

[225] Szirmai, A., W. Naude, and M. Goedhuys, eds. 2011. *Entrepreneurship, Innovation and Economic Development*, 26–27. Oxford: Oxford University Press.

[226] Baumol, W. 1990. "Entrepreneurship—Productive, Unproductive, and Destructive." *Journal of Political Economy* 98, no. 5, pp. 893–921, as cited in Welter, F. 2010. "Entrepreneurship and Development—Do We Really Know Which Entrepreneurship Types Contribute (Most)?" Strategic Entrepreneurship—The Promise for Future Entrepreneurship, Family Business and SME Research? Papers Presented to the Beitrage zu den Rencontres de St-Gall 2010, St. Gallen: KMU-Verlag HSG.

depends heavily on the rules of the game—the reward structure in the economy—that happen to prevail.[227]

Welter explained that "[p]roductive entrepreneurship includes any activity that indirectly or directly contribute to economic output or the capacity of the economy to produce additional output," while unproductive, or "destructive" entrepreneurship "includes, but is not limited to, rent seeking, illegal activities, and shadow activities or different forms of corruption."[228] This distinction is sometimes simplified by assuming that the activities of legal, registered businesses are productive and that the activities of illegal, informal businesses are unproductive and, in fact, destructive in those instances where they attract followers that engage in wholesale circumvention and defiance of the legal and normative framework of the society.[229] Assuming all of this is true, policymakers developing tools to encourage and support "entrepreneurship" need to have a good understanding of just what types of entrepreneurial activities are likely to have the most positive impact on economic development.

While much of the research regarding entrepreneurship and economic development assumes that there is a direct correlation between the success of the entrepreneurial activities at the "micro," or venture, level and the contribution of those activities to society at the "macro" level, it is useful to analyze a particular set of activities using the model developed by Davidsson and Wiklund, which allows for the fact that entrepreneurial activities may have either positive or negative outcomes at both the venture (i.e., micro) and societal (i.e., macro) levels.[230] The result is a typology of four different enterprises that can be described as follows:

- "Hero" or "success" enterprises, which have positive
  societal and venture level outcomes, generally as a result

---

[227] Id.

[228] Id.

[229] Id.

[230] Davidsson, P., and J. Wiklund. 2001. "Levels of Analysis in Entrepreneurship Research: Current Research Practice and Suggestions for the Future." *Entrepreneurship: Theory & Practice* 25, no. 4, p. 81.

of introducing new products or services and creating personal income and wealth.

- "Robber" or "re-distributive" enterprises, which are successful at the venture level, yet contribute nothing at the societal level since their success is tied to the use of strategies that Baumol would classify as "unproductive."
- "Catalyst" enterprises, which may not be successful at the venture level, yet do make a positive contribution at the societal level. An example would be a venture that develops ideas and methods that do not generate profit for that venture but which eventually are successfully imitated and productively exploited by others in the future.
- "Failed" enterprises, which are unsuccessful at both the venture and societal levels.

However, this model does not fully explain how things work in the "real economy." For example, Davidsson pointed out that ". . . we have to live with the fact that in real economies 'legal, yet re-distributive' and 'illegal, yet societal beneficial' are both possible."[231] In addition, even enterprises that eventually are found to fall within the "hero" category may sometimes engaged in activities generally thought to be "unproductive" from a societal level at some point during their development. Even "failed" enterprises cannot be totally dismissed since it is feasible to imagine that the entrepreneurs involved with these enterprises may have learned from their failures and applied this knowledge to new enterprises that were more successful.[232]

Other researchers have found evidence that entrepreneurs "switch" between "proprietorship" behavior, which focuses primarily on income and survival for the individual entrepreneur and his or her family, and

---

[231] Davidsson, P. 2004. *Researching Entrepreneurship*. New York, NY: Springer.

[232] Sauka, A., and F. Welter. 2007. "Productive, Unproductive and Destructive Entrepreneurship in an Advanced Transition Setting: The Example of Latvian Small Enterprises." In *Empirical Entrepreneurship in Europe: New Perspectives*, eds. M. Dowling and J. Schmude, 87–105. Cheltenham, UK, Northampton, MA: Elgar.

so-called *opportunity-based* or *dynamic* entrepreneurship that is more focused on growth and business development and discussed elsewhere in this chapter. For example, while entrepreneurs may have the skills and desire to oversee growth-oriented ventures, their initial goals may be largely necessity-based as they struggle to create a basic income for themselves and limit their activities to satisfying local demand. As time goes by, however, and they are more confident in the sustainability of their venture they may shift toward strategies that are most consistent with opportunity-based entrepreneurship. In addition, researchers analyzing entrepreneurship in the transitional economies of the former socialist countries in Eastern Europe have concluded that most new and small companies are engaged in both productive and unproductive activities at the same time, a situation that the researchers attribute to the lack of formal laws and regulations in those countries and the corresponding need of entrepreneurs to engage in "defiance and avoidance strategies," particularly rent seeking, in order to simply survive in a turbulent, ambiguous, and uncertain environment.[233] Welter concluded that analyzing entrepreneurship using just

---

[233] Welter, F. 2010. "Entrepreneurship and Development—Do We Really Know Which Entrepreneurship Types Contribute (Most)?" *Strategic Entrepreneurship—The Promise for Future Entrepreneurship, Family Business and SME Research?* Papers presented to the Beitrage zu den Rencontres de St-Gall 2010, St. Gallen: KMU-Verlag HSG, (citing Manolova, T., and A. Yan. 2002. "Institutional Constraints and Entrepreneurial Responses in a Transforming Economy: The Case of Bulgaria." *International Small Business Journal* 20, no. 2, pp. 163–84); Rehn, A., and S. Taalas. 2004. "Znakomstva I Svyazi' (Acquaintances and connections)-Blat, the Soviet Union, and Mundane Entrepreneurship." *Entrepreneurship and Regional Development* 16, no. 3, pp. 235–50; Smallbone, D., and F. Welter. 2001. "The Distinctiveness of Entrepreneurship in Transition Economies." *Small Business Economics* 16, no. 4, pp. 249–62; Smallbone, D., and F. Welter. 2009. *Entrepreneurship and Small Business Development in Post-socialist Economies.* London: Routledge; Welter, F., and D. Smallbone. 2009. "The Emergence of Entrepreneurial Potential in Transition Environments: A Challenge for Entrepreneurship Theory or a Developmental Perspective?" In *Entrepreneurship and Growth in Local, Regional and National Economies: Frontiers in European Entrepreneurship Research*, eds. D. Mallbone, L. Hans and D. Jones-Evans, 339–53. Cheltenham, UK, Northampton, MA: Edward Elgar; Yan, A., and T. Manolova. 1998. "New and Small Players on Shaky Ground: A Multi-case Study of Emerging

assessments of "activities" (i.e., productive or unproductive) or measures of output provides an incomplete picture and that it is necessary to take into account both activities and output in a nonjudgmental fashion and consider the environment in which the entrepreneur is operating and the likelihood that strategies may change over time.[234] Welter also pointed out that it could reasonably be assumed that once entrepreneurs in these economies have survived the initial stages of formation and organization using any means possible some of them may "develop their activities from simply trading toward more substantial businesses."

Entrepreneurial Firms in a Transforming Economy." *Journal of Applied Management Studies* 7, no. 1, pp. 139–43.

[234] Welter, F. 2010. "Entrepreneurship and Development—Do We really Know Which Entrepreneurship Types Contribute (Most)?" *Strategic Entrepreneurship— The Promise for Future Entrepreneurship, Family Business and SME Research?* Papers presented to the Beitrage zu den Rencontres de St-Gall 2010, St. Gallen: KMU-Verlag HSG.

CHAPTER 2

Research on Entrepreneurship

Introduction

Entrepreneurship has emerged as a popular career option across the globe and there has been an intense interest in the subject shown by researchers and policymakers in both developed and developing countries. Research relating to entrepreneurship has been expanding rapidly and the researchers have dwelt on a diverse range of issues. In 2003, for example, Richtermeyer published the results of her review of 77 abstracts of articles published then recently in academic journals and then compiled the following extensive list of the areas of emerging research on entrepreneurship at that time: culture/ethnicity; economic growth; education/learning; entrepreneurship theory and practice; ethics; family-owned businesses; finance; firm performance/planning; gender; human resources; intrapreneurship versus entrepreneurship; international entrepreneurship, cross-national comparisons, and individual country studies; internationalization, exporting, and small business; motivation/firm creation or dissolution/founder characteristics; quality systems; resource-based views of the firm; social networks, business groups, and alliances; strategic planning and product development; supply chain management and distribution; teams; technology and technology-based firms; and venture capital.[1] In addition, the interest in entrepreneurship is no longer confined to developing countries and it is now well established that encouragement

---

[1] Richtermeyer, G. 2003. *Emerging Themes in Entrepreneurship Research.* University of Missouri, Business Research and Information Development Group. Richtermeyer also includes a comprehensive list of the articles that were reviewed.

of entrepreneurial activities, including new venture formation, can and should be an important policy tool for governments in emerging markets looking to stimulate economic growth and development.[2]

According to Austin et al., it is possible to identify three streams of research relating to entrepreneurship that focus on the results of entrepreneurship, the causes of entrepreneurship, and entrepreneurial management.[3] A well-known example of research on the results and impact of entrepreneurship is Schumpeter's theory of the entrepreneur as a "change agent" who identifies and attacks opportunities to harness innovation to engage in "creative destruction" that overturns the way business is being done in entire industries and markets.[4] Research on the causes of entrepreneurship includes work on understanding the personal drives and motivations of entrepreneurs and relies heavily on psychology and sociology.[5]

---

[2] See, for example, Harper, M. 1991. "The Role of Enterprise in Poor Countries." *Entrepreneurship Theory and Practice* 15, no. 4, pp. 7–11.
Gibb, A. 1993. "Small Business Development in Central and Eastern Europe—Opportunity for a Rethink?" *Journal of Business Venturing* 8, pp. 461–86.
Audretsch, D. 1991. The Role of Small Business in Restructuring Eastern Europe. Vaxjo, Sweden: 5th Workshop for Research in Entrepreneurship. Other studies that have identified entrepreneurship as a critical factor in national economic development include Birley, S. 1987. "New Ventures and Employment Growth." *Journal of Business Venturing* 2, no. 2, pp. 155–65;
Reynolds, P. 1987. "New Firms: Societal Contributions Versus Survival Potential." *Journal of Business Venturing* 2, no. 3, pp. 231–46; Morris, M., and P. Lewis. 1991. "Entrepreneurship as a Significant Factor in Societal Quality of Life." *Journal of Business Research* 23, no. 1, pp. 21–36; and Shane, S., L. Kolvereid, and P. Westhead. 1991. "An Exploratory Examination of the Reasons Leading to New Firm Formation across Country and Gender (Part 1)." *Journal of Business Venturing* 6, no. 6, pp. 431–46.
[3] Stevenson, H., and J. Jarillo. 1991. "A New Entrepreneurial Paradigm" In *Socio-economics: Toward a New Synthesis*, eds. A. Etzioni and P. Lawrence, 185. Armonk, NY: M. E. Sharpe.
[4] Schumpeter, J. 1934. *The Theory of Economic Development*. Cambridge, MA: Harvard University Press.
[5] See, for example, Collins, O., and D. Moore. 1964. *The Enterprising Man*. East Lansing, MI: Michigan State University and McClelland, D. 1961. *The Achieving Story*. Princeton, NJ: D. Van Nostrand.

Research on entrepreneurial management focuses on the practical steps that must be taken to execute exploitation of opportunities in an entrepreneurial manner and includes research on the dynamics of startups and venture capital,[6] intrapreneurship (i.e., entrepreneurial innovation inside established companies),[7] organizational life cycles,[8] and predictors of entrepreneurial success.[9]

Austin et al. were particularly interested in the last of three research streams mentioned above, which they described as the "how" of entrepreneurship (i.e., how opportunities are recognized, the process of committing to an opportunity, the steps taken to gain control over resources, the steps taken to generate success and new information that can be used in the pursuit of additional resources, management of a network of resources that may or may not be within a single hierarchy, and the decision made about allocating rewards among the participants).[10] They suggested that in order to better understand the process of entrepreneurial management reference should be made to an analytical framework proposed by

[6] See, for example, Timmons, J., and W. Bygrave. 1986. "Venture Capital's Role in Financing Innovation for Economic Growth." *Journal of Business Venturing* 1, p. 161.

[7] See, for example, Burgelman, R. 1983. "Corporate Entrepreneurship and Strategic Management: Insights from a Process Study." *Management Science* 29, p. 1349. and Burgelman, R. 1984. "Designs for Corporate Entrepreneurship in Established Firms." *California Management Review* 26, p. 154.

[8] See, for example, Quinn, R., and K. Cameron. 1983. "Organizational Life Cycles and Shifting Criteria of Effectiveness." *Management Science* 29, p. 33.

[9] See, for example, Cooper, A., and A. Bruno. August 1975. "Predicting Performance in New High-Technology Firms." *Academy of Management, Proceedings of the 35th Annual Meeting*, 426; and Dollinger, M. 1984. "Environmental Boundary Spanning and Information Processing Effects on Organizational Performance." *Academy of Management Journal* 27, p. 351.

[10] Stevenson, H. 1985. "The Heart of Entrepreneurship." *Harvard Business Review* 63, p. 85; and Stevenson, H., and J. Jarillo. 1991. "A New Entrepreneurial Paradigm." In *Socio-Economics: Toward a New Synthesis,* eds. A. Etzioni, and P. Lawrence, 185. Armonk, NY: M.E. Sharpe.

Sahlman, which is based on four interrelated elements that are crucial for entrepreneurial activity[11]:

- *People*: This element is defined as those who actively participate in the venture or who bring resources to the venture and includes both those within the organization and those outside the organization who must be involved in order for the venture to be successful. This element includes not only the personal characteristics of the entrepreneur such as his or her skills, attitudes, contacts, goals, and values, but also the cumulative skills, attitudes, knowledge, contacts, goals, and values of all participants who provide the mix of resources that contribute to the success of the venture.

- *Context*: This element includes relevant factors that are generally outside of the control of the entrepreneur but which are expected to have an impact on his or her activities. Examples include the general economy, taxes, and other regulations and the sociopolitical institutions in the areas in which the entrepreneur intends to operate. Specific contextual factors identified by Austin et al. included economic environment, taxation policies, employment levels, technological advances, and social movements such as those involving labor, religion, and politics. Entrepreneurs need to understand that context frames the opportunities and risks for every new venture and need to determine which factors must be consciously addressed from a strategic perspective and which are best left to play out as they will since the entrepreneur has limited

---

[11] Adapted from Austin, J., H. Stevenson, and J. Wei-Skillern. 2006. "Social and Commercial Entrepreneurship: Same, Different, or Both?" *Entrepreneurship Theory and Practice* 30, no. 1, p. 1; citing Sahlman, W. 1996. "Some Thoughts on Business Plans." In *The Entrepreneurial Venture*, eds. W. Sahlman, H. Stevenson, M. Roberts, and A. Bhide, 138. Boston, MA: Harvard Business School Press, and van Eijck, P. 2012. *Sustainable Entrepreneurship: Institutional Profile and Cross-Country Comparison: Denmark & US and Its Viability*. Rotterdam: Bachelor Thesis in Entrepreneurship, Strategy and Organizations Economics from Erasmus School of Economics.

time and ability to attend to everything that might have an impact on the venture.

- *Deal*: Austin et al. used the term "deal" to refer to the substance of the bargain that defines who among the participants in a venture gives what, who among the participants in the venture gets what, and how and when those deliveries and receipts will take place. The deal emerges from a bargaining process that normally addresses topics such as economic benefits, social recognition, autonomy and decisions rights, satisfaction of deep personal needs, social interactions, fulfillment of generative and legacy desires, and delivery on altruistic goals.[12]

- *Opportunity*: In order for the entrepreneur to spring into action he or she must perceive an opportunity, which Austin et al. defined as "any activity requiring the investment of scarce resources in hopes of a future return."[13] The entrepreneur must have a vision of a future that is better for him or her and must be able to develop and implement a credible path to change the current situation to that desired future state. Austin et al. observed that "change" is generally difficult and it is challenging for entrepreneurs to bring followers together to agree on a common definition of opportunity and change that can be shared and used as a motivation for joint action by the multiple constituencies that must work together in order to create the desired change. For example, change usually impacts power relationships, economic interests, personal networks, and even the self-image of participants.

---

[12] Martin, R., and S. Osberg. Spring 2007. "Social Entrepreneurship: The Case for Definition." *Stanford Social Innovation Review*, p. 28.

[13] Austin, J., H. Stevenson, and J. Wei-Skillern. 2006. "Social and Commercial Entrepreneurship: Same, Different, or Both?" *Entrepreneurship Theory and Practice* 30, no. 1, p. 5; citing Sahlman, W. 1996. "Some Thoughts on Business Plans." In *The Entrepreneurial Venture*, eds. W. Sahlman, H. Stevenson, M. Roberts, and A. Bhide, 138, 140. Boston, MA: Harvard Business School Press.

While each element of the framework above, which is often referred to as the "PCDO" model, is introduced and described separately, Austin et al. made it clear that they must be understood and applied as being interdependent and situationally determined and that the fit among them are continuously changing and must be carefully monitored. For example, Austin et al. pointed out that changes in "context" often require bringing in new people with different skill sets and jettison other people whose skills have become obsolete and that these changes will usually trigger the need for bargaining around a restructured "deal" among the new group of participants. Changes in context can also cause entrepreneurs to perceive new opportunities that require a different strategy and path to change that will impact each of the other elements.

Mueller and Thomas have observed that while entrepreneurship has clearly become a popular topic around the world a number of interesting and important questions regarding entrepreneurial activities and formation of new ventures remain to be answered with respect to countries other than the United States.[14] In fact, one of the most interesting and promising areas of entrepreneurship research is "international entrepreneurship," which Oviatt and McDougall defined as "(...) the discovery, enactment, evaluation, and exploitation of opportunities—across national borders—to create future goods and services."[15] Hessels has explained that, as a field of research, international entrepreneurship involves "research into entrepreneurship in multiple countries (cross-country comparisons of the nature and extent of entrepreneurial activity) and research into cross-border entrepreneurship (international activity of SMEs and new ventures)."[16]

---

[14] Mueller, S., and A. Thomas. 2001. "Culture and Entrepreneurial Potential: A Nine Country Study of Locus of Control and Innovativeness." *Journal of Business Venturing* 16, no. 1, pp. 51–75, 53.

[15] Oviatt, B., and P. McDougall. 2005. "Defining International Entrepreneurship and Modeling the Speed of Internationalization." *Entrepreneurship Theory and Practice* 29, no. 5, pp. 537–53.

[16] Hessels, J. 2008. "International Entrepreneurship: An Introduction, Framework and Research Agenda Zoetermeer." *The Netherlands: Scientific Analysis of Entrepreneurship and SMEs* 4; citing Lu, J., and P. Beamish. 2001. "The Internationalization and Performance of SMEs." *Strategic Management Journal* 22, nos. 6/7, pp. 565–86; Coviello, N., and M. Jones. 2004. "Methodological Issues

It is believed that international entrepreneurship first appeared in the literature in the late 1980s and began as a response to evidence that technological advances and cultural awareness were driving new ventures beyond their more familiar domestic environments toward entering previously untapped foreign markets.[17] McDougall and Oviatt noted research activities under the umbrella of international entrepreneurship expanded beyond "new venture internationalization" to include topics such as national culture,[18] alliances and cooperative strategies,[19] small and medium-sized company internationalization,[20] top management

---

in International Entrepreneurship Research." *Journal of Business Venturing* 19, no. 4, pp. 485–508, and Oviatt. B., and P. McDougall. 2005. "Defining International Entrepreneurship and Modeling the Speed of Internationalization." *Entrepreneurship Theory and Practice* 29, no. 5, pp. 537–53. McDougall and Oviatt explained that "The Scholarly Field of International Entrepreneurship Examines and Compares—Across National Borders—how, by whom, and with what effects those opportunities are acted upon." McDougall, P., and B. Oviatt. 2012. *Some Fundamental Issues in International Entrepreneurship*. United States Association for Small Business and Entrepreneurship. http://usasbe.org/knowledge/whitepapers/mcdougall2003.pdf (accessed March 31, 2012).

[17] Morrow, M. 1988. "International Entrepreneurship: A New Growth Opportunity, 3 New Mgmt." pp. 59–61; Zahra, S., and G. George. 2002. "International Entrepreneurship: The Current Status of the Field and Future Research Agenda." In *Strategic Entrepreneurship: Creating a New Mindset*, eds. M. Hitt, R.D. Ireland, S. Camp, and D.L. Sexton.

[18] McGrath, R., and I. MacMillan. 1992. "More Like Each Other than Anyone Else? A Cross-Cultural Study of Entrepreneurial Perceptions." *Journal of Business Venturing* 7, no. 5, pp. 419–29; Thomas, A., and S. Mueller. 2000. "A Case for Comparative Entrepreneurship: Assessing the Relevance of Culture." *Journal of International Business Studies* 31, no. 2, pp. 287–301.

[19] Steensma, H., L. Marino, M. Weaver, and P. Dickson. 2000. "The Influence of National Culture in the Formation of Technology Alliances by Entrepreneurial Firms." *Academy of Management Journal* 43, no. 5, pp. 951–73; Li, H., and K. Atuahene-Gima. 2001. "Product Innovation Strategy and the Performance of New Technology Ventures in China." *Academy of Management Journal* 44, no. 6, pp. 1123–134.

[20] Lu, J., and P. Beamish. 2001. "The Internationalization and Performance of SMEs." *Strategic Management Journal* 22, nos. 6–7, pp. 565–86.

teams,[21] entry modes, cognition,[22] country profiles,[23] corporate entrepreneurship,[24] exporting,[25] knowledge management,[26] venture financing,[27] technological learning,[28] and entrepreneurship in developing countries. They also reported that international entrepreneurship research had quickly become multidisciplinary and attracted the interest and resources of researchers in the areas of international business, entrepreneurship, anthropology, economics, psychology, finance, marketing, and sociology. Another indicator of growing interest in international entrepreneurship has been the increased coverage of the topic in leading academic journals and the launch of a completely new journal, the *Journal of International*

---

[21] Reuber, A., and E. Fischer. 1997. "The Influence of the Management Team's International Experience on the Internationalization Behavior of SMEs." *Journal of International Business Studies* 28, no. 4, pp. 807–25.

[22] Mitchell, R., K. Smith, W. Seawright, and E. Morse. 2000. "Cross-Cultural Cognitions and the Venture Creation Decision." *Academy of Management Journal* 43, no. 5, pp. 974–93.

[23] Busenitz, L.W., C. Gomez, and J.W. Spencer. 2000. "Country Institutional Profiles: Unlocking Entrepreneurial Phenomena." *Academy of Management Journal* 43, no. 5, pp. 994–1003.

[24] Birkinshaw, J. 1997. "Entrepreneurship in Multinational Corporations: The Characteristics of Subsidiary Initiatives." *Strategic Management Journal*, pp. 207–29.

[25] Bilkey, W.J., and G. Tesar. 1977. "The Export Behavior of Smaller-Sized Wisconsin Manufacturing Firms." *Journal of International Business Studies* 8, no. 1, pp. 93–98.

[26] Kuemmerle, W. 2002. "Home Base and Knowledge Management in International Ventures." *Journal of Business Venturing* 17, pp. 99–122.

[27] Roure, J., R. Keeley, and T. Keller. 1992. "Venture Capital Strategies in Europe and the U.S. Adapting to the 1990's." In *Frontiers of Entrepreneurship Research*, eds. N. Churchill et al., 345–59.

Zahra, S., R. Ireland, and M. Hitt. 2000. "International Expansion by New Venture Firms: International Diversity, Mode of Market Entry, Technological Learning and Performance." *Academy of Management Journal* 43, pp. 925–50.

[28] Zahra, S., R. Ireland, and M. Hitt. 2000. "International Expansion by New Venture Firms: International Diversity, Mode of Market Entry, Technological Learning and Performance." *Academy of Management Journal* 43, pp. 925–50.

Entrepreneurship, dedicated specifically to the field.[29] In any event, international entrepreneurship is a field that remains relatively new and immature from a research perspective and holds great promise for informing policymakers and educators about how best to encourage meaningful new business formation that contributes to economic growth and development.

Global Entrepreneurship Monitor

The Global Entrepreneurship Monitor (GEM) is a partnership between the London Business School and Babson College that administers a comprehensive research program to produce annual assessments of national levels of entrepreneurial activity. The project was first launched in 1999, when it covered just 10 countries, and has since grown to cover as many as 85 countries in subsequent years and is recognized as the largest ongoing study of entrepreneurial dynamics in the world. The main objectives of the GEM program are measurement of differences in the level of entrepreneurial activity between countries, uncovering the factors that lead to appropriate levels of entrepreneurship, and making suggestions for policies that may lead to enhancement of national levels of entrepreneurial activity. The GEM, like other models, has always been focused on exploration of the link between entrepreneurship and economic development and its original model attempted to integrate several variables thought necessary to enable business activity including entrepreneurial capacity, entrepreneurial opportunities, and certain "entrepreneurial framework conditions" discussed in more detail below. Recently, the GEM model was revised to take into account that the contribution of entrepreneurs to an economy varies according to its phase of economic development, with

---

[29] For useful reviews of international entrepreneurship literature and research issues, see McDougall, P., and B. Oviatt. 1997. "International Entrepreneurship Literature in the 1990s and Directions for Future Research." In *Entrepreneurship 2000*, eds. D. Sexton and R. Smilor, 291; Zahra, S., and G. George. 2002. "International Entrepreneurship: The Current Status of the Field and Future Research Agenda." In *Strategic Entrepreneurship: Creating a New Mindset*, eds. M. Hitt, R. Ireland, S. Camp, and D. Sexton.

those phases being defined in the manner suggested by Porter et al. and described elsewhere in this chapter, namely "factor-driven economies," "efficiency-driven economies," and "innovation-driven economies." A large amount of information regarding the work of the GEM researchers is available at the program's website and in addition to the annual global reports, such as the one for 2011 referred to herein, there are a number of country-specific "national reports" that provide international benchmarking, local context, and recommendations for national entrepreneurship policies.

The GEM is based on a conceptual model of the institutional environment and its effect on entrepreneurship. The model recognizes the importance of the social, cultural, and political context in which entrepreneurial activities occur and assumes that these contextual factors influence three sets of conditions: basic requirements, which include institutions, infrastructure, macroeconomic stability, health, and primary education; "efficiency enhancers," which include higher education, goods and labor market efficiency, financial market sophistication, technological readiness, and market size; and the "entrepreneurial framework conditions" discussed below. Entrepreneurship itself is measured by looking at the entrepreneurship profile of prospective and actual entrepreneurs, including their attitudes, activities, and aspirations, and at the entrepreneurship process itself. The GEM researchers acknowledge that entrepreneurship is a process that extends over multiple phases, thus allowing opportunities for assessing the state of entrepreneurship in a particular society at different phases. These entrepreneurship phases are briefly summarized as follows[30]:

- *Potential entrepreneurs*: These are persons who see opportunities in their areas, believe they have the abilities and resources to start businesses to pursue those opportunities, and who are not deterred by fear of failure in pursuing those opportunities. The level of broader societal support for entrepreneurship is

---

[30] Kelley, D., S. Singer, and M. Herrington. 2012. *Global Entrepreneurship Monitor: 2011 Global Report*, 5. Babson Park, MA: Global Entrepreneurship Research Association.

also important at this phase. The GEM survey uses a variety of measures of entrepreneurial perceptions, intentions, and societal attitudes including perceived opportunities, perceived capabilities, fear of failure, entrepreneurial intentions, entrepreneurship as a "good career choice," high status to successful entrepreneurs, and media attention for entrepreneurship.

- *Expected entrepreneurs*: Expected entrepreneurs are those persons who have not yet started a business but who have expressed an expectation that they would start a business within the next three years.
- *Nascent activity*: This phase covers the first three months after the entrepreneur establishes a new business to pursue the identified opportunities.
- *New business owners*: These are persons who have successfully emerged from the nascent phase and have been in business more than three months but less than three and one-half years.
- *Established businesses*: These are businesses that have been operating for more than three and one-half years, thus moving beyond "new business owner" status.
- *Discontinued businesses*: Discontinued businesses, regardless of how long they were operating, are factored into the analysis because they are a source of experienced entrepreneurs who may start new businesses and/or use their expertise and experience to support other entrepreneurs (e.g., by providing financing and/or business advice).

Data collection for the GEM project includes a minimum of 2,000 adult (i.e., 18–64 years of age) population surveys in each GEM country to track the entrepreneurial attitudes, activity, and aspirations of individuals; and input and assessment from a minimum of 36 experts in each GEM country on "entrepreneurial framework conditions" (EFCs) that are thought to reflect major features of a country's socioeconomic milieu that are expected to have a significant impact on the entrepreneurial sector. The adult population surveys provide a means for measuring individual involvement in venture creation, identifying the motives of entrepreneurs, measuring the aspirations of entrepreneurs with respect to pursuing high growth and/or activities in foreign markets, and understanding the societal climate for entrepreneurship. The "climate for entrepreneurship" includes not only the perceptions of prospective entrepreneurs regarding the availability of opportunities around them, their ability to start businesses, and the value of doing so but also the availability of positive support from others regarding entrepreneurship as measured by "societal perceptions" of entrepreneurship and the willingness of vendors and investors to supply tangible and financial resources. The national expert surveys measure the following nine EFCs:

- *Finance*: The availability of financial resources—equity and debt—for small and medium enterprises (SMEs) (including grants and subsidies);
- *Government policies*: The extent to which taxes or regulations are either size-neutral or encourage SMEs;
- *Government programs*: The presence and quality of direct programs to assist new and growing firms at all levels of government (national, regional, municipal);
- *Entrepreneurial education and training*: The extent to which training in creating or managing SMEs is incorporated within the education and training system at all levels (primary, secondary, and postschool);
- *R&D transfer*: The extent to which national research and development will lead to new commercial opportunities and is available to SMEs;
- *Commercial and professional infrastructure*: The presence of property rights and commercial, accounting, and other legal services and institutions that support or promote SMEs;
- *Entry regulation*: Contains two components including "market dynamics," which is the level of change in markets from year to year, and "market openness," which is the extent to which new firms are free to enter existing markets;
- *Physical infrastructure and services*: Ease of access to physical resources—communication, utilities, transportation, land, or space—at a price that does not discriminate against SMEs; and

- *Cultural and social norms*: The extent to which social and cultural norms encourage or allow actions leading to new business methods or activities that can potentially increase personal wealth and income.

The GEM researchers measure the total early-stage entrepreneurial activity (TEA) for each country by identifying and combining entrepreneurs who are either engaged in nascent activities or acting as new business owners. In addition to a TEA rate for each country, the GEM researchers also score and rank countries with respect to established business ownership rate, discontinuation of businesses, necessity-driven entrepreneurship as a percentage of TEA, and improvement-driven opportunity entrepreneurship as a percentage of TEA. Countries are grouped by their phase of economic development so that comparisons can be made among comparable countries and researchers can also track how entrepreneurial activities change as countries develop economically and socially. As noted above, the GEM researchers borrowed from Porter by suggesting that countries go through three stages of economic development: a factor-driven stage; an efficiency-driven stage; and, finally, an innovation-driven stage.[31] Acs and Szerb have provided the following brief descriptions of each of these stages[32]:

- The factor-driven stage is marked by high rates of agricultural self-employment and countries in this stage generally compete based on low-cost efficiencies in the production of commodities or low value-added products. Countries in this stage do not create knowledge that can be used for innovation nor do they use knowledge to engage in exporting activities. In the 2011 GEM survey, for example, seven of the 54 countries fell into the factor-driven stage including Guatemala (with the

---

[31] Porter, M. 2002. *Global Competitiveness Report*. Geneva: World Economic Forum.

[32] Acs, Z., and L. Szerb. June 2010. "The Global Entrepreneurship and Development Index (GEDI)." Paper Presented at Summer Conference 2010 on "Opening Up Innovation: Strategy, Organization and Technology." Imperial College London Business School.

highest TEA among the group) and Pakistan (with the lowest TEA among the group).[33]

- The efficiency-driven stage requires that countries engage in efficient productive practices in large markets so that firms are able to achieve and exploit economies of scale. Industries in this stage are generally manufacturing-based and focused on the production and distribution of basic goods and services. Self-employment tends to decline during this stage and capital, labor, and technology begin to emerge as the key drivers of productivity. In the 2011 GEM survey, for example, 24 of the 54 countries fell into the efficiency-driven stage including China, Chile, and Peru with the highest TEA rates among the group and Hungary, Malaysia, and Russia with the lowest TEA rates among the group.[34]

- In the innovation-driven stage, the key input is "knowledge" and decisions about embarking on new projects are based primarily on expected net returns and the likelihood that economic activities can generate high value-added products and services. In the 2011 GEM survey, for example, 23 of the 54 countries fell into the efficiency-driven stage including Australia and the United States with the highest TEA rates among the group and Denmark, Japan, and Slovenia with the lowest TEA rates among the group.[35]

As discussed below, as countries transition between stages of development there will be changes in their entrepreneurship profile. Even among comparable countries, countries at the same stage of economic development, the rate and profile of entrepreneurship may vary significantly due to environmental constraints that are specific to a given country. For example, a country may have a high rate of startup activity but

[33] Kelley, D., S. Singer, and M. Herrington. 2012. *Global Entrepreneurship Monitor: 2011 Global Report*, 10. Babson Park, MA: Global Entrepreneurship Research Association.

[34] Id. at pp. 10–11.

[35] Id. at p. 11.

fail to maintain that rate at the established business phase due to societal factors that make it difficult for nascent entrepreneurs to maintain their momentum and get their businesses to the point where they are sustainable. In addition, the GEM researchers have often cautioned that higher TEAs do not necessarily imply better economic conditions. For example, certain nations with higher levels of TEA, such as the United Arab Emirates, Iceland, and Greece, experienced severe economic distress in the early 2010s and some innovation-driven economies, such as Japan, have historically had low levels of TEA.

For 2011 survey results obtained from interviewing over 140,000 adults in 54 countries led the GEM researchers to make the following estimates[36]:

- There were 388 million entrepreneurs who were actively engaged in starting and running new businesses.
- There were 163 million women early-stage entrepreneurs; however, in most of the surveyed countries the entrepreneurship rates for women were significantly lower than for men.
- There were 165 million young early-stage entrepreneurs (i.e., between the ages of 18 and 35) and, in general, early-stage entrepreneurs tended to be young to mid-career (i.e., from ages 25 to 44) and entrepreneurs tended to be younger in the efficiency-driven economies.
- 141 million of the early-stage entrepreneurs expected to create at least five new jobs in the next five years.
- 65 million of the early-stage entrepreneurs expected to create 20 or more new jobs in the next five years.
- 69 million of the early-stage entrepreneurs offered innovative products and services that are new to customers and have few other competitors.
- 18 million of the early-stage entrepreneurs sell at least 25 percent of their products and services internationally.

---

[36] Id at p. 4.

The results reported by the GEM researchers reflect some of the nuances in their assessment of entrepreneurial activity. In particular, the researchers who prepared the results of the 2011 GEM survey noted the interest in identifying the "profile of entrepreneurs," rather than just the number of entrepreneurs, and that the report focused on three profile factors: inclusiveness, including the availability of entrepreneurial activities to women and people of various ages; industry, realizing that the skills and other attributes of entrepreneurs will differ from industry to industry; and, finally, impact, which looks at the role of innovation in an entrepreneurial endeavor and the aspirations of the entrepreneur with respect to internationalization and growth.[37]

The 2011 GEM survey also generated data that allowed the researchers to reach various conclusions regarding entrepreneurial activities in the 54 countries that were part of the survey. Highlights included the following[38]:

- With regard to potential entrepreneurship, countries included among the factor-driven economies displayed higher average perceptions about entrepreneurial activities in their area than countries falling into the other two development levels and also displayed higher perceived capabilities to start a business than countries classified as efficiency- or innovation-driven economies. The researchers explained that these differences could be attributed to individuals having different ideas about what kind of businesses to establish based on their level of development and noted that consumer-oriented businesses were the most popular in factor-driven economies while innovation-driven economies had a higher proportion of business services enterprises than countries in the other two development levels.
- Potential entrepreneurship varied significantly among countries in the same level of economic development. For example, the researchers pointed out that while

---

[37] Id. at pp. 6, 15–21.
[38] Id at pp. 7–18.

Bangladesh, a factor-driven economy, scored highly on perceived opportunities, the pool of entrepreneurs in that country was reduced by a high lack of confidence in ability to start a business and a high fear of failure. On the other hand, another factor-driven economy, Venezuela, displayed only an average level of perceived opportunities but had strong positive opinions regarding ability to start a business and a low fear of failure.

- A number of European countries who had been pummeled by adverse economic conditions at the time of the survey had relatively low perceptions of opportunities, and low rates of opportunities and capabilities were also found in some of the innovation-driven Asian economies such as Japan, Korea, and Singapore. The score from the respondents from the United States with respect to perceived opportunities fell near the average of the innovation-driven economies; however, they were generally quite confident of their abilities to start a new business and had a relatively low fear of failure.

- The researchers asked respondents whether they felt that entrepreneurship was a "good career choice" and found that the percentage of respondents answering affirmatively declined as economic development improved. This finding was supported by the fact that perceptions about the status of entrepreneurs were higher in the factor-driven economies than in the other two development levels.

- Entrepreneurial intentions, as measured by the percentages of individuals who had not yet started a business but had expressed an intention to start a business within the next three years, were highest in factor-driven economies. Entrepreneurial intentions declined as the level of development increased. There was evidence that entrepreneurial intentions were influenced by the types of economic activities typically carried out in a country, with countries that placed a high emphasis on extractive resources (i.e., Russia and the United Arab Emirates) having relatively low entrepreneurial intention rates.

- From 2010 to 2011, there was a significant increase in TEA rates in many economies across all development levels, an interesting trend given the turbulent economic conditions that countries all over the world were experiencing during that time.

- Consumer-oriented business (e.g., retail enterprises) tended to dominate entrepreneurial activities at the factor-driven and efficiency-driven stages; however, business services, which rely and compete on knowledge and technology, were the most prominent among entrepreneurs in the innovation-driven economies.[39]

- Among factor-driven economies necessity- and improvement-driven opportunism as a percentage of total TEA is roughly the same; however, as the level of development increased, the necessity-driven opportunism became less important as a motivator to start a new business and improvement-driven opportunism became more important as a motivator.[40]

- Comparing TEA rates to the rate of established business ownership, the GEM researchers found that TEA rates were highest in the factor-driven economies and decreased as the level of development increased and necessity-driven entrepreneurship declined. There were significantly more early-stage entrepreneurs than established business owners in the factor-driven economies; however, on average, by the time

---

[39] Id. at p. 18. In addition to consumer-oriented businesses and business services, the GEM survey also tracked extractive and transforming activities.

[40] The GEM defined "necessity-driven" entrepreneurs as those persons who start new businesses because they have no other work options and need a source of income while improvement-driven entrepreneurs are defined as those persons interested in pursuing an opportunity and who do so in order to improve their incomes and/or independence in their work. Id. at p. 13. For further discussion of necessity-driven entrepreneurship and other methods for classifying "types of entrepreneurship," see "Definitions and Types of Entrepreneurship" in "Entrepreneurship: A Library of Resources for Sustainable Entrepreneurs" prepared and distributed by the Sustainable Entrepreneurship Project (www.seproject.org).

a country reached the innovation-driven stage it could be expected that the TEA rate would drop slightly and the level of established business ownership would go up.

• Business discontinuance declined as the level of economic development increased, a finding attributed, at least in part, to the higher proportion of entrepreneurs at the earlier development phases and the higher levels of risk that those entrepreneurs must overcome. Business closings among factor- and efficiency-driven economies were often blamed on a lack of profitability and sources of financing while business discontinuances in the innovation-driven economies were more likely due to retirement, sale, or the desire to pursue another opportunity.

The GEM researchers also focused on three other important measures of entrepreneurship: entrepreneur's expectations regarding growth in terms of number of persons who will be employed in five years, the degree of "innovation" involved in the entrepreneur's product or service and "internationalization" (i.e., the extent to which entrepreneurs sell to customers in foreign countries).[41] Innovation was measured by looking at the extent to which an entrepreneur's product or service was new to some or all customers of the entrepreneur and whether there were few or no other businesses offering the same product or service. Measured in this way innovation is context-dependent and determined by the entrepreneur's main customer market. Accordingly a product or service offered for the first time in one country would be deemed innovative with respect to that country even if the product or service is commonly sold by number of competitors in other countries. Internationalization was measured by looking at what percentage of the entrepreneurs in a given country had at least 25 percent of their customers in foreign countries.

The survey results included growth expectations for the 54 countries at three levels: 0–4 employees in five years (low growth expectations), 5–19

---

[41] Kelley, D., S. Singer, and M. Herrington. 2012. *Global Entrepreneurship Monitor: 2011 Global Report*, 18–21. Babson Park, MA: Global Entrepreneurship Research Association.

employees in five years (medium growth expectations), and 20 or more employees in five years (high growth expectations). While factor-driven economies had more entrepreneurs, most of them were in the low-growth category. On the other hand, innovation-driven economies had a lower percentage of entrepreneurs but those entrepreneurs were much more likely to have high growth expectations. As for innovativeness, it is not surprising that the researchers found that it increased along with the level of economic development. Finally, internationalization, like innovation, was lowest in the factor-driven economies but rose as economic development improved. Internationalization appeared to be influenced by factors other than just economic development such as the size of the population and land mass in the "home country" and the size and diversity of the local market.

The GEM researchers suggest that the nature of entrepreneurship and its contribution to the national economy changes as economies grow and development should be accompanied by changes in the emphasis of governmental policies. For example, since economic development in factor-driven economies is largely driven by the "basic requirements" in the GEM conceptual model of the relationship between the institutional context and entrepreneurship, emphasis during that phase should be placed on development of institutions, infrastructure, macroeconomic stability, and health and primary education. Once an economy transitions into the efficiency-driven phase, government policies should be focused "efficiency enhancers" including the proper (i.e., "efficient") functioning of goods and labor markets, development of higher education systems, enhancement of technological readiness, and increasing the scope and sophistication of financial markets. While these initiatives may not have an immediate direct impact on entrepreneurship, they will provide the foundation for attracting and enabling higher levels of entrepreneurship in the future. Finally, economies in, or about to enter, the innovation-driven phase requires governmental attention to each of the various EFCs mentioned above in order to create jobs and spur technical innovation.

The highest ratings for EFCs in the 2011 GEM survey came from the experts in the innovation-driven economies, which confirmed the assumption that the basic requirements and efficiency enhancers included the GEM theoretical model are more developed in those economies and thus it is appropriate to focus on the EFCs. Three of the EFCs were also considered to be quite important by experts from the factor-driven economies: postschool entrepreneurship education; internal market dynamics; and cultural and social norms for entrepreneurship. Significant differences between innovation-driven economies and factor-driven economies were found with respect to the following EFCs: government programs, physical infrastructure, R&D transfer, finance, and national policy.[42]

Global Entrepreneurship and Development Index

Acs and Szerb believed that the GEM project and its focus on the business formation process in a large number of countries, while impressive and valuable, fell short due to its failure to incorporate the different impacts of new businesses and its ranking of countries based primarily on the number of new businesses without regard to their success from a financial perspective or in terms of job creation, improving the local knowledge base, and increasing the level of development and innovation.[43] Specifically, they were critical of the tendency of empirical investigations of entrepreneurship to take "simple, one-dimensional approaches" even as modern research theories implicitly acknowledged that entrepreneurship required a multidimensional definition.[44] For example, they argued that indexes such as GEM's TEA that are based solely or primarily on measures of "self-employment," business ownership, new business creation, or the percentage of the adult population willing to engage in "entrepreneurial" activity[45] neglected important differences in the "quality"

[42] Id. at pp. 22–23.

[43] Acs, Z., and L. Szerb. June 2010. "The Global Entrepreneurship and Development Index (GEDI)." Paper presented at Summer Conference 2010 on "Opening Up Innovation: Strategy, Organization and Technology." Imperial College London Business School.

[44] Id.

[45] With regard to self-employment, see Acs, Z., D. Audretsch, and D. Evans. 1994. "Why Does the Self-Employment Rate Vary Across Countries and Over Time?" CEPR Working Paper No., 871. Center for Economic Policy Research; Blanchflower, D., A. Oswald, and A. Stutzer. 2001. "Latent Entrepreneurship Across Nations." *European Economic Review* 45, nos. 4–6, pp. 680–91; and Grilo,

of entrepreneurial activity (e.g., skills, innovation, and high growth); differences in environmental factors; and the efficiency and level of the society's institutional setup (e.g., property rights, size and role of government, and regulatory conditions to new venture formation). Acs and Szerb believed that it was important to distinguish entrepreneurship from small businesses, self-employment, craftsmanship, and "usual businesses" and defined entrepreneurship as "a dynamic interaction or entrepreneurial attitudes, entrepreneurial activity, and entrepreneurial aspiration that vary across stages of economic development."[46]

Using their definition of entrepreneurship, Acs and Szerb set out to address and overcome the above-described shortcomings of the GEM project and other then-existing measures of national entrepreneurship based primarily on business formation by creating the Global Entrepreneurship and Development Index (GEDI).[47] They explained that their

---

I., and R. Thurik. 2008. "Determinants of Entrepreneurship in Europe and the US." *Industrial and Corporate Change* 17, no. 6, pp. 1113–145. With regard to business ownership Rate, see Carree, M., A. van Stel, R. Thurik, and S. Wennekers. 2002. "Economic Development and Business Ownership: An Analysis Using Data of 23 OECD Countries in the Period 1976–1996." *Small Business Economics* 19, no. 3, pp. 271–90; and Cooper, A., and W. Dunkelberg. 1986. "Entrepreneurship and Paths to Business Ownership." *Strategic Management Journal* 7, no. 1, pp. 53–68. With regard to new venture creation, see Gartner, W. 1985. "A Conceptual Framework for Describing the Phenomenon of New Venture Creation." *The Academy of Management Review* 10, no. 4, pp. 696–706 and Reynolds, P., and D. Storey, and P. Westhead. 1994. "Cross-National Comparisons of the Variation in New Firm Formation Rates." *Regional Studies* 28, no. 4, pp. 443–56. For information on the TEA, see Acs, Z., P. Arenius, M. Hay, and M. Minniti. 2005. *Global Entrepreneurship Monitor: 2004 Executive Report.* Babson Park, MA: Babson College and London: London Business School and Bosma, Jones, N., E. Autio, and J. Levie. 2008. *GEM Executive Report 2007.* Babson College, London Business School, and Global Entrepreneurship Research Consortium.

[46] Acs, Z., and L. Szerb. June 2010. "The Global Entrepreneurship and Development Index (GEDI)." Paper Presented at Summer Conference 2010 on "Opening Up Innovation: Strategy, Organization and Technology." Imperial College London Business School.

[47] Id. Acs and Szerb. did note that the original GEM model had been updated to incorporate a number of "contextual" factors that impact entrepreneurship including education, infrastructure, government support, venture capital, and research and development transfer and that the GEM was also beginning to

goal in constructing the GEDI was to contribute to the understanding of economic development by providing a measuring tool that "captures the essence of the contextual features of entrepreneurship and fills a gap in the measure of development."[48] The initial GEDI covered 71 countries around the world and was based on both the quality and quantity of the business formation process in those countries and designed to incorporate both individual and institutional level variables.[49] In a report prepared for the U.S. Small Business Administration Acs and Szerb explained that the GEDI captures the contextual features of entrepreneurship by focusing on three broad areas referenced in their definition of "entrepreneurship" referred to above: "The first is entrepreneurial attitudes, a society's basic attitudes toward entrepreneurship through education and social stability. The second area of focus is entrepreneurial activity, what individuals are actually doing to improve the quality of human resources and technological efficiency. The final area is entrepreneurial aspirations, how much of the entrepreneurial activity is being directed toward innovation, high-impact entrepreneurship, and globalization."[50]

---

recognize individual differences in the "quality" of new ventures (i.e., "startups"). Bosma, N., K. Jones, E. Autio, and J. Levie. 2008. *GEM Executive Report 2007.* Babson College, London Business School, and Global Entrepreneurship Research Consortium; Bosma, N., Z. Acs, E. Autio, A. Coduras, and J. Levie. 2009. *GEM Executive Report 2008.* Babson College, Universidad del Desarrollo, and Global Entrepreneurship Research Consortium.

[48] Acs, Z., and L. Szerb. June 2010. "The Global Entrepreneurship and Development Index (GEDI)." Paper Presented at Summer Conference 2010 on "Opening Up Innovation: Strategy, Organization and Technology." Imperial College London Business School.

[49] Acs and Szerb explained that all of the institutional variables used in compiling the indexes that are part of the GEDI were taken from the Global Competitiveness Index. For further information on the Global Competitiveness Index, see Sala-I-Martin, X., B. Bilbao-Osorio, J. Blanke, M. Hanouz, and T. Geiger. 2011. "The Global Competitiveness Index 2011–2012: Setting the Foundations for Strong Productivity." In *The Global Competitiveness Report 2011–2012*, ed. K. Schwab, 3–50. Geneva: World Economic Forum.

[50] Acs, Z., and L. Szerb. September 2010. *Global Entrepreneurship and the United States.* Washington, DC: U.S. Small Business Administration Office of Advocacy. http://sba.gov/content/global-entrepreneurship-and-united-states (accessed April 30, 2011).

The GEDI created by Acs and Laszlo was a "super-index" based on societal scores on three subindexes measuring activity, aspiration, and attitudes[51]:

- The entrepreneurial attitude subindex (ATT) focuses on identifying and measuring "entrepreneurial attitudes" associated with a society's entrepreneurship-related behavior. Among the areas of interest with respect to ATT are the potential for perceiving novel business opportunities, "fear of failure," "startup skills," and personal networks. Acs and Laszlo believed that several institutional factors would influence ATT including the size of the market, education, business risk, Internet usage, and culture.
- The entrepreneurial activity subindex (ACT) makes the GEDI distinguishable from other empirical measures of entre-preneurship through its focus on measuring "high growth potential start-up activity." Among the factors taken into account are "opportunity start-up motives," sophistication or intensity of technology involved, level of education, and product/service uniqueness. Acs and Laszlo believed that the relevant institutional factors relating to ACT included ease of doing business (referred to as "business freedom"), the avail-ability and absorption of the latest technology, and the level of human development (i.e., education and training).
- The entrepreneurial aspiration subindex (ASP) relates to what Acs and Laszlo called "the distinctive, qualitative, strategy related nature of entrepreneurial activity" and incorporates "the efforts of the early-stage entrepreneur to introduce new products and services, develop new production processes,

---

[51] Acs, Z., and L. Szerb. June 2010. "The Global Entrepreneurship and Develop-ment Index (GEDI)." Paper Presented at Summer Conference 2010 on "Open-ing Up Innovation: Strategy, Organization and Technology." Imperial College London Business School. The article includes an extensive discussion of the methodology used in compiling and weighting the indexes and a description of the institutional variables used in the indexes.

penetrate foreign markets, substantially increase the number of firm employees, and finance the business with either formal or informal venture capital, or both."[52]

Acs and Szerb concluded that public policymakers must take steps to strengthen institutions before a country's entrepreneurial resources can be fully deployed.[53] Thus, for example, steps must be taken to increase "business freedom" by easing restrictions on the ability of entrepreneurs to start, operate, and close a business and making governmental processes with respect to business approvals more efficient and transparent. In addition, the government must take appropriate action to improve the society's human capital, through education and training to increase the capacity to absorb and apply new technologies, and reduce corruption and business risk by creating a legal framework that provides investors with a higher level of trust in entering into business transactions. Institutional building should also be targeted toward activities that have been identified as drivers of development such as technology-based ventures and enterprises that pursue distinctive business strategies and seek to become fully integrated into a global marketplace.

Acs and Szerb, like others,[54] observed that an understanding of entrepreneurship requires going beyond the traits and characteristics of the individual entrepreneur to also consider institutional variables and they noted that "[t]he dynamics of the [entrepreneurial] process can be vastly

---

[52] Acs, Z., and E. Autio. 2011. "The Global Entrepreneurship and Development Index: A Brief Explanation." www.imperial.ac.uk/business-school (accessed April 30, 2011). One of the institutional variables used by Acs and Szerb was "business strategy" and referred to "the ability of companies to pursue distinctive strategies, which involves differentiated positioning and innovative means of production and service delivery." See Acs, Z., and L. Szerb. June 2010. "The Global Entrepreneurship and Development Index (GEDI)." Paper Presented at Summer Conference 2010 on "Opening Up Innovation: Strategy, Organization and Technology." Imperial College London Business School.

[53] Id.

[54] See, for example, Busenitz, L., and J. Spencer. 2000. "Country Institutional Profiles: Unlocking Entrepreneurial Phenomena." *Academy of Management Journal* 43, no. 5, pp. 994–1003.

different depending on the institutional context and level of development within an economy."[55] They explained that entrepreneurship occurs within an environment that is influenced by economic development and that development directly impacts and strengthens institutions that eventually affect characteristics that are considered to be vitally important to the phenomenon of entrepreneurship such as quality of governance, access to capital and other resources, the perceptions of entrepreneurs, and incentive structures for prospective entrepreneurs. Researchers have found evidence that the strengthening of institutions causes more entrepreneurial activity to be shifted toward "productive entrepreneurship," which, in turn, strengthens economic development.[56] Entrepreneurial activity reaches its highest level of intensity as countries go through the innovation-driven stage and eventually levels off as institutions are fully developed and the country has achieved a high level of innovation.[57]

Acs and Szerb reported the rankings of the 71 countries in their survey and noted that their findings were significantly and highly correlated with other well-known measurement tools such as the Global Entrepreneurship Index, Index of Economic Freedom, and Global Competitiveness Index. When reporting the rankings Acs and Szerb placed the countries into their appropriate stage of development using the aforementioned categories developed by Porter (i.e., factor-driven, efficiency-driven, and innovation-driven).[58] Acs and Szerb pointed out the following notable findings from the 2010 rankings:

---

[55] Acs, Z., and L. Szerb. June 2010. "The Global Entrepreneurship and Development Index (GEDI)." Paper Presented at Summer Conference 2010 on "Opening Up Innovation: Strategy, Organization and Technology." Imperial College London Business School.

[56] Acemoglu, D., and S. Johnson. 2005. "Unbundling Institutions." *Journal of Political Economy* 113, no. 5, pp. 949–95.

[57] Fukuyama, F. 1989. "The End of History?" *The National Interest* 16, pp. 3–18.

[58] For further discussion of the views of Acs and Szerb on the contributions of entrepreneurship to development and relative importance of institutional factors in promoting entrepreneurship at different stages of economic development, see "Factors Influencing Entrepreneurial Activities." In "Entrepreneurship: A Library of Resources for Sustainable Entrepreneurs." Prepared and distributed by the Sustainable Entrepreneurship Project (www.seproject.org).

- Nordic and Anglo-Saxon countries in the innovation-driven stage of development were in the front ranks. Denmark and Sweden led the GEDINDEX, Iceland and Norway joined them in the top 10, and Finland was 13th overall. The United States and Canada were third and fourth and Australia, Ireland, and Switzerland also did well although they were weak in at least one of the subindexes.
- The most populous EU countries were in the middle part of the rankings, with the United Kingdom at 14th, Germany at 16th, France at 18th, Italy at 27th, and Spain at 28th. Acs and Szerb suggested that there was a relationship between low levels of entrepreneurship in those countries and their relatively weak economic performance over the decade leading up to the rankings.
- The bottom of the rankings hosted a number of low GDP-level factor-driven countries such as Jamaica, Bosnia-Herzegovina, Venezuela, Brazil, Philippines, Iran, Bolivia, Ecuador, and Uganda.

Entrepreneurial performance of the innovation-driven countries was significantly different from the efficiency-driven countries, with the largest differences observed with respect to indicators of new products, "non-fear of failure," internationalization, and risk capital. Factor-driven and efficiency-driven countries were more similar regarding entrepreneurship indicators, but notable differences could be identified with respect to attitudinal indicators of "non-fear of failure" and "cultural support."

Acs and Szerb also used "cluster analysis" to divide the surveyed countries into five country groups that possessed similar entrepreneurial features. The first group included most of the factor-driven economies in the survey with low scores on measures of international connections and development of human resources. A number of the efficiency-driven economies were in the next cluster and Acs and Szerb noted that these economies were involved in trying to increase entrepreneurship from what was currently a relatively low level of development. The remaining three clusters were home to most of the innovation-driven economies and broke down into innovation leaders, such as the United States and the

Scandinavian countries that topped the list for several reasons including the availability of formal and informal venture finance and excellence in technology application and adaptation; innovation followers that generally took a "follower" approach in identifying and pursuing innovation strategies first launched within the "leader" group; and innovation challengers who possessed some relative advantages that would allow them to compete with the leaders in certain instances. The most significant differences among the three "innovation" clusters could be found in the area of "entrepreneurial attitudes," which included opportunity perception, startup skills, "non-fear of failure," networking, and cultural support.

In general, the innovation leaders were the same countries who led the GEDINDEX rankings; Latin American countries appeared in the factor-driven cluster; and most of the Eastern European and Balkan countries and five out of six of the African countries appeared in the efficiency transformers cluster. An interesting, although not totally surprising, finding was the tremendous diversity among the Asian countries with respect to entrepreneurship. Acs and Szerb observed that the poorer Asian countries fell into the resource- or factor-driven clusters while highly populated Asian countries such as China, India, and Indonesia could be found in the efficiency-driven cluster. Among the richer Asian countries, Hong Kong was an innovation challenger and Japan, Korea, and Singapore were innovation followers. None of the Asian countries appeared in the innovation leader cluster. Acs and Szerb concluded that the cluster analysis provided further confirmation of a strong and positive relationship between economic development and entrepreneurship.

In 2010 the five highest ranking countries on the entrepreneurial attitude subindex (ATT) were, in order, New Zealand, Australia, Canada, Sweden, and Denmark. The United States was the sixth. The five lowest ranking countries were Guatemala, Indonesia, Russia, Syria, and Uganda. The five highest ranking countries on the entrepreneurial activity subindex (ACT) were, in order, Denmark, Canada, Puerto Rico, Ireland, and Norway. The United States was eighth. The five lowest ranking countries were Bosnia and Herzegovina, Morocco, the Philippines, Serbia, and Uganda. The five highest ranking countries on the entrepreneurial aspiration subindex (ASP) were, in order, the United States, Iceland, Singapore, Israel, and Sweden. The five lowest ranking countries were Bolivia, Guatemala,

Iran, Kazakhstan, and the Philippines. Subindex scores of a few of the other major global economic players were as follows: China 54th on ATT, 53rd on ACT, 26th on ASP, and 40th overall on GEDI; Japan 47th on ATT, 23rd on ACT, 22nd on ASP, and 29th overall on GEDI; and India 62nd on ATT, 51st on ACT, 40th on ASP, and 53rd overall on GEDI. Not surprisingly, there were several instances of significant deviations, upward and downward, on one of the subindexes in relation to the other subindexes and overall GEDI. For example, Germany was placed 7th on the ASP but its ranking of 24th on ATT drove its overall GEDI placement down to 16th. Israel, not surprisingly, was 4th in ASP but its placement as 38th and 21st in ATT and ACT, respectively, led to an overall GEDI for this famously entrepreneurial society as 21st.

Research Issues in Cross-Country Comparisons of Entrepreneurial Activities

It has generally been assumed that entrepreneurship plays an important role in national economies and is particularly important as a mechanism for national economic development to the extent that the creation of new economic activity by entrepreneurial actors contributes to increases in employment and greater innovation. However, researchers focusing on cross-country comparisons of entrepreneurial activities have found considerable differences between countries on a variety of factors including the extent to which entrepreneurship is "growth" or "innovation" oriented.[59] As a result, commentators have recommended that it is essential for scientists, policymakers, and entrepreneurs to collect and analyze additional information on the factors that influence the emergence of

---

[59] Hessels, J. 2008. *International Entrepreneurship: An Introduction, Framework and Research Agenda,* 4. Zoetermeer, The Netherlands: Scientific Analysis of Entrepreneurship and SMEs citing Autio, E. 2007. *Global Entrepreneurship Monitor: 2007 Global Report on High Growth Entrepreneurship.* Wellesley, MA and London: Babson College and London Business School. and Hessels, J., M. van Gelderen, and A. Thurik. 2008. "Drivers of Entrepreneurial Aspirations at the Country Level: The Role of Start-up Motivations and Social Security." *International Entrepreneurship and Management Journal* 4, pp. 401–17.

the various types of entrepreneurship and the economic outcomes of each type.[60]

Mueller and Thomas noted that much work needs to be done in understanding whether various theories regarding human motivation and performance developed in North America can be usefully applied in other countries where cultural, social, and economic conditions are quite different.[61] Another interesting question they raised is the need to identify whether, at the national and regional level, there is an adequate supply of "prospective entrepreneurs" (i.e., individuals with the requisite personal characteristics and ambitions to identify and exploit opportunities and initiate new business ventures) to justify programs that might be implemented to encourage entrepreneurial activities.[62] Unfortunately, at least in the eyes of researchers such as Mueller and Thomas, "with a few exceptions, international comparative studies of entrepreneurship are rare, hampered by barriers such as difficulty in gaining access to entrepreneurs in other countries, high expense, and lack of reliable secondary data."[63]

---

[60] Id.

[61] Mueller, S., and A. Thomas. 2000. "Culture and Entrepreneurial Potential: A Nine Country Study of Locus of Control and Innovativeness." *Journal of Business Venturing* 16, no. 1, pp. 51–75, 53. For further discussion of cross-cultural transfer of management theories, see "Globalization: A Library of Resources for Sustainable Entrepreneurs." Prepared and distributed by the Sustainable Entrepreneurship Project (www.seproject.org). See also Adler, N. 1991. *International Dimensions of Organizational Behavior*, 2nd ed. Boston, MA: Kent Publishing and Boyacigiller, N., and N. Adler. 1991. "The Parochial Dinosaur: Organizational Science in a Global Context." *Academy of Management Review* 16, pp. 262–90.

[62] Mueller, S., and A. Thomas. 2000. "Culture and Entrepreneurial Potential: A Nine Country Study of Locus of Control and Innovativeness." *Journal of Business Venturing* 16, no. 54, pp. 51–75 (citing Schumpeter's observation that the overall rate of new venture creation and entrepreneurial activity depends not only on the presence of an "entrepreneurial climate" but also the availability of prospective entrepreneurs).

[63] Mueller, S., and A. Thomas. 2000. "Culture and Entrepreneurial Potential: A Nine Country Study of Locus of Control and Innovativeness." *Journal of Business Venturing* 16, no. 53, pp. 51–75. Mueller and Thomas did cite the following examples of cross-cultural studies that had been completed: Shane, S. 1992. "Why Do Some Societies Invent More than Others?" *Journal of Business*

One example of an attempt to conduct a cross-border comparative study of entrepreneurship is the work done by Kantis. He proposed a conceptual framework to be used to analyze and understand the "entrepreneurial process" and facilitate comparison of the conditions confronting prospective entrepreneurs in different countries.[64] As part of this framework, Kantis suggested that a model of an "entrepreneurial development system" could be created that takes into account a combination of elements and factors that have an impact, both positive and negative, on the process and, ultimately, on the efficient development of entrepreneurs and entrepreneurial firms. Kantis grouped these factors into a short list of categories, which included social and economic conditions, societal culture, productive structure and dynamism, personal aspects, networks, factor markets, and regulations and policies.[65] These factors then served as the basis for analyzing data collected from several comparative studies of entrepreneurial activities and development overseen by the Inter-American Development Bank, including an extensive study reported in 2005 that involved the following countries: Argentina, Brazil, Chile, Costa Rica, El Salvador, Mexico, and Peru in Latin America; Japan, Singapore, South Korea, and Taiwan in East Asia; and Italy and Spain in southern

Venturing 7, no. 1, pp. 29–46; Shane, S. 1993. "Cultural Influences on National Rates of Innovation." *Journal of Business Venturing*, pp. 59–73; McGrath, R., I. MacMillan, and S. Scheinberg. 1992. "Elitists, Risk-Takers, and Rugged Individualists—An Exploratory Analysis of Cultural Differences Between Entrepreneurs and Non-entrepreneurs." *Journal of Business Venturing* 7, no. 2, pp. 115–35; Baum, J., J. Olian, M. Erez, E. Schnell, K. Smith, H. Sims, J. Scully, and K. Smith. 1993. "Nationality and Work Role Interactions: A Cultural Contrast of Israeli and U.S. Entrepreneur's Versus Manager's Needs." *Journal of Business Venturing* 8, pp. 499–512; Huisman, D. 1985. "Entrepreneurship: Economic and Cultural Influences on the Entrepreneurial Climate." *European Research* 13, no. 4, pp. 10–17.

[64] Kantis, H. 2005 "A Systematic Approach to Enterprise Creation." In *Developing Entrepreneurship: Experience in Latin America and Worldwide,* ed. H. Kantis, 17–27. Washington, DC: Inter-American Development Bank.

[65] For further discussion of each of these categories, see "Factors Influencing Entrepreneurial Activities." In "Entrepreneurship: A Library of Resources for Sustainable Entrepreneurs." Prepared and distributed by the Sustainable Entrepreneurship Project (www.seproject.org).

Europe.[66] Kantis provided the following description of the some of the key differences among the countries in the study[67]:

- Based on output per capita and income distribution patterns, it was apparent that socioeconomic conditions are extremely dissimilar and this likely explained differences among the countries with respect to the level and profile of demand, the scope for business opportunities, and the supply of opportunity-based entrepreneurs. New Latin American enterprises were less dynamic (i.e., growth-focused) than firms created in other regions based on a variety of measures include overall sales and sales per employee.

- Opportunity-based entrepreneurship was lower in areas, such as Latin America, where individuals did not have ready access to the information and savings necessary for successful and effective opportunity-based entrepreneurship and were forced by lack of work options to settle on necessity-based entrepreneurship.

- As discussed elsewhere in this publication, there were differences between countries on cultural dimensions identified with entrepreneurship. The "entrepreneurial spirit" was stronger in those countries where cultural values tolerated higher levels of risk and celebrated individualism; however, countries in Latin America tended to have cultural characteristics that are deemed unfavorable to entrepreneurship. Especially in East Asia, the mass media frequently publicized

---

[66] For a detailed discussion of the study, see Kantis, H., ed. 2005. *Developing Entrepreneurship: Experience in Latin America and Worldwide.* Washington, DC: Inter-American Development Bank.

[67] Kantis, H. 2005. "A Systematic Approach to Enterprise Creation." In *Developing Entrepreneurship: Experience in Latin America and Worldwide*, ed. H. Kantis, 17–27, 22–25. Washington, DC: Inter-American Development Bank and Kantis, H. 2005. "The Entrepreneurial Process: Main Contrasts Between Latin America and East Asia, Italy and Spain." In *Developing Entrepreneurship: Experience in Latin America and Worldwide*, ed. H. Kantis, 47, 47–60, 59–60. Washington, DC: Inter-American Development Bank.

entrepreneurial models and business opportunities, thereby helping to forge entrepreneurial vocations and identify ambitious business ideas. In Italy, the desire to create a business to continue the family tradition is a strong motivating factor, especially when the widespread presence of family businesses in that country is taken into account. In Latin America, such sources of motivation are much less powerful, reflecting the limitations of the sociocultural context for igniting entrepreneurial vocations.

- The projects undertaken by entrepreneurial firms in various regions could be differentiated in terms of their initial scale and also in the profile of opportunities on which they are based. Knowledge-based, subcontracting, or export businesses were significantly less common in Latin American countries and they also had less of an edge on their competitors with respect to differentiation (quality, service, or marketing), which is the main source of opportunities for creating dynamic enterprises. Latin American teams tended to be smaller and their networks are both less stable and more restricted to the immediate social circle and the data indicated that building teams and networks depended largely on predominant attitudes and values in society.

- Export sales were considerably greater among firms from the Asian countries, Italy, and Spain as opposed to those from Latin America. In the same vein, the technical content of exports and sophistication of design features were higher in Asia and Europe than in Latin America. These findings were consistent with the much higher ratio of personnel in research and development to the total population in East Asia when compared to Latin America.

- Small- and medium-sized firms from the East Asian countries and some regions in Italy and Spain had achieved international competitiveness and were strongly involved in complex networks that linked them with major firms; however, the productive sector in Latin America generally was fragmented and lacked integration between large firms and small- and medium-sized firms.

- Latin American firms were severely disadvantaged in relation to Asian firms with respect to access to financing, such as venture capital and bank loans, and the ease of formally starting new businesses (i.e., registration procedures). As a result, Latin American entrepreneurs were forced to scale down their projects in terms of startup size or technology level, and to seek alternative financing sources, such as credit from suppliers and customers or purchasing used equipment.

- The importance of the middle class, and the emergence of entrepreneurs from lower socioeconomic strata, was more limited in Latin America than in East Asia, where social mobility is fostered more. There are fewer first-time entrepreneurs in Latin America than in East Asia, and hence their contribution to spreading the entrepreneurial base is more limited.

- Variations among countries were identified with respect to the primary sources of learning for entrepreneurial activities. For example, in Latin America universities played a more important role in the acquisition of technical knowledge than on-the-job training; however, in other countries the companies in which entrepreneurs had worked previously were the main source of this kind of learning.

The results of the survey led to the following recommendation to policymakers in Latin America interested in promoting entrepreneurship[68]:

- Broaden the social and gender bases from which dynamic enterprises emerge.
- Expand the number and quality of business opportunities.
- Facilitate potential entrepreneur's access to work experience.

---

[68] Kantis, H., P. Angelelli, and J. Llisterri. 2005. "Conclusions and Policy Implications." In *Developing Entrepreneurship: Experience in Latin America and Worldwide,* ed. H. Kantis, 101–107, 105. Washington, DC: Inter-American Development Bank.

- Foster the development of entrepreneur teams and networks.
- Improve access to financing.
- Enhance the entrepreneurial process in local areas.
- Take advantage of the transformation power of knowledge-based businesses.
- Generate environmental conditions more favorable to the growth of new enterprises.
- Adopt a systematic approach based on complementary efforts between different areas and levels of government, with strong leadership from the private sector.
- Make development of entrepreneurs a social investment with a long-term vision.

Research Issues in Cross-Border Entrepreneurship

A number of scholars have observed a widespread increase in cross-border entrepreneurship in the last decades and commented that, for a variety of reasons, the acceleration of international trade and investment has been fueled more by SMEs and new ventures as opposed to the multinational corporations that had previously dominated in this area.[69] They have attributed this phenomenon to what Hessels described as "substantial changes that took place in the past decades and that resulted in a reduction of transaction costs for undertaking international business."[70] Among the changes most commonly cited are reduction of trade and investment barriers in the context of the World Trade Organization and

---

[69] Moen, Ø., and P. Servais. 2002. "Born Global or Gradual Global? Examining the Export Behavior of Small and Medium-Sized Enterprises." *Journal of International Marketing* 10, no. 3, pp. 49–72; Oviatt, B., and P. McDougall. 1994. "Toward a Theory of International New Ventures." *Journal of International Business Studies* 25, no. 1, pp. 45–64; Rennie, M. 1993. "Global Competitiveness: Born Global." *The McKinsey Quarterly* 4, pp. 45–52 and Reynolds, P. 1997. "New and Small Firms in Expanding Markets." *Small Business Economics* 9, no. 1, pp. 78–84.

[70] Hessels, J. 2008. *International Entrepreneurship: An Introduction, Framework and Research Agenda,* 5. Zoetermeer, The Netherlands: Scientific Analysis of Entrepreneurship and SMEs.

regional economic cooperation agreements; technological advancements, such as the Internet and e-mail, that have increased communication and the flow of timely information around the globe; and decreased in transportation costs.[71] Taken together, it is now possible for small and new ventures everywhere to collect information about foreign markets and identify niches in those markets for their products and services, communicate with foreign customers and other business partners, and gain access to resources in foreign markets that they can use in both their domestic activities and in building their international businesses. In fact, the forces of change have been so strong that internationalization is occurring at an increasingly faster pace and this is not expected to abate given that firms are now vulnerable to foreign competition in their home markets and must therefore aggressively pursue opportunities outside of those markets in order to survive and grow.[72]

---

[71] Id. citing also Autio, E. 2005. "Creative Tension: The Significance of Ben Oviatt's and Patricia McDougall's Article 'Toward a Theory of International New Ventures.'" *Journal of International Business Studies* 36, no. 1, pp. 9–19; and Reynolds, P. 1997. "New and Small Firms in Expanding Markets." *Small Business Economics* 9, no. 1, pp. 78–84.

[72] Acs, Z., L.P. Dana, and M. Jones. 2003. "Toward New Horizons: The Internationalisation of Entrepreneurship." *Journal of International Entrepreneurship* 1, no. 1, pp. 5–12; McDougall, P., and B. Oviatt. 2000. "International Entrepreneurship: The Intersection of Two Research Paths." *Academy of Management Journal* 43, no. 5, pp. 902–6; and Root, F. 1994. *Entry Strategies for International Markets*. Lexington, MA: Lexington Books. Within the research path focusing on cross-border entrepreneurship there has been a steady increase in the attention paid to "new venture internationalization," as opposed to "SME Internationalization." SME internationalization, which first became the subject of research in the 1970s, is concerned with the expansion of international activities by firms that were initially formed with a domestic focus while new venture internationalization, which caught the interest of researchers beginning in the late 1980s, includes firms "that, for inception, [seek] to derive significant competitive advantage from the use of resources and the sale of outputs in multiple countries." Acs, Z., L.P. Dana, and M. Jones. 2003. "Toward New Horizons: The Internationalisation of Entrepreneurship." *Journal of International Entrepreneurship* 1, no. 1, pp. 5–12. Definition of "new venture internationalization" provided by Oviatt, B., and P. McDougall. 1994. "Toward a Theory of International New Ventures." *Journal of International Business Studies* 25, no. 1, pp. 45–64, 49.

During the decades following the end of World War II, the internationalization process for most firms was generally thought to follow the linear path of the product life cycle. Under this model, companies initially developed their products for the domestic market and once the products had been successfully introduced in that market they began to look for export opportunities and, if all went well, eventually moved on to foreign product and distribution activities.[73] This progression, often referred to as "incremental internationalization," was the foundation of the well-known "Uppsala model" developed by Johanson and Vahlne based on their study of manufacturing firms in Sweden in the 1970s.[74] Those researchers were interested in how the firms in their study approached their internationalization activities and observed that firms tended to begin by focusing on physically close markets using simple and less risky methods of entry, such as exporting. Once the firms had become experienced in foreign markets and increased their knowledge they were then sufficiently confident to increase their international commitments and expand their activities into markets that were located farther away from their home market.

McDougall and Oviatt commented that the incremental internationalization model may no longer be universally applicable in light of factors such as growing regional and global integration of trade and production and accelerating changes in technology that have allowed companies all around the world to enter into global trading activities more quickly and efficiently. In particular, they noted that researchers have documented numerous cases of new ventures that skipped the incremental stages in the traditional model described above and/or became "international"

---

[73] Vernon, R. 1966. "International Investment and International Trade in the Product Cycle." *Quarterly Journal of Economics* 80, pp. 190–207 and Vernon, R. 1979. "The Product Cycle Hypothesis in a New International Environment." *Oxford Bulletin of Economics and Statistics* 41, pp. 255–68.

[74] Johanson, J., and J.E. Vahlne. 1977. "The Internationalization Process of the Firm: A Model of Knowledge Development and Increasing Foreign Market Commitment." *Journal of International Business Studies* 4, pp. 20–29; Johanson, J., and J.E. Vahlne. 1990. "The Mechanism of Internationalization." *International Marketing Review* 7, pp. 11–24.

from the very moment they were launched.[75] These ventures have been referred to by various names such as "international new ventures,"[76] "born globals,"[77] "infant multinationals,"[78] "instant internationals,"[79] and "global startups."[80] Oviatt and McDougall attempted to identify some of the elements associated with the accelerated internationalization of "international new ventures" and their initial list included ownership of certain valuable assets, use of alliances and network structures to control a relative large percentage of vital assets, and control over a unique resources that provided a sustainable advantage and was transferable to a

---

[75] McDougall, P., and B. Oviatt. 2012. "Some Fundamental Issues in International Entrepreneurship." *United States Association for Small Business and Entrepreneurship.* http://usasbe.org/knowledge/whitepapers/mcdougall2003.pdf (accessed March 31, 2012). The McDougall and Oviatt article includes extensive citations that should be reviewed for further information on the cited research.

[76] McDougall, P., S. Shane, and B. Oviatt. 1994. "Explaining the Formation of International New Ventures: The Limits of Theories from International Business Research." *Journal of Business Venturing* 9, pp. 469–87. These ventures were defined by Oviatt and McDougall as "a business organization that, from inception, seeks to derive significant competitive advantage from the use of resources and the sale of outputs in multiple countries." Oviatt, B., and P. McDougall. 1994. "Toward a Theory of International New Ventures." *Journal of International Business Studies* 25, no. 1, pp. 45–64, 49.

[77] Knight, G., and S. Cavusgil. 1996. "The Born Global Firm: A Challenge to Traditional Internationalization Theory." *Advances in International Marketing* 8, pp. 11–26 and Madsen, T., and P. Servais. 1997. "The Internationalization of Born Globals: An Evolutionary Process." *International Business Review* 6, pp. 561–83.

[78] Lindqvist, M. 1991. "Infant Multinationals: The Internationalization of Young." *Technology-Based Swedish Firms.* Stockholm School of Economics, Stockholm: Unpublished doctoral dissertation.

[79] Preece, S., G. Miles, and M. Baetz. 1999. "Explaining the International Intensity and Global Diversity of Early-Stage Technology-Based Firms." *Journal of Business Venturing* 14, pp. 259–81.

[80] Oviatt, B., and P. McDougall. 1994. "Toward a Theory of International New Ventures." *Journal of International Business Studies* 25, no. 1, pp. 45–64.

foreign location.[81] In a later article, however, they noted that this list of static elements did not provide much insight into the dynamic process of formation of international new ventures and commented that a useful process theory would likely need to take into account factors such as changes in communications and transportation technology, the political and economic environment, industry conditions, firm effects, and the management team.[82]

Hessels observed that "[e]xisting research on cross-border entrepreneurship is concentrated on investigating antecedents of internationalization at the micro-level and pays only limited attention to outcomes of internationalization."[83] Antecedents of internationalization include both facilitating and inhibiting factors and were divided by Hessels into three categories with the following descriptions[84]:

---

[81] Id. Oviatt and McDougall hypothesized that since international new ventures lacked sufficient resources to control many assets through outright ownership, they needed to rely on alternative means of control that might be available through participation in network exchange structures that allowed them to gain access to valuable resources without incurring the often prohibitive expense associated with vertical integration.

[82] McDougall, P., and B. Oviatt. 2012. "Some Fundamental Issues in International Entrepreneurship." United States Association for Small Business and Entrepreneurship. http://usasbe.org/knowledge/whitepapers/mcdougall2003.pdf (accessed March 31, 2012). The McDougall and Oviatt article includes extensive citations that should be reviewed for further information on the cited research.

[83] Hessels, J. 2008. *International Entrepreneurship: An Introduction, Framework and Research Agenda*, 11. Zoetermeer, The Netherlands: Scientific Analysis of Entrepreneurship and SMEs.

[84] Id. citing Antoncic, B., and R. Hisrich. 2000. "An Integrative Conceptual Model." In *Global Marketing Co-operation and Network*, ed. L.P. Dana, 17–35. New York, NY: International Business Press. Ford, I., and L. Leonidou. 1999. "Research Developments in International Marketing." In *New Perspectives on International Marketing*, ed. S.J. Paliwoda, 3–32. London: Routledge; and Ibeh, K. 2006. "Internationalisation and the Small Business." In *Enterprise and Small Business: Principles, Practice and Policy*, eds. S. Carter and D. Jones-Evans, 465–84. Harlow, UK: Pearson Education.

- Individual- or entrepreneur-specific factors, which are normally factors related to characteristics of the entrepreneur such as demographic characteristics (i.e., age and the level of education)[85] and factors relating to the knowledge and experience of the entrepreneur and/or his or her top management team with respect to international business and foreign institutions (i.e., foreign laws, norms, standards, and languages).[86]
- Firm-specific factors, which might include firm size, as measured by number of employees and sales volume,[87] firm resources such as possession of a unique product, and/or a proprietary technology, and the possession of specific management capabilities.[88]

---

[85] Westhead, P. 1995. "Exporting and Non-Exporting Small Firms in Great Britain." *International Journal of Entrepreneurial Behavior and Research* 1, no. 2, pp. 6–36 and Simpson, C., and D. Kujawa. 1974. "The Export Decision Process: An Empirical Inquiry." *Journal of International Business Studies* 5, no. 1, pp. 107–17.

[86] Bloodgood, J., H. Sapienza, and J. Almeida. 1996. "The Internationalization of New High-Potential U.S. Ventures: Antecedents and Outcomes." *Entrepreneurship Theory and Practice* 20, no. 4, pp. 61–76; Eriksson, K., J. Johanson, A. Majkgård, and D. Sharma. 1997. "Experiential Knowledge and Cost in the Internationalization Process." *Journal of International Business Studies* 28, no. 2, pp. 337–60; Oviatt, B., and P. McDougall. 1995. "Global Start-Ups: Entrepreneurs on a Worldwide Stage." *Academy of Management Executive* 9, no. 2, pp. 30–44 and Reuber, A., and E. Fischer. 1997. "The Influence of the Management Team's International Experience on the Internationalization Behaviors of SMEs." *Journal of International Business Studies* 28, no. 4, pp. 807–25.

[87] Chetty, S., and R. Hamilton. 1993. "Firm Level Determinants of Export Performance: A Meta-Analysis." *International Marketing Review* 10, no. 3, pp. 26–34; Lefebvre, E., and L.A. Lefebvre. 2002. "Innovative Capabilities as Determinants of Export Performance and Behaviour: A Longitudinal Study of Manufacturing SMEs." In *Innovation and Firm Performance: Econometric Explorations of Survey Data*, eds. A. Kleinknecht and P. Mohnen, 281–309. London: Palgrave and Westhead, P. 1995. "Exporting and Non-Exporting Small Firms in Great Britain." *International Journal of Entrepreneurial Behavior and Research* 1, no. 2, pp. 6–36.

[88] Akoorie, M., and P. Enderwick. 1992. "The International Operations of New Zealand Companies." *Asia Pacific Journal of Management* 9, no. 1, pp. 51–69;

- Environment-specific factors, which can include conditions
  in both domestic and foreign markets such as a fall
  in production costs in the home market, which allow
  domestically manufactured products to become competitive
  in global markets, and size limitations in the home market,
  which dictate that internationalization is the only way
  to expansion.[89]

As for the outcomes of cross-border entrepreneurship, Hessels suggested that it is useful to look at three levels of analysis: the individual level, which focuses on development of human and social capital; the firm level, which can be measured by looking at profitability, employment growth, and innovation; and, finally, the "macro" level, which includes an assessment of national employment and economic growth and improvements in the innovative capacity of national economies.[90] It is clear that more emphasis should be placed on researching outcomes of cross-border entrepreneurship and Hessels suggested that "adding a multi-country

---

Cavusgil, T., and J. Nevin. 1981. "Internal Determinants of Export Marketing Behavior: An Empirical Investigation." *Journal of Marketing Research* 18, no. 1, pp. 114–19; Keeble, D., C. Lawson, H. Smith, B. Moore, and F. Wilkinson. 1988. "Internationalisation Processes, Networking and Local Embeddedness in Technology-Intensive Small Firms." *Small Business Economics* 11, no. 4, pp. 327–42 and Roberts, E., and T. Senturia. 1996. "Globalizing the Emerging High-Technology Company." *Industrial Marketing Management* 25, no. 6, pp. 491–506.

[89] Axinn, C. 1988. "Export Performance: Do Managerial Perceptions Make a Difference?" *International Marketing Review* 5, no. 5, pp. 67–71 and Rasmussen, E., T. Madsen, and F. Evangelista. 2001. "The Founding of the Born Global Company in Denmark and Australia: Sensemaking and Networking." *Asia Pacific Journal of Marketing and Logistics* 13, no. 3, pp. 75–107.

[90] Hessels, J. 2008. *International Entrepreneurship: An Introduction, Framework and Research Agenda*, 12. Zoetermeer, The Netherlands: Scientific Analysis of Entrepreneurship and SMEs. For more discussion of the research on outcomes of SME and new venture internationalization, see Lu, J., and P. Beamish. 2006. "Partnering Strategies and Performance of SME's International Joint Ventures." *Journal of Business Venturing* 21, no. 4, pp. 461–86 and Zahra, S. 2005. "A Theory of International New Ventures: A Decade of Research." *Journal of International Business Studies* 36, no. 1, pp. 20–28.

perspective to research on cross-border entrepreneurship . . . will help to increase our understanding of the economic benefits and drivers of entrepreneurship across countries . . . [and] . . . increase the ability to generalize findings."[91]

Research on Entrepreneurship in Developing Countries

Entrepreneurship has been continuously linked to economic development of countries and has often been championed as a key path for transforming developing countries toward greater economic growth, innovation, competitiveness, and alleviation of poverty.[92] However, researchers have bemoaned the fact that, as described by Lingelbach et al., ". . . entrepreneurship in developing countries is arguably the least studied significant economic and social phenomenon in the world today."[93] For example, while as of 2004 there were literally hundreds of millions of "entrepreneurs," generally defined as owners of managers of new firms, in developing countries as opposed to just under 18 million entrepreneurs in the United States,[94] leading books on entrepreneurship research often had no more than a handful of pages on entrepreneurship in important developing countries such as China and India.[95] Research on entrepreneurship in developing countries is important for a number of reasons, not

---

[91] Id. at p. 15.

[92] Landes, D. 1998. *The Wealth and Poverty of Nations.* New York, NY: W.W. Norton.

[93] Lingelbach, D., L. De La Vina, and P. Asel. 2005. *What's Distinctive about Growth-Oriented Entrepreneurship in Developing Countries?* San Antonio, TX: UTSA College of Business Center for Global Entrepreneurship Working Paper No. 11. For detailed discussion of the scope of research conducted in the field of international entrepreneurship, see "Entrepreneurship: A Library of Resources for Sustainable Entrepreneurs." Prepared and distributed by the Sustainable Entrepreneurship Project (www.seproject.org).

[94] Reynolds, P., W. Bygrave, and E. Autio. 2004 *Global Entrepreneurship Monitor: 2003 Executive Report.*

[95] Bhidé, A. 2000. *The Origin and Evolution of New Businesses.* New York, NY: Oxford University.

the least of which is providing policymakers with a better idea of how to encourage entrepreneurship as part of an overall strategy for private sector development in developing countries. A strictly Western model of entrepreneurship is not likely to work well in developing countries due not only to differences in societal culture but also the distinctive nature of entrepreneurship in emerging markets where resources readily available in developed countries are scarce or even nonexistent.[96]

Decolonization was the trigger for the first attempts to study entrepreneurship in developing countries and most researchers have, until recently, focused their attention on small-scale industrialization[97] and microenterprises.[98] As time has gone by, and initiatives such as the GEM were launched, the analysis of entrepreneurship in developing countries has become more nuanced and it is now recognized that entrepreneurial firms in those countries can fall into one of several different categories such as newly established, established but not growing, established but growing slowly, and graduates to a larger size.[99] This movement has opened the door for studying a small, yet very important, subset of businesses in developing countries: new firms formed with a growth orientation and strategies tied to entry into global markets. It is apparent that there are now a number of promising areas for further research with respect to entrepreneurship in developing countries, all with important policy implications for governments looking to stimulate economic growth

---

[96] For a discussion of the influence of societal culture on entrepreneurship, see "Factors Influencing Entrepreneurial Activities." In "Entrepreneurship: A Library of Resources for Sustainable Entrepreneurs." Prepared and distributed by the Sustainable Entrepreneurship Project (www.seproject.org).

[97] See, for example, Schmitz, H. 1992. "Growth Constraints on Small-scale Manufacturing in Developing Countries: A Critical Review." *World Development* 10, no. 6, pp. 429–50.

[98] See, for example, Robinson, M. 2001–2002. *The Microfinance Revolution.* Washington, DC: World Bank.

[99] Liedholm, C., and D. Mead. 1999. *Small Enterprises and Economic Development.* London: Routledge.

and development.[100] Lingelbach et al., for example, offered the following list as a suggested research agenda for entrepreneurship in developing countries[101]:

- Increased focus on new and growth-oriented firms in developing countries, which are important given that these firms are most likely to contribute to economic growth and provide new sources of higher quality employment in developing countries;
- Analysis of the dynamics of firm creation and destruction in developing countries;
- Analysis of the strategies used by entrepreneurs in developing countries to overcome poor access to finance including the use of funds provided by personal savings and intrafamilial financial linkages;
- Further exploration of the link, if any, between the general business environment and the level of entrepreneurial activities in poorer countries;

---

[100] See, for example, Harper, M. 1991. "The Role of Enterprise in Poor Countries." *Entrepreneurship Theory and Practice* 15, no. 4, pp. 7–11; Gibb, A. 1993. "Small Business Development in Central and Eastern Europe—Opportunity for a Rethink?" *Journal of Business Venturing* 8, pp. 461–86; Audretsch, D. 1991. *The Role of Small Business in Restructuring Eastern Europe.* Vaxjo, Sweden: 5th Workshop for Research in Entrepreneurship. Other studies that have identified entrepreneurship as a critical factor in national economic development include Birley, S. 1987. "New Ventures and Employment Growth." *Journal of Business Venturing* 2, no. 2, pp. 155–65; Reynolds, P. 1987. "New firms: Societal Contributions Versus Survival Potential." *Journal of Business Venturing* 2, no. 3, pp. 231–46; Morris, M., and P. Lewis. 1991. "Entrepreneurship as a Significant Factor in Societal Quality of Life." *Journal of Business Research* 23, no. 1, pp. 21–36 and Shane, S., L. Kolvereid, and P. Westhead. 1991. "An Exploratory Examination of the Reasons Leading to New Firm Formation across Country and Gender (Part 1)." *Journal of Business Venturing* 6, no. 6, pp. 431–46.
[101] Lingelbach, D., L. De La Vina, and P. Asel. 2005. *What's Distinctive about Growth-Oriented Entrepreneurship in Developing Countries?* 7–8. San Antonio, TX: UTSA College of Business Center for Global Entrepreneurship Working Paper No. 1.

- Development of more information on "models of success" among entrepreneurs in developing countries in order to provide a better picture of the common features of successful entrepreneurship in developing countries and the extent to which those features differ from successful entrepreneurship in the United States and other developed countries;
- Development of strategies for designing markets for entrepreneurial finance in developing countries including introduction of various methods for managing risk such as hedging and insurance;
- Application of behavioral economics and finance to entrepreneurship in developing countries to determine how cognitive biases identified by researchers in those fields vary in entrepreneurs in developing countries; and
- Development of models of entrepreneurship that adequately take into account how entrepreneurship is carried out in developing countries.[102]

---

[102] Lingelbach et al. commented that most of the models of entrepreneurship, such as the uncertainty/investment/profit diagram developed by Bhide, are based primarily on research conducted in the United States and other developed countries. Id. at 2 citing Bhide, A. 2000. *The Origin and Evolution of New Businesses.* New York, NY: Oxford University.

CHAPTER 3

Factors Influencing Entrepreneurial Activities

Introduction

Shane et al. were particularly interested in improving the quality and conciseness of research on how human motivations influence entrepreneurship; however, they suggested a model that may well have a broader application in the design of an analytical framework for studying the various factors that influence entrepreneurship.[1] Shane et al. believed that entrepreneurship was best viewed as a "process" that occurred over an extended period of time, rather than an isolated event or moment in time when a person decides whether he or she should become an "entrepreneur." This process included a number of stages, including recognition of opportunities, development of ideas about how to pursue the opportunity by turning it into new products or services, and, finally, execution of the activities required to harvest the desired profits from the opportunities. The execution phase involved an array of tasks and activities such as evaluating the feasibility of the opportunity, product or service development, assembly of human and financial resources, organizational design, and "market making" (i.e., identification and pursuit of customers). In their model, the success or failure of the entire entrepreneurial process, and the decisions made along the way are influenced by several important factors. The motivational traits of the prospective entrepreneur is one of them; however, in order to get a complete picture it is necessary to also take into account other factors that Shane et al. felt had been ignored by previous

---

[1] Shane, S., E. Locke, and C. Collins. 2003. "Entrepreneurial Motivation." *Human Resource Management Review* 13, no.2, pp. 257–79, 274–76.

researchers such as cognitive factors, the nature of the opportunity, and environmental conditions.[2]

In order to address the concerns described above regarding the inadequacies of previous research on the relationship between human motivation and entrepreneurship, Shane et al. devised their own "model of entrepreneurial motivation and the entrepreneurial process" that focused on the factors that came into play at various points where individuals (i.e., "entrepreneurs") transitioned from one stage of the entrepreneurial process to the next. It was assumed that at each "transition point," such as moving from "opportunity recognition" to "idea development," influences might come from one or more categories of factors: entrepreneurial motivations, entrepreneurial opportunities, and conditions and cognitive factors.[3] However, the mix of influences in play at a particular stage was not fixed, nor was the relative importance of specific factors. Interestingly, the model did not attempt to identify relationships between any of the factors and traditional measures of "success" or "performance," such as profitability or growth rates, but simply focused on sensitizing researchers to the influences on the actions that entrepreneurs must take as they pursue development and commercialization of their ideas. In other words, in contrast to earlier models and assumptions, Shane et al. recognized that the most relevant effects of factors such as "entrepreneurial motivations" on venture performance and growth may actually be more "indirect" than "direct."[4]

---

[2] Id. at p. 258 ("In our arguments, we explicitly assume that all human action is the result of both motivational and cognitive factors, the latter including ability, intelligence and skills. We also assume that entrepreneurship is not solely the result of human action; external factors also play a role . . .")

[3] This view was consistent with the observations of others such as Aldrich and Zimmer, who wrote that entrepreneurial activity "can be conceptualized as a function of opportunity structures and motivated entrepreneurs with access to resources." See Aldrich, H., and C. Zimmer. 1986. "Entrepreneurship through Social Networks." In *The Art and Science of Entrepreneurship*, eds. D. Sexton and R. Smilor, 3–23, 3. Cambridge, MA: Ballinger.

[4] Shane, S., E. Locke, and C. Collins. 2003. "Entrepreneurial Motivation." *Human Resource Management Review* 13, pp. 257–79, 276. ("Motivations might be more or less stronger than these other factors in the degree that they influence

The elements of the analytical framework suggested by Shane et al. were similar in many ways to those used by Baum et al. in studying the growth of small companies in the architectural woodworking industry.[5] Baum et al. analyzed 29 variables divided among five different domains, including "traits and motivations," which included motivational factors similar to those described by Shane et al., such as hard work, tenacity, and drive; situation-specific motivation, such as goals and self-efficacy; cognitive skills; business strategies; and environmental factors. Interestingly, consistent with the arguments made by Shane et al., Baum et al. found that motivational factors did have an effect on the growth of the ventures included in their study but that the effects were "indirect," meaning that motives came into play as influencers of other domains such as cognitive skills, situation-specific motivation, and business strategies.[6] The sections that follow combine the various factors and domains identified by Shane et al. and Baum et al. to describe an analytical model of the entrepreneurial process that would incorporate several key factors: entrepreneurial motivations, cognitive factors, entrepreneurial opportunities, environmental conditions, competitive strategies, and, finally, certain nonmotivational individual differences that have been shown to play an important role on the willingness of people to engage in entrepreneurial activities.

While not explicitly incorporated into the sections below, notice should also be taken of the "entrepreneurial process model," which is a conceptual framework proposed by Kantis to analyze and understand the "entrepreneurial process" and facilitate comparison of the conditions confronting prospective entrepreneurs in different countries.[7] While conceding, as others have done, that the entrepreneurial process does not

---

particular transitions points. In addition, there might be important and interesting interaction effects between motivations and opportunities, [knowledge, skills and abilities] and environmental factors.")

[5] Baum, J., E. Locke, and K. Smith. 2001. "A Multi-Dimensional Model of Venture Growth." *Academy of Management Journal* 44, no. 2, pp. 292–303.

[6] Shane, S., E. Locke, and C. Collins. 2003. "Entrepreneurial Motivation." *Human Resource Management Review* 13, pp. 257–79, 273.

[7] Kantis, H. 2005. "A Systematic Approach to Enterprise Creation." In *Developing Entrepreneurship: Experience in Latin America and Worldwide*, ed. H. Kantis, 17–27. Washington, DC: Inter-American Development Bank.

necessarily follow a linear sequence, Kantis suggested that it was useful to analyze that process as three stages of events, which, hopefully, lead to the creation of entrepreneurs and entrepreneurial firms.[8] The first stage was "inception of the entrepreneurial venture" and involved three key activities and related questions. First, the prospective entrepreneur needs to acquire the motivation and skills needed to become an entrepreneur and this raises the following questions: what are the motivating factors that first lead a person to think about becoming an entrepreneur? how does the entrepreneur's immediate social context influence the motivational process? and where does an individual find the motivation and skills needed to become an entrepreneur? Second, the business opportunity for the new enterprise must be identified and researchers would like to know the principal sources of business opportunities and how entrepreneurs find and identify these opportunities? Finally, business planning is required during the preparatory phase and the inquiries focus on what information and planning tools do entrepreneurs use? The second stage is "company startup" and begins with the final decision to begin entrepreneurial activity. Kantis suggested that it is important to understand how entrepreneurs make the final decision to start a new business. Once the decision has been made, the inquiry turns to understanding how entrepreneurs access and mobilize the financial and nonfinancial resources needed to launch a business. The last of the three stages is early development of the firm including introduction to the market of the firm's goods and services and management of the firm during the early years. The key questions for this stage include what factors influence market entry; what are the main problems confronting entrepreneurs during this phase and how to they deal with those problems; and how do entrepreneurs finance firm operations and growth?

Having defined and explained the "entrepreneurial process," Kantis suggests that a model of an "entrepreneurial development system" can be created by adding in a combination of elements and factors that have an impact, both positive and negative, on the process and, ultimately, on the efficient development of entrepreneurs and entrepreneurial firms. Kantis

---

[8] Id. at pp. 19–21.

grouped these factors into a short list of categories, which he introduced and described as follows[9]:

- *Social and economic conditions* reflect the profile of the households from which potential entrepreneurs emerge and take into factors such as the degree of social fragmentation, access to education, flow of information relevant to entrepreneurial activity, income levels, and overall macroeconomic conditions such as the behavior of demand or the degree of economic stability;
- *Societal culture*, which is discussed extensively in this book, influences the formation of the "entrepreneurial spirit" and cultural values impact important factors such as the social value ascribed to the entrepreneur and attitudes toward the risk of failure;
- *Productive structure and dynamism* refers to the sector and regional profile and the size of the existing enterprises and institutions and is considered important because it determines the type of work and professional experience, including opportunities for the development of entrepreneurial skills and networks of relationships (see below), which individuals can obtain prior to becoming entrepreneurs;
- *Personal aspects,* which refers to sociodemographic profile of the entrepreneur—which are influenced by his or her family, educational and work environments—and his or her entrepreneurial skills (e.g., propensity to assume risk, tolerance for hard work, managerial capacities, and creativity);
- *Networks*, which include the assistance provided through his or her social networks (i.e., friends and family), institutional networks (i.e., business associations, institutions of higher

---

[9] The summary description of each of the categories is based on Kantis, H. 2005. "A Systematic Approach to Enterprise Creation." In *Developing Entrepreneurship: Experience in Latin America and Worldwide*, ed. H. Kantis, 17–27, 20–22. Washington, DC: Inter-American Development Bank.

learning and/or development agencies), and commercial networks (i.e., suppliers and customers);

- *Factor markets,* which provide entrepreneurs with access to financial resources (e.g., bank loans, venture capital, and/or government financing), skilled labor, and professional services (accountants, consultants, etc.) and suppliers of inputs and equipment; and

- *Regulations and policies* that have an impact on enterprise creation, such as taxes, procedural requirements for formally establishing a new firm, and initiatives and programs to develop entrepreneurship.

In many ways, the list of factors developed by Kantis was similar to those discussed in the following sections. For example, the issues consumed in personal aspects and networks can also be found in the discussion of entrepreneurial motivations, cognitive factors, and nonmotivational individual differences. In addition, social and economic conditions and societal culture are part of the relevant environmental conditions and productive structure and dynamism determine entrepreneurial opportunities and competitive strategies. As noted above, Kantis himself deployed his model as a tool for cross-border comparison of entrepreneurial activities and policies.

Entrepreneurial Motivations

The "entrepreneurial motivations" that Shane et al. included in their model were similar to those that they had identified and analyzed in their survey of previous research discussed above and were separated into "general" and "task-specific." Motivations classified as "general" included nAch, locus of control, "vision," desire for independence, passion, and drive. The motivations classified as "task-specific" included "goal-setting" and "self-efficacy" and were similar to those analyzed in the "situation-specific motivation" domain of the Baum et al. study.[10] Once again, it

_____

[10] Shane, S., E. Locke, and C. Collins. 2003. "Entrepreneurial Motivation." *Human Resource Management Review* 13, pp. 257–79, 274.

is important to emphasize the Shane et al. believed that the influence of any of these motivations varied depending upon the stage of the entrepreneurial process:

> In some cases, all of the motivations might matter. In other cases, only some of the motivations might matter. The relative magnitudes of how much each motivation matters will likely vary, depending on the part of the process under investigation. In fact, it is quite plausible that motivations that influence one part of the process have all of their effects at that stage in the process and have no effects on later stages in the process.[11]

Baum et al. tested for the influence of traits and motives of entrepreneurs on venture success.[12] They noted that several important personality theorists, such as McClelland, had argued that personality predispositions were important predictors of the success of entrepreneurial ventures[13] and observed that venture capitalists, whose job it is to "pick winners" among all the proposals and opportunities presented to them by would-be entrepreneurs, had consistently emphasized how much weight they gave to "entrepreneur characteristics" as key indicators of profitable investments.[14] The problem, from a research perspective, was that studies had shown a relatively weak relationship between the traits and motives of entrepreneurs and venture performance and that traits and motives were not nearly as important to venture success as organizational and industry

---

[11] Id. at p. 275.

[12] Baum, J., E. Locke, and K. Smith. 2001. "A Multi-dimensional Model of Venture Growth." *Academy of Management Journal* 44, no. 2, pp. 292–303.

[13] Hollenbeck, J., and E. Whitener. 1988. "Reclaiming Personality Traits for Personnel Selection." *Journal of Management* 14, no. 1, pp. 81–91; and McClelland, D. 1965. "N-Achievement and Entrepreneurship: A Longitudinal Study." *Journal of Personality and Social Psychology* 1, no. 4, pp. 389–92.

[14] MacMillan, I., R. Siegel, and P. SubbaNarisimha. 1985. "Criteria Used by Venture Capitalists to Evaluate New Venture Proposals." *Journal of Business Venturing* 1, no. 1, pp. 119–28.

variables.[15] Baum et al. believed that the influence of individual-level traits and motives of entrepreneurs had not been properly recognized because they did not work in isolation from other factors and the previous studies had not included the proper traits.[16] In their study they supplemented the pool of entrepreneurial traits by adding tenacity, pro-activity, and passion and tested not only for a direct relationship of traits and motives on venture growth but also for the relationship that traits and motives had on other influencers of venture growth (i.e., "indirect effects"). While they did not find support for the hypothesis that, with all other antecedents of venture growth controlled, the greater the tenacity, pro-activity, and passion for work of a venture's CEO, the greater the venture's growth, they did find evidence that these individual-level traits and motives *did* have a strong influence on several other factors relevant to venture growth, including general competencies, situation-specific motivation, and competitive strategies.[17]

As mentioned above, Baum et al. created and tested a separate dimension for several situational-specific motivations, including "vision," growth goals, and self-efficacy.[18] These motivations were distinguished from the other entrepreneurial traits and motives because they had previously demonstrated "significant empirical relationships with business performance" and had been celebrated by researchers as important for planning and venture performance.[19] Baum et al. did indeed find confirmation for

---

[15] Begley, T., and D. Boyd. 1987. "Psychological Characteristics Associated with Performance in Entrepreneurial Firms and Smaller Businesses." *Journal of Business Venturing* 2, no. 1, pp. 79–93; Low, M., and I. MacMillan. 1988. "Entrepreneurship: Past Research and Future Challenges." *Journal of Management* 14, no. 2, pp. 139–61; Sandberg, W., and C. Hofer. 1987. "Improving New Venture Performance: The Role of Strategy, Industry Structure and the Entrepreneur." *Entrepreneurship Theory and Practice* 16, no. 1, pp. 73–90.

[16] Baum, J., E. Locke, and K. Smith. 2001. "A Multi-Dimensional Model of Venture Growth." *Academy of Management Journal* 44, no. 2, pp. 292–303, 292.

[17] Id. at pp. 299–300.

[18] Id. at p. 293.

[19] Low, M., and I. MacMillan. 1988. "Entrepreneurship: Past Research and Future Challenges." *Journal of Management* 14, no. 2, pp. 139–61; and Bird, B. 1989. *Entrepreneurial Behavior*. Glenview, IL: Scott, Foresman. Also, one of the

the hypothesis that "[t]he greater the situationally specific motivation of a venture's CEO with respect to vision, growth goals, and self-efficacy, the greater the venture's growth."[20] Apparently, these traits and motivations had a much greater direct effect on venture growth than the more "general" traits and motives tested by Baum et al.; however, those general traits and motives did have a significant influence on the strength of the situational-specific motivations.[21] The general competencies of entrepreneurs also had a large influence on their situational-specific motivations. Situational-specific motivations also had a significant influence on elements of the competitive strategies selected by entrepreneurs, which, in turn, ultimately influenced venture growth. Specifically, Baum et al. argued that organizations led by highly motivated entrepreneurs often reflected the character of these entrepreneurs as evidenced by the choices made regarding organizational structures and processes and the bias toward recruiting goal-oriented employees.[22]

Cognitive Factors

According to Locke, all action is a result of the integration or combination of motivational and cognitive factors and thus it was necessary and appropriate for Shane et al. to include certain cognitive factors—knowledge, skills, and abilities ("KSAs")—in their analytical framework.[23] They

---

core elements of motivation in charismatic leadership theory is "vision." See Bass, B. 1990. *Handbook of Leadership.* New York, NY: Free Press.

[20] Baum, J., E. Locke, and K. Smith. 2001. "A Multi-Dimensional Model of Venture Growth." *Academy of Management Journal* 44, no. 2, pp. 292–303, 293, 297, 301 (citing Bandura, A. 1997. *Self-efficacy: The Exercise of Control.* New York, NY: W.H. Freeman.); and Locke, E., and G. Latham. 1990. *A Theory of Goal Setting and Task Performance.* Englewood Cliffs, NJ: Prentice-Hall.

[21] Id. at pp. 294–299 (confirming hypothesis that "[t]he greater the tenacity, proactivity, and passion for work of a venture's CEO, the greater his or her situationally specific motivation with respect to vision, goals, and self-efficacy").

[22] Id. at p. 301 (citing Hambrick, D., and P. Mason. 1984. "Upper Echelons: The Organization as a Reflection of Its Top Managers." *Academy of Management Review* 9, no. 2, pp. 193–206).

[23] Id. at p. 275.

explained that entrepreneurs must have "some knowledge," particularly knowledge about the industry and markets in which they are involved and the technology that is relevant to the projected success of the entrepreneurial activities. In addition, entrepreneurs must have certain skills, the range of which depends on the circumstances, which can be called upon during the various stages of entrepreneurial process. Shane et al. listed skills such as "selling and bargaining, leadership, planning, decision making, problem solving, team building, communication and conflict management." Shane et al. mentioned that entrepreneurs can hire persons to fill in gaps in their own "skill set"; however, they believed that entrepreneurs cannot rely on others for the knowledge about the industry and technology that is crucial for setting the right course during the entrepreneurial process. Finally, entrepreneurs needed certain abilities, such as intelligence, in order to acquire and process the knowledge and develop and use the skills referred to above.

As with the "entrepreneurial motivations," the KSAs are needed in order for entrepreneurs to navigate the entrepreneurship process and Shane et al. noted that not only did the KSAs come into play in making the best decisions at each stage of the process but also in the development of an overriding "vision" for entrepreneurial activities, including formulation of a viable strategy for the firm.[24] Inclusion of these cognitive factors in the model was consistent with the findings of other researchers that have highlighted the importance of certain types of knowledge and skills on various phases of the entrepreneurial process, particularly the startup and resource assembly and organization stages.[25] Motivations are linked

---

[24] Locke referred to "vision" as the "capacity of the human mind to discover, through creative thought, solutions that had not existed before" and noted that vision often stepped in when traditional financial methods of assessing and mapping an opportunity would not be helpful (e.g., when Jobs first developed the mass market for personal computers or Walton planted the seeds for discount retailing). Id. at p. 263 (citing Locke, E. 2000. *The Prime Movers: Traits of the Great Wealth Creators*. New York, NY: AMACOM).

[25] Id. at p. 275 (citing Bates, T. 1990. "Entrepreneur Human Capital Inputs and Small Business Longevity." *Review of Economics and Statistics* 72, no. 4, pp. 551–59; and Schoonhoven, C., K. Eisenhardt, and K. Lyman. 1990. "Speeding Products to Market: Waiting Time to First Product Introduction in New Firms." *Administrative Science Quarterly* 35, pp. 177–207).

to cognitive factors in that motivations provide entrepreneurs with the incentive and drive to acquire the necessary KSAs and take the actions necessary to implement the vision and associated strategies.

KSAs were also part of the foundational principles for the "individual competencies" domain in the Baum et al. model.[26] Baum et al. actually broke out this domain into two categories: "general" competencies, which included an array of so-called *organizational competencies* such as oral presentation skills, decision-making ability, conceptualization ability, diagnostic use of concepts, use of power, and "opportunity recognition"; and "specific competencies," which included technical skills and industry skills.[27] They found that the general competencies of a venture's CEO, particularly with respect to organizational skills and opportunity recognition, did not have a material positive relationship on venture growth; however, they did influence situation-specific motivations and the selection process for competitive strategies. On the other hand, specific competencies were found to have a direct positive relationship with, and effect on, venture growth.[28] In their own words, Baum et al. explained:

> We speculate that an entrepreneur's technical and industry competencies are an important form of expert power that facilitates the implementation of the entrepreneur's vision and strategy. We can further hypothesize that these entrepreneurial skills may serve as sources of competitive advantage that rivals find difficult to identify and imitate.[29]

---

[26] Id. at p. 293.

[27] Id. (citing Bird, B. 1989. *Entrepreneurial Behavior*. Glenview, IL: Scott, Foresman); Boyatzis, R. 1982. *The Competent Manager*. New York, NY: Wiley; Chandler, G., and E. Jansen. 1992. "The Founder's Self-Assessed Competence and Venture Performance." *Journal of Business Venturing* 7, pp. 223–36; and Herron, L., and R. Robinson. 1990. "Entrepreneurship Skills: An Empirical Study of the Missing Link Connecting the Entrepreneur with Venture Performance." Paper Presented at the annual meeting of the Academy of Management, San Francisco.

[28] Id. at pp. 299–301.

[29] Id. at pp. 300–301.

Notice should be taken of the work of Nassif et al., who studied entrepreneurship from a dynamic perspective in order to gain a better understanding of the values, characteristics, and actions over time as they launch and develop their businesses.[30] Based on their analysis of work by various researchers on the types and characteristics of Brazilian small business entrepreneurs, Nassif et al. developed an entrepreneurial process dynamics framework that included and distinguished "affective aspects," which were most important during the earliest stages of the entrepreneurial process, and "cognitive aspects," which became more important relative to the affective aspects as time went on and the business matured. The affective aspects included perseverance, courage, willpower, initiative, willingness to take risks, personal motivation, facing challenges, passion for the business, autonomy, self-confidence, and independence. Cognitive aspects included assumption of calculated risks, ability to establish partnerships, defining goals and planning skills, knowing one's limits, and eloquent communication skills.

Entrepreneurial Opportunities

Shane et al. argue that the nature of entrepreneurship, including the decisions made with regard to entrepreneurial actions and even deciding whether or not entrepreneurship is an appropriate and desired path, depends upon the specific "opportunity" confronting the would-be entrepreneur.[31] They defined "entrepreneurial opportunities" as "situations in which new goods, services, raw materials, and organizing methods can be introduced and sold at greater than the cost of their production."[32] The problem, of course, is coming up with a reasonable estimate of the "expected value" of an opportunity since, by definition, an opportunity

---

[30] Nassif, V., A. Ghobril, and N.S.D. Silva. April/June 2010. "Understanding the Entrepreneurial Process: A Dynamic Approach." *Brazilian Administrative Review* 7, no. 2, pp. 213–26.

[31] Shane, S., E. Locke, and C. Collins. 2003. "Entrepreneurial Motivation." *Human Resource Management Review* 13, no. 2, pp. 257–79, 269.

[32] Id. at pp. 260–61 (citing Shane, S., and S. Venkataraman. 2000. "The Promise of Entrepreneurship as a Field of Research." *Academy of Management Review* 25, no. 1, pp. 217–26, 220).

is all about potential rather than guarantees. One issue, of course, is that there is wide range of activities that would fit within this definition of opportunity: grand and bold initiatives that seek to establish whole new industries (e.g., the early biotechnology firms) as well as more modest undertakings such as starting a new business in an established industry to exploit a small, yet potential profitable, market niche.[33] In addition, the value of opportunities not only varies across industries but one also finds variations in opportunity values within industries. Still another factor that must be considered is how the entrepreneur "interprets" the opportunity. The Internet, for example, has generated a wide array of new business models from e-tailing targeting millions of potential customers to sole proprietors looking to make their mark through website design or consulting on online advertising. Finally, "solutions" clearly matter—if an entrepreneur develops a product, service, or method that creates more sales and/or lower production costs than he or she can rightly assign a high value to that opportunity.

It is assumed that an individual will generally not pursue opportunities unless they have value to the individual and a "valuable opportunity for an individual is one that generates a level of profit that exceeds the entrepreneur's opportunity cost, a premium for the illiquidity of money, time and effort expended, and a premium for bearing risk and uncertainty."[34] Obviously, this formulation allows that some opportunities will have more value than others for a particular entrepreneur and that the same opportunity may be valued differently by different entrepreneurs.[35]

---

[33] Established industries may also be reenergized and transformed by entrepreneurs testing new business models, such as Sam Walton's disruptive activities in the retail sector and the new organizing models in that same sector deployed by a wide array of "e-tailors." Id. pp. 261–62.

[34] Id. (citing Venkataraman, S. 1997. "The Distinctive Domain of Entrepreneurship Research: An Editor's Perspective." In *Advances in Entrepreneurship, Firm Emergence and Growth*, eds. J. Katz and R. Brockhaus, 119–38. vols. Greenwich, CT: JAI Press).

[35] Shane et al. observed that variations in the opportunities that various entrepreneurs might pursue were not being taken into account by researchers studying the effects of motivation on entrepreneurial decisions. They suggested, among other things, that "researchers could explore settings in which potential entrepreneurs

It does not necessarily mean that entrepreneurs will always choose the opportunity that has the highest "value" since that decision will be influenced by the motivations that are most important in the entrepreneur's decision-making process at the particular time; however, studies have shown that entrepreneurs are more likely to pursue an opportunity based on a condition or asset that is likely to generate extraordinary returns (e.g., patented technology, large market opportunity, and/or high margins).[36]

Ultimately, the value of entrepreneurial opportunities only becomes clear in hindsight once the entrepreneurial process has played out and each of the stages in that process have been navigated and completed. At each point along the way information is gathered, and decisions are made, which influence the assessment of the value of the opportunity and there could arise a possibility where an opportunity ceases to be "valuable" for the entrepreneur because, for example, the anticipated level of profits no longer exceeds the entrepreneur's estimate of the opportunity costs that will need to be borne over the remaining stages of the entrepreneurial process. All of this does necessarily dissuade the boldest of innovators from moving forward in situations where it is impossible to quantify the value of an opportunity simply because what is being attempted has never been done before. Shane et al. reminded that Steve Jobs in the PC industry and Sam Walton in retailing were able to take advantage of opportunities through entrepreneurial actions that turned nothing more than a potential market for a product or service that had not been created into tangible industries in which values could eventually be assigned to the anticipated outputs of their actions. For Jobs, he not only had to develop the technical solution (i.e., a computer with a reasonable design cost) he also had to create a new "mass market" through a combination of

---

pursue reasonably identical opportunities," such as comparing the motivations of persons interested in purchasing a McDonald's franchise against those of persons preferring to tapped to manage a company-owned McDonald's outlet. Id. at p. 270.

[36] Shane, S., 2001. "Technology Opportunities and New Firm Creation." *Management Science* 47, no. 2, pp. 205–20. For further discussion of the "characteristics of entrepreneurial opportunities," see Christiansen, C. 1997. *The Innovator's Dilemma*. Cambridge, MA: Harvard Business School Press.

design features, easy-to-use software, pricing, and marketing. Walton had to test and prove the viability of his "discounting" strategy and fend off the responses of his existing competitors as well as new competitors who entered the market after Walton took the first steps.[37]

Environmental Conditions

A large amount of research had been done on the impact of environmental conditions on entrepreneurship and many of these studies have found indications that the success of an entrepreneurial activity, as measured by the firm growth, is influenced by things such as

> (1) political factors (e.g., legal restrictions, quality of law enforcement, political stability and currency stability); (2) market forces (e.g., structure of the industry, technology regime, potential barriers to entry, market size, and population demographics); and (3) resources (e.g., availability of investment capital, labor market including skill availability, transportation infrastructure, and complimentary technology).[38]

Shane et al. argued that it would be interesting and useful to study whether the motivations of entrepreneurs led to different types of entrepreneurial actions and decisions under different environmental conditions.[39] They also noted that in order to gain a clearer understanding of the influence of motivations on the entrepreneurial process and the impact of environmental conditions would need to be controlled, perhaps

---

[37] Shane, S., E. Locke, and C. Collins. 2003. "Entrepreneurial Motivation." *Human Resource Management Review* 13, pp. 257–79, 261–62.

[38] Id. at pp. 260, 275–76. Other environmental factors mentioned by Shane et al. included the age of the industry, the condition of capital markets, and the overall health of the economy. See also, for example, Aldrich, H., and G. Wiedenmayer. 1993. "From Traits to Rates: An Ecological Perspective on Organizational Foundings." In *Advances in Entrepreneurship, Firm Emergence, and Growth*, eds. J. Katz and R. Brockhaus, Sr. 1 vols. Greenwich, CT: JAI Press, 145–95; and Aldrich, H. 2000. *Organizations Evolving*. Beverly Hills, CA: Sage.

[39] Id.

by limiting sampling to firms in the same industry pursuing comparable market and technological opportunities.

Baum et al. also analyzed environmental conditions and focused on three dimensions relating to the environment: dynamism, which is the level of environmental predictability, including the rate of market and industry change and the level of uncertainty that firms must endure due to forces that are out of their control; munificence, which refers to the support provided by the environment for organizational growth; and complexity, which is measured by the concentration or dispersion of organizations in the environment.[40] Somewhat surprisingly, Baum et al. did not find sufficient evidence to support their hypothesis that a firm's environment is related to venture growth. Specifically, operating in a stable, munificent, and simple environment did not guarantee that a firm would achieve the highest growth.[41] Environmental factors did have a significant, positive influence on competitive strategies but not as much as the traits, general competencies, and situation-specific motivations of the entrepreneurs leading the firms.[42] Baum et al., noting the somewhat surprising "relatively low impact of the environmental domain on venture growth," suggested that perhaps CEOs of smaller firms have more control over the growth and performance of their firms than had previously been suggested by several "macro theories" such as those posited by Hannan and Freeman and Pfeffer and Salancik.[43]

---

[40] Id. at pp. 293–94 (citing Dess, G., and P. Davis. 1984. "Porter's (1980) Generic Strategies as Determinants of Strategic Group Membership and Organizational Performance." *Academy of Management Journal* 27, no. 3, pp. 467–88; and Aldrich, H., and G. Wiedenmayer. 1993. "From Traits to Rates: An Ecological Perspective on Organizational Foundings." In *Advances in Entrepreneurship, Firm Emergence, and Growth*, eds. J. Katz and R. Brockhaus, Sr. 1 vols. 145–95. Greenwich, CT: JAI Press.

[41] Id. at p. 301.

[42] Id. at p. 299.

[43] Id. at p. 301 (citing Hannan, M., and J. Freeman. 1977. "The Population Ecology of Organizations." *American Journal of Sociology* 82, no. 5, pp. 929–64; and Pfeffer, J., and G. Salancik. 1978. *The External Control of Organizations*. New York, NY: Harper & Row).

Competitive Strategies

Shane et al. argued that it was important for researchers to study and analyze the role that individual motivations played in the specific decisions that entrepreneurs made at certain points during the entrepreneurial process—in other words, how do the motivations of the entrepreneurs influence the choices that they make regarding "business strategies."[44] Shane et al. offered several scenarios. First, they suggested that an inventor with a high level of self-efficacy might be more likely to take an aggressive approach regarding exploitation of his or invention, such as going through the trouble of forming their own firm, while an inventor with an invention of equal "value" but lower self-efficacy might prefer to pursue profits indirectly through the efforts of others by selecting a strategy of licensing the invention to others who take on the additional tasks found along the path of the entrepreneurial process. Another example would be the influence of the entrepreneur's "need for independence" on financing strategies: entrepreneurs scoring high on the measure might be more motivated to self-finance their firms to avoid having to put up with the "interruptions" from outside investors while entrepreneurs scoring lower on that measure would not be uncomfortable with giving up some control over their businesses in exchange for capital (e.g., venture capital investment).

Baum et al. studied the relationship of a firm's competitive strategy to its performance. They conceived of "competitive strategy" in terms of three broad business-level choices suggested by Porter as alternative viable approaches for dealing with environmental forces: "focus" strategies, which target a particular set of customers, segment of a product line or geographic market; "low-cost" strategies, which involve construction of efficient-scale facilities and aggressive pursuit of cost reductions; and "differentiation" strategies, which are based on attempting to create and market innovative, high-quality products and/or services industry-wide.[45] According to Porter, in order for firms to have a chance at being successful

---

[44] Id. at p. 272.

[45] Id. at p. 293 (citing Porter, M. 1980. *Competitive Strategy*. New York, NY: Free Press); and Dess, G., and P. Davis. 1984. "Porter's (1980) Generic Strategies as Determinants of Strategic Group Membership and Organizational Performance." *Academy of Management Journal* 27, no. 3, pp. 467–88.

they need to pick and follow one of these strategies and failure to do leaves them "stuck in the middle" and doomed to failure.[46] Baum et al. found evidence supporting Porter's proposition (i.e., that a firm's competitive strategy will be related to performance and that the firms with the highest growth were those that emphasized either a focus, low-cost, or differentiation strategy).[47] Interestingly, they also found that choices regarding competitive strategy were heavily influenced by the traits, general competencies, and situation-specific motivations of the entrepreneurs responsible for making the decisions about firm strategy.[48] This finding was consistent with theories holding that personal characteristics of entrepreneurs are determinants of their personal strategies and that these personal strategies are, in turn, determinants of the strategies of the organizations that they found and lead.[49]

Nonmotivational Individual Differences

While Shane et al. focused on motivational differences among prospective entrepreneurs, they acknowledged that nonmotivational individual differences have been shown to play an important role in the willingness of people to pursue entrepreneurial activities. For example, researchers have found evidence that a person's decision to become an "entrepreneur" may depend on such factors as the person's opportunity cost,[50] which is actually built into the definition of "entrepreneurial opportunity" used by Shane et al.; his or her stocks of financial capital[51]; the

---

[46] Id. at p. 293 (citing Porter, M. 1980. *Competitive Strategy*, 42. New York, NY: Free Press.)

[47] Id. at pp. 297, 301.

[48] Id. at p. 301.

[49] Id. (citing Bandura, A. 1997. *Self-efficacy: The Exercise of Control*. New York, NY: W.H. Freeman.); and Locke, E., and G. Latham. 1990. *A Theory of Goal Setting and Task Performance*. Englewood Cliffs, NJ: Prentice-Hall.

[50] Amit, R., E. Meuller, and I. Cockburn. 1995. "Opportunity Costs and Entrepreneurial Activity." *Journal of Business Venturing* 10, no. 2, pp. 95–106.

[51] Evans, D., and L. Leighton. 1989. "Some Empirical Aspects of Entrepreneurship." *American Economic Review* 79, pp. 519–35.

social ties that he or she may have with investors[52]; and the person's career experience.[53] There does not, however, appear to be much research on how these nonmotivational factors specifically influence particular stages of the entrepreneurial process. Presumably a large stock of personal financial capital and/or close social ties with investors would be helpful in procuring capital for the firm but these "advantages" may be of value during other stages of the process.

Societal Culture and Entrepreneurship

While a good deal of the research regarding entrepreneurship has focused on questions such as identifying individual traits and values that are positively associated with entrepreneurial activities, it is generally conceded that societal culture also plays an important role in entrepreneurship.[54] In fact, as Mueller and Thomas put it,

> culture, as the underlying system of values peculiar to a specific group or society, shapes the development of certain personality traits and motivates individuals in a society to engage in behaviors that may not be as prevalent in other societies . . . [e]ntrepreneurial activity (i.e., new venture creation) may be one of these behaviors

---

[52] Aldrich, H., and C. Zimmer. 1986. "Entrepreneurship through Social Networks." In *The Art and Science of Entrepreneurship*, eds. D. Sexton and R. Smilor, 3–23. Cambridge, MA: Ballinger.

[53] Cooper, A., C. Woo, and W. Dunkleberg. 1989. "Entrepreneurship and the Initial Size of Firms." *Journal of Business Venturing* 4, no. 5, pp. 97–108.

[54] See, for example, Holt, D. 1997. "A Comparative Study of Values among Chinese and USA Entrepreneurs: Pragmatic Convergence between Contrasting Cultures." *Journal of Business Venturing* 12, no. 6, pp. 483–505; McGrath, R., I. MacMillan, and S. Scheinberg. 1992. "Elitists, Risk-takers, and Rugged Individualists—An Exploratory Analysis of Cultural-Differences between Entrepreneurs and Non-Entrepreneurs." *Journal of Business Venturing* 7, no. 2, pp. 115–35; Peterson, R. 1988. "Understanding and Encouraging Entrepreneurship Internationally." *Journal of Small Business Management* 26, no. 2, pp. 1–7; and Huisman, D. 1985. "Entrepreneurship: Economic and Cultural Influences on the Entrepreneurial Climate." *European Research* 13, no. 4, pp. 10–17.

which varies across countries due to differences in cultural values and beliefs.[55]

Mueller and Thomas also noted that while there are many factors underlying entrepreneurial behavior that are common across all cultures, such as economic incentives that serve as motivators for entrepreneurship, differences in societal cultures influence other relevant factors by reinforcing certain characteristics related to entrepreneurship, and penalizing other characteristics, thus leading to variations among societies with respect to how closely they are aligned with an entrepreneurial orientation.[56]

Representative Studies of Influence of Societal Culture on Entrepreneurship

While there has been a relative dearth of research on the relationship between culture and entrepreneurship, particularly cross-border comparisons, studies have provided strong evidence that some cultures produce more innovation and entrepreneurship than others.[57] R. Bouncken et al. provided a short summary of some of the research that has been done on cultural aspects of entrepreneurial intentions.[58] They noted, for example,

---

[55] Mueller, S., and A. Thomas. 2000. "Culture and Entrepreneurial Potential: A Nine Country Study of Locus of Control and Innovativeness." *Journal of Business Venturing* 16, no. 1, pp. 51–75, 58.

[56] Id. at p. 59.

[57] Baumol, W. 1990. "Entrepreneurship: Productive, Unproductive, and Destructive." *Journal of Political Economy* 98, no. 5, pp. 893–921; Shane, S. 1995. "Uncertainty Avoidance and the Preference for Innovation Championing Roles." *Journal of International Business Studies* 26, no. 1, pp. 47–68; Shapero, A., and L. Sokol. 1982. "The Social Dimensions of Entrepreneurship." In *Encyclopedia of Entrepreneurship*, ed. K. Vesper, 72–90. Englewood Cliffs, NJ: Prentice Hall.

[58] Bouncken, R., J. Zagvozdina, and A. Golze. 2009. "A Comparative Study of Cultural Influences on Intentions to Found a New Venture in Germany and Poland." *International Journal of Business and Globalisation* 3, no. 1, pp. 47–65, 51–52.

that dissimilarities of entrepreneurship across cultures had been identified by researchers such as Erez and Early[59] and that other researchers had analyzed issues such as the impact of values and culture on entrepreneurial motivations and the generation and success of new ventures. In addition, they cited a number of studies that appeared to confirm that entrepreneurship and the associated new venture generation are influenced by culture. For example, McGrath et al. found that high scores of power distance, individualism, and masculinity, and low scores of uncertainty avoidance, appeared to increase entrepreneurship.[60] However, they also noted that other researchers had found contrary indications with regard to some of the cultural dimensions and concluded that the direction of the influence of culture uncovered in the research community has often been somewhat unclear and conflicting.[61]

---

[59] Erez, M., and P. Earley. 1993. *Culture, Self-Identity, and Work.* New York, NY: Oxford University Press.

[60] McGrath, R., I. MacMillan, and S. Scheinberg. 1992. "Elitists, Risk-takers, and Rugged Individualists—An Exploratory Analysis of Cultural-Differences between Entrepreneurs and Non-entrepreneurs." *Journal of Business Venturing* 7, no. 2, pp. 115–35.

[61] See, for example, McGrath, R., I. MacMillan, and S. Scheinberg. 1992. "Elitists, Risk-takers, and Rugged Individualists—An Exploratory Analysis of Cultural-Differences between Entrepreneurs and Non-entrepreneurs." *Journal of Business Venturing* 7, no. 2, pp. 115–35; Busenitz, L., and C. Lau. 1996. "A Cross-Cultural Cognitive Model of Venture Creation." *Entrepreneurship: Theory and Practice* 20, no. 4, pp. 25–39; Mitchell, R., B. Smith, K. Seawright, and E. Morse. 2000. "Cross-Cultural Cognitions and the Venture Creation Decision." *Academy of Management Journal* 43, no. 5, pp. 974–93; Morris, M., D. Davis, and J. Allen. 1994. "Fostering Corporate Entrepreneurship—Cross-cultural Comparisons of the Importance of Individualism Versus Collectivism." *Journal of International Business Studies* 25, no. 1, pp. 65–89; and Takyi-Asiedu, S. 1993. "Some Socio-Cultural Factors Retarding Entrepreneurial Activity in Sub-Saharan Africa." *Journal of Business Venturing* 8, no. 2, pp. 91–98. The discussion of the various cultural dimensions herein assumes familiarity with the topic, which is introduced and discussed in "Globalization: A Library of Resources for Sustainable Entrepreneurs" prepared and distributed by the Sustainable Entrepreneurship Project (www.seproject.org).

As noted above, McGrath et al. found that a high score on power distance appeared to increase entrepreneurship[62]; however, several other researchers have found that a high score on that cultural dimension actually decreased entrepreneurship.[63] The hypothesis that low power distance is more conducive to entrepreneurship appears to be supported by other studies relating to some of the organizational characteristics associated with increased levels of innovativeness, often mentioned as a core element of entrepreneurship. For example, it is well accepted that innovation is more likely to occur in organic organizational structures, which feature lower power distance, than in higher power distance mechanistic structures.[64] In addition, greater equality of prestige, rewards, and social power has been found to increase innovation.[65] Finally, it has been observed that decentralization, which is associated with low power distance, promotes innovation because upper and lower level staff members are able to communicate more easily.[66] On balance, it appears that cross-cultural

---

[62] McGrath, R., I. MacMillan, and S. Scheinberg. 1992. "Elitists, Risk-takers, and Rugged Individualists—An Exploratory Analysis of Cultural-Differences between Entrepreneurs and Non-entrepreneurs." *Journal of Business Venturing* 7, no. 2, pp. 115–35.

[63] See, for example, Aiken, M., and J. Hage. 1971. "The Organic Organization and Innovation." *Sociology* 5, no. 1, pp. 63–82; Burns, T., and G. Stalker. 1961. *The Management of Innovation*. London: Tavistock; Thompson, J. 1967. *Organizations in Action*. New York, NY: McGraw-Hill; and Zaltman, G., R. Duncan, and J. Holbek. 1973. *Innovations and Organizations*. New York, NY: A Wiley-Interscience Publication.

[64] Burns, T., and G. Stalker. 1961. *The Management of Innovation*. London: Tavistock.

[65] Id. The relative "equality" associated with a low power distant environment also increase opportunities for the formation of coalitions that are useful in combining the resources required for innovation. See, for example, Thompson, J. 1967. *Organizations in Action*. New York, NY: McGraw-Hill.

[66] Aldrich, H. 1979. *Organizations and Environments*. Englewood Cliffs, NJ.: Prentice Hall; and Aiken, M., and J. Hage. 1971. "The Organic Organization and Innovation." *Sociology* 5, no. 1, pp. 63—82. Other researchers have also found that the more innovative organizations in surveys conducted in the United States and Japan were those that created mechanisms for freer communications throughout the organization. See, for example, Shane, S. 1993. "Cultural

research should identify differences between low and high power distance countries with respect to entrepreneurial motivations, with high power distance having a negative impact on such motivations.[67]

There are a number of indicators that individualism should be positively associated with entrepreneurial activities and, in fact, researchers have uncovered evidence that higher levels of individualism in an entrepreneur increase the chances of his or her success.[68] McGrath et al. found that a high societal culture score on individualism appeared to increase entrepreneurship in that society.[69] Individualistic societies tend to be nurturing environments for several of the individual personality traits thought to be positively associated with a bent toward entrepreneurship. For example, Shane found that autonomy and independence are more common in individualistic societies[70] and studies have confirmed that these traits are found more frequently among entrepreneurs than non-entrepreneurs.[71] In addition, Mueller and Thomas speculated, based on several research studies, that:

Influences on National Rates of Innovation." *Journal of Business Venturing*, pp. 59–73; and Thompson, J. 1967. *Organizations in Action*. New York, NY: McGraw-Hill.

[67] Bouncken, R., J. Zagvozdina, and A. Golze. 2009. "A Comparative Study of Cultural Influences on Intentions to Found a New Venture in Germany and Poland." *International Journal of Business and Globalisation* 3, no. 1, pp. 47–65, 51.

[68] Peterson, R. 1980. "Entrepreneurship and Organization." In *Handbook of Organizational Design*, eds. P. Nystrom and W. Starbuck. Oxford, UK: Oxford University Press.

[69] McGrath, R., I. MacMillan, and S. Scheinberg. 1992. "Elitists, Risk-takers, and Rugged Individualists—An Exploratory Analysis of Cultural-Differences between Entrepreneurs and Non-entrepreneurs." *Journal of Business Venturing* 7, no. 2, pp. 115–35.

[70] Shane, S. 1992. "Why Do Some Societies Invent More than Others?" *Journal of Business Venturing* 7, no. 1, pp. 29–46.

[71] For an extensive discussion of the various "trait" theories of entrepreneurship, see "Motivational Traits of Prospective Entrepreneurs" in "Entrepreneurship: A Library of Resources for Sustainable Entrepreneurs" prepared and distributed by the Sustainable Entrepreneurship Project (www.seproject.org).

. . . [s]ince individualistic cultures are more supportive of individual action and more tolerant of independent action than are
collectivist cultures, we would expect that an internal locus of
control orientation would be less prevalent in collectivist cultures
than in individualistic cultures.[72]

However, researchers have suggested that the traditional approach of a
single dimension with individualism and collectivism at opposite ends of
the pole should be modified to take into account that both individualism
and collectivism are necessary for successful entrepreneurship[73] and, in
fact, studies have shown that collectivism increases motivation to form
new ventures and also facilitates the team-based entrepreneurship that
often eases the path to innovation.[74]

McGrath et al. found that low scores of uncertainty avoidance
appeared to increase entrepreneurship.[75] In turn, Dwyer et al. found that
a person's intent to engage in new venture creation will be negatively

---

[72] Mueller, S., and A. Thomas. 2000. "Culture and Entrepreneurial Potential:
A Nine Country Study of Locus of Control and Innovativeness." *Journal of
Business Venturing* 16, pp. 51–75, 60 (including citations). Research has generally
confirmed that firm founders are more "internal" than the general public with
regard to locus of control.

[73] Bouncken, R., J. Zagvozdina, and A. Golze. 2009. "A Comparative Study of
Cultural Influences on Intentions to Found a New Venture in Germany and
Poland." *International Journal of Business and Globalisation* 3, no. 1, pp. 47–65,
52 (citing Tiessen, J. 1997. "Individualism, Collectivism and Entrepreneur-
ship: A Framework for International Comparative Research." *Journal of Business
Venturing* 12, no. 5, pp. 367–84).

[74] Id. (citing Shane, S. 1992. "Why Do Some Societies Invent More than
Others?" *Journal of Business Venturing* 7, no. 1, pp. 29–46; and Shane, S. 1993.
"Cultural Influences on National Rates of Innovation." *Journal of Business Ventur-
ing* 8, no. 1, pp. 59–73).

[75] McGrath, R., I. MacMillan, and S. Scheinberg. 1992. "Elitists, Risk-takers,
and Rugged Individualists—An Exploratory Analysis of Cultural-Differences
between Entrepreneurs and Non-entrepreneurs." *Journal of Business Venturing* 7,
no. 2, pp. 115–35.

influenced by things such as uncertainty avoidance and the fear of over-coming new and unfamiliar barriers (e.g., technological bureaucracy).[76] Mueller and Thomas speculated that

> [s]ince low uncertainty avoidance cultures are more accepting of non-traditional behaviors, it follows that entrepreneurs in those contexts enjoy greater freedom and legitimacy than their counter-parts in high uncertainty avoidance cultures where the "deviance" of entrepreneurs would be viewed with suspicion.[77]

Tuunanen et al. found that preferences for innovation among entre-preneurs were higher among entrepreneurs in the United States, a rela-tively low uncertainty avoidance country, than among entrepreneurs in Finland, a relatively high uncertainty avoidance country.[78] Shane tested the "per capita rate of innovation" among 33 countries and concluded that the rate declined as uncertainty avoidance increased.[79]

Mueller and Thomas conducted a multicultural survey of third-and fourth-year university students in nine countries to analyze the rela-tionship between two common cultural dimensions: individualism-collectivism and uncertainty avoidance, and internal locus of control and innovativeness, two traits that are often associated with entrepreneurial

---

[76] Dwyer, S., H. Mesak, and H. Maxwell. 2005. "An Exploratory Examination of the Influence of National Culture on Cross-national Product Diffusion." *Journal of International Marketing* 13, no. 2, pp. 1–28.

[77] Mueller, S., and A. Thomas. 2000. "Culture and Entrepreneurial Potential: A Nine Country Study of Locus of Control and Innovativeness." *Journal of Business Venturing* 16, pp. 51–75, 61.

[78] Tuunanen, M., and K. Hyrsky. 1997. "Innovation Preferences among Finnish and U.S. Entrepreneurs." *Academy of Entrepreneurship Journal* 3, no. 1, pp. 1–11.

[79] Shane, S. 1993. "Cultural Influences on National Rates of Innovation." *Journal of Business Venturing* 8, pp. 59–73 (innovation rates determined by reference to number of trademarks granted to nationals of the 33 countries included in the survey). See also Shane, S. 1995. "Uncertainty Avoidance and the Preference for Innovation Championing Roles." *Journal of International Business Studies* 26, no. 1, pp. 47–68.

potential.[80] As they had expected, the results confirmed that "some cultures are more conductive for entrepreneurship than others."[81] Specifically, they found that an increased likelihood on internal locus of control orientation in individualistic cultures and also found that what they referred to as "entrepreneurial orientation," defined as a combination of internal locus of control and innovativeness, was more likely to be found in individualistic, low uncertainty avoidance cultures than in collectivistic, high uncertainty avoidance cultures. Mueller and Thomas argued that their results provided support for the notion that creating a "supportive" societal culture may have positive benefits for increasing entrepreneurial potential and suggested that business training efforts include not only technical areas but also lessons that assist prospective entrepreneurs in realizing and cultivating psychological characteristics such as self-reliance, independent action, creativity, and flexible thinking. Mueller and Thomas conceded that other traits associated with entrepreneurial behavior and not included in their study could also have an important impact and that other contextual factors (e.g., other dimensions of societal culture, educational systems, political economy, and stage of economic development) should also be integrated into expanded investigations.

Bouncken et al. set out to "investigate the cultural antecedents of new venture generation" by focusing on several cultural dimensions, power distance, individualism, and collectivism, and searching for differences in cultural influences on entrepreneurship between Germany and Poland.[82]

---

[80] Mueller, S., and A. Thomas. 2000. "Culture and Entrepreneurial Potential: A Nine Country Study of Locus of Control and Innovativeness." *Journal of Business Venturing* 16, no. 1, pp. 51–75. While students in 15 countries were surveyed the cultural analysis was limited to those nine countries within that group that were in 1980 survey conducted by Hofstede: the United States, Croatia and Slovenia (former Yugoslavia), Canada, Ireland, Belgium, Germany, Singapore, and China (PRC).

[81] Id. at p. 52.

[82] Bouncken, R., J. Zagvozdina, and A. Golze. 2009. "A Comparative Study of Cultural Influences on Intentions to Found a New Venture in Germany and Poland." *International Journal of Business and Globalisation* 3, no.1, pp. 47–65. The authors noted that the cultural profiles of the two countries based on Hofstede's four cultural dimensions were as follows: power distance— Germany "low" and Poland "high"; uncertainty avoidance—both "high";

They concluded that their hypothesis that influences on entrepreneur-ship across cultures was supported by Germany and Poland. For example, Bouncken et al. surveyed a sample of 450 MBA students in the two coun-tries and found that among the German students, power distance, which is lower in Germany than in Poland, had a negative impact on entre-preneurial motivation while the same cultural dimension had a positive impact among the Poles. Bouncken et al. speculated that the results for the Germans, which were consistent with prior research on the relation-ship of power distance to entrepreneurship, was due to individuals in that country being more comfortable with being subordinates in organizations with less power distance across organizational levels. On the other hand, people in Poland, weary of hierarchical constraints created by long-stand-ing political conditions, might have a strong desire to break these old ties and increase their social status and freedom through entrepreneurship. Bouncken et al. also found differences between Germany and Poland with respect to the influence of individualism and collectivism, which they believed were best treated as two separate dimensions rather than points on a continuum of a single dimension for purposes of entrepreneurship, on both motivation to form a new venture and actual intention to form a new venture.[83] Finally, Bouncken et al. noted that although motivation to engage in entrepreneurship influenced intent to form a new venture in each country, the likelihood of new venture formation was influenced by noncultural factors such as the economic environment and that this led to a finding that the likelihood of new venture formation was higher in Germany than in Poland.

---

individualism-collectivism—Germany "individualist" and Poland "collectivist"; and masculine-feminine: both "masculine". Id. at p. 50.

[83] Bouncken et al. commented that collectivism is important to certain aspects of successful entrepreneurship such as leveraging resources internally, establish-ing external ties and effective teamwork among members of a group involved in launching a new venture. They noted that their results for Poland, a "collectivist" society as opposed to the "individualism" associated with Germany, explicitly identified the positive impact of collectivism as a motivator for entrepreneurship and thus suggested that it was best for "research to move from the single dimen-sional measures of individualism to two dimensional measures of individualism and collectivism." Id. at pp. 60–61.

Hyrsky et al. compared entrepreneurial behavior between entrepreneurs and small business owners in the United States and Finland, with a specific focus on two personality traits generally associated with potential for entrepreneurship: "innovativeness" and "risk taking."[84] Their results showed that the respondents from the United States scored higher on both "risk taking" propensity and on innovation than their counterparts in Finland. Another interesting finding was that while U.S. founders of their own businesses scored higher on risk taking than those U.S. respondents who had purchased or inherited their businesses (referred to as "nonfounders" by Hyrsky et al.) the situation in Finland was reversed with nonfounders scoring higher on risk taking than Finns who founded their own businesses. The countries scored the same with respect to several other issues. For example, in the combined sample of United States and Finnish respondents the females had higher levels of innovation preference than the males but males scored significantly higher than females with respect to risk taking. In addition, in both the United States and Finland, the respondents who scored highest on innovativeness and risk taking were more likely to take the time to create formal, written plans for developing and growing their businesses. Finally, in both countries there was a correlation between innovativeness and risk taking on the one hand and an orientation toward pursuing profits and growth as opposed to simply earning family income.

Another study by Abbey focused on identifying differences between entrepreneurs in the United States, generally recognized as a highly individualistic societal culture, and the relatively collectivist society of Ghana.[85] The survey results uncovered statistically significant differences

---

[84] Hyrsky, K., M. Tuunanen, and M. Koiranen. March 22, 2012. "Innovativeness and Risk-Taking Propensity: A Cross-Cultural Study of Finnish and U.S. Entrepreneurs and Small Business Owners." lta.hse.fi/1999/3/lta_1999_03_s2.pdf (accessed March 22, 2012).

[85] Abbey, A. 2002. "Cross-Cultural Comparison of the Motivation for Entrepreneurship." *Journal of Business and Entrepreneurship* 14, no. 1, pp. 69–82. The researcher noted that Ghana's place as a more collectivist society on the Hofstede individualism-collectivism scale was consistent with other countries in West Africa where there is a strong emphasis on extended familial relationships and traditional values that persist even in the face of the influences of modernization. See, for example, Sadowsky, R. 1989. *The Things We Lose.* Columbia,

were found between the entrepreneurs in the two countries on entrepreneurial motivations such as the desire for independence, need for economic security, social standing, and opportunity to contribute; however, no difference between entrepreneurs in the United States and Ghana were found on other entrepreneurial motivational factors such as the desire for recognition, innovativeness, and challenge. Abbey cited his results as confirmation that certain motivational factors may be common to entrepreneurs from different cultural backgrounds (i.e., "universal") and that there are also differences between countries caused by differences in the cultural frame of reference of the entrepreneurs in those countries. Abbey observed that recognition of cultural differences is important for policymaking creating economic development policies for collectivist societies such as Ghana since those policies are not likely to be effective if they are based on a Western model that solely or heavily encourages individualist values such as individual initiative and need for individual achievement. Abbey urged policymakers to "focus on how to use the cultural orientation of the people to foster entrepreneurship."[86]

Universality and Cultural Specificity of Entrepreneurial Cognitions

As noted above, there appears to be little opposition to the notion that societal culture plays an important role in entrepreneurial activity.[87] However, as in other areas of leadership and management studies, "universality" has long been debated among scholars and researchers involved in

---

MO: University of Missouri Press; and McFadden, J., and K. Gbekobou. 1984. "Counseling African Children in the United States." *Elementary School Guidance and Counseling* 18, pp. 223–30. The researcher conducted his own assessment among the respondents in his survey to confirm the differences between the two groups of entrepreneurs on various indicators used to measure placement on the individualist-collectivist pole.

[86] Abbey, A. 2002. "Cross-Cultural Comparison of the Motivation for Entrepreneurship." *Journal of Business and Entrepreneurship* 14, no. 1, pp. 69–82.

[87] See, for example, Huisman, D. 1985. "Entrepreneurship: Economic and Cultural Influences on the Entrepreneurial Climate." *European Research* 13, no. 4, pp. 10–17; and Wittman, D. 1989. "Why Democracies Produce Efficient Results." *Journal of Political Economy* 97, no. 6, pp. 1395–424.

international studies of entrepreneurship and there is inconclusive evidence on whether universal reasons exist for entrepreneurship. Mitchell et al., for example, suggested that some part of entrepreneurial thinking may be "universal" due, in part to the increasing similarity of the global environment for business and the need for entrepreneurs everywhere to confront and overcome many of the same challenges along the road to new venture creation.[88] Other researchers, however, have cautioned that any "universal" values and norms attributed to entrepreneurs must be tempered by culture-specific values and norms that heavily influence behaviors in particular countries.[89] Accordingly, while there seems to be a growing consensus that entrepreneurship is an important driving force for new infrastructure, technology, and job creation around the world,[90] the development of a new global system based on entrepreneurship will be impacted by both cultural homogenization and cultural clashes.[91]

Researchers have conducted studies in multiple countries in an effort to identify reasons for new business formation and have found

---

[88] Mitchell, R., B. Smith, K. Seawright, and E. Morse. 2000. "Cross-Cultural Cognitions and the Venture Creation Decision." *Academy of Management Journal* 43, no. 5, pp. 974–93. Other researchers have found similarities across countries with respect to certain predictors of success of small firms including staffing, level of education, and use of professional advice and planning. Lussier, R., and S. Pfeifer. July 1, 2001. "A Cross-National Prediction Model for Business Success." *Journal of Small Business Management* (comparing small firms in the United States and in Central Eastern Europe).

[89] Busenitz, L., C. Gomez, and J. Spencer. 2000. "Country Institutional Profiles: Unlocking Entrepreneurial Phenomena." *Academy of Management Journal* 43, no. 5, pp. 994–1003.

[90] Arzeni, S. Dec 1997/Jan 1998. "Entrepreneurship and Job Creation." *The OECD Observer* 209, pp. 18–20; Bates, T., and C. Dunham. 1993. "Asian-American Success in Self-Employment." *Economic Development Quarterly* 7, no. 2, pp. 199–214; and McDougall, P., and B. Oviatt. 1997. "International Entrepreneurship Literature in the 1990s and Directions for Future Research." In *Entrepreneurship 2000*, 291–320. eds. D. Sexton and R. Smilor, Chicago, IL: Upstart Publishing.

[91] King, R., and T. Craig. 2002. "Asia and Global Popular Culture: The View from He Yong's Garbage Dump." In *Global Goes Local: Popular Culture in Asia*, eds. R. King and T. Craig, 1–11. Vancouver: UBC Press.

indications that entrepreneurs in many countries act out of needs for approval, personal wealth, personal development, independence, social status, and escape.[92] A study conducted by McGrath et al. provided support for the idea that entrepreneurs share a common set of values despite differences in cultural background.[93] Shane et al. identified the "desire for job freedom" as a universal reason for new business formation.[94] A study of entrepreneurs in the United States and Ghana led Abbey to conclude that it was likely that "desire for independence" was a universal reason for new business formation.[95] However, other results from the same study caused Abbey to conclude that there are also differences between countries caused by differences in the cultural frame of reference of the entrepreneurs in those countries. Shapero and Sokol also observed that entrepreneurial activity varies from society to society because of cultural beliefs about entrepreneurship.[96]

One interesting exploration of universality versus culture-specificity was grounded in entrepreneurial cognition research, which focuses on identifying and analyzing entrepreneur's distinctive ways of thinking as

---

[92] Ray, D., and D. Turpin. 1987. "Factors Influencing Entrepreneurial Events in Japanese High Tech Venture Business." In *Frontiers of Entrepreneurship Research*, eds. N. Churchill et al. Wellesley, MA: Babson College; and Scheinberg, S., and I. MacMillan. 1988. "An Eleven-country Study of the Motivation to Start a Business." In *Frontiers of Entrepreneurship Research*, eds. B. Kirchoff, W. Long, W. McMullan, K. Vesper and W. Wetzel. Wellesley, MA: Babson College.

[93] McGrath, R., I. MacMillan, and S. Scheinberg. 1992. "Elitists, Risk-takers, and Rugged Individualists? An Exploratory Analysis of Cultural Differences between Entrepreneurs and Non-entrepreneurs." *Journal of Business Venturing* 7, no. 2, pp. 115–35.

[94] Shane, S., L. Kolvereid, and P. Westhead. 1991. "An Exploratory Examination of the Reasons Leading to New Firm Formation across Country and Gender (Part 1)." *Journal of Business Venturing* 6, no. 6, pp. 431–46.

[95] Abbey, A. 2002. "Cross-Cultural Comparison of the Motivation for Entrepreneurship." *Journal of Business and Entrepreneurship* 14, no. 1, pp. 69–82.

[96] Shapero, A., and L. Sokol. 1982. "The Social Dimensions of Entrepreneurship." In *Encyclopedia of Entrepreneurship*, eds. C. Kent, D. Sexton and K. Vesper, 72–88. Englewood Cliffs, NJ: Prentice Hall.

a way of addressing issues related to the entrepreneurship phenomena.[97] Entrepreneurial cognitions have been shown to be useful in explaining a number of aspects of entrepreneurial activity including, for example, differentiation between entrepreneurs and nonentrepreneurs,[98] opportunity identification,[99] success in the startup process,[100] and making the venture-creation decision.[101] Specifically, Mitchell et al. conducted a comprehensive study of 990 entrepreneurs and business managers in 11 countries, including the members of what was then known as the G7 (i.e., the United States, Canada, the United Kingdom, Germany, France, Italy, and Japan) and four Pacific Rim countries—Australia, Chile, Mexico, and China.[102] The researchers explained that they had identified two cognitive scripts of entrepreneurs, which were generally referred to as

---

[97] Ho, M., and M. Wilson. March 31, 2012. "Cognitive Mapping Methodologies for Entrepreneurial Cognition Research." http://swinburne.edu.au/lib/ir/onlineconferences/agse2008/000022.pdf (accessed March 31, 2012). For further discussion of the "cognitive view" of entrepreneurship, see Meyer, D., W. Gartner, and S. Venkataraman. 2000. "The Research Domain of Entrepreneurship." *Entrepreneurship Division Newsletter* 15, no. 6; Stevenson, H., and J. Jarillo. 1990. "A Paradigm of Entrepreneurship: Entrepreneurial Management." *Strategic Management Journal* 11, no. 1, pp. 17–27; and Venkataraman, S. 1997. "The Distinctive Domain of Entrepreneurship Research." In *Advances in Entrepreneurship, Firm Emergence and Growth*, ed. J. Katz, 119–38. 3 vols. Greenwich, CT: JAI Press.

[98] Baron, R. 1998. "Cognitive Mechanisms in Entrepreneurship: Why and When Entrepreneurs Think Differently than Other People." *Journal of Business Venturing* 13, no. 4, pp. 275–94.

[99] Krueger, N. 2000. "The Cognitive Infrastructure of Opportunity Emergence." *Entrepreneurship Theory and Practice* 24, no. 3, pp. 5–23.

[100] Gatewood, E., K. Shaver, and W. Gartner. 1995. "A Longitudinal Study of Cognitive Factors Influencing Start-up Behaviors and Success at Venture Creation." *Journal of Business Venturing* 10, no. 5, pp. 371–91.

[101] Mitchell, R., B. Smith, K. Seawright, and E. Morse. 2000. "Cross-Cultural Cognitions and the Venture Creation Decision." *Academy of Management Journal* 43, no. 5, pp. 974–93.

[102] Mitchell, R., J. Smith, E. Morse, A. Peredo, and B. McKenzie. 2002. "Are Entrepreneurial Cognitions Universal? Assessing Entrepreneurial Cognitions across Cultures." *Entrepreneurship Theory and Practice* 26, no. 4, pp. 9–32.

"entry" and "doing."[103] The "entry" phase required attention to making "arrangements" for embarking on the entrepreneurial activities. Once those arrangements have been completed, the entrepreneur then moves to the "doing" phase, which requires that the entrepreneur have the "willingness" and the "ability" to take the actions necessary to achieve the goal of successfully engaging in the entrepreneurial activities. Mitchell et al. briefly described the three conditions, mindsets, and skills that must be present in order for entrepreneurship to be successful as follows:

- *Arrangements*: Arrangements include seeking and finding a supportive environment in relation to an opportunity and organizing the resources available from that environment (e.g., capital, social networks (i.e., contacts and relationships), plant and equipment, labor, etc.) that would allow the entrepreneur to capitalize on the opportunity.[104]
- *Willingness*: Willingness includes a commitment to venturing and receptivity to the idea of starting a new venture,[105] readiness to commit,[106] motivation to seek an opportunity,[107] and eagerness to act versus missing an opportunity.[108]

---

[103] Leddo, J., and R. Abelson. 1986. "The Nature of Explanations." In *Knowledge Structures*, eds. J. Galambos, R. Abelson and J. Black, 103–22. New Jersey, NJ: Lawrence Erlbaum Associates.

[104] Vesper, K. 1996. *New Venture Experience*. Seattle, WA: Vector Books; and Mitchell, R., B. Smith, K. Seawright, and E. Morse. 2000. "Cross-Cultural Cognitions and the Venture Creation Decision." *Academy of Management Journal* 43, no. 5, pp. 974–93.

[105] Id.

[106] Ghemawat, P. 1991. *Commitment: The Dynamics of Strategy*. New York, NY: The Free Press; and Hisrich, R., and A. Jankowicz. 1990. "Intuition in Venture Capital Decisions: An Exploratory Study Using a New Technique." *Journal of Business Venturing* 5, no. 1, pp. 49–62.

[107] Kirzner, I. 1982. "The Theory of Entrepreneurship in Economic Growth." In *Encyclopedia of Entrepreneurship*, eds. C. Kent, D. Sexton and K. Vesper, 272–76. Englewood Cliffs, NJ: Prentice Hall; and Krueger, N., and D. Brazeal. Spring 1994. "Entrepreneurial Potential and Potential Entrepreneurs." *Entrepreneurship Theory and Practice* 19, pp. 91–104.

[108] Sexton, D., and N. Bowman-Upton. 1985. "The Entrepreneur: A Capable Executive and More." *Journal of Business Venturing* 1, no. 1, pp. 129–40.

- *Ability*: Ability refers to the knowledge structures or scripts[109] that individuals have to support the capabilities, skills, knowledge, norms, and attitudes required to create a venture[110] and recognize, capture, and protect an opportunity.[111]

Mitchell et al. assumed that a high amount of cognitions were a threshold condition for entrepreneurship and then went on to suggest the following four entrepreneurial archetypes based on the levels of the other two cognitive categories—willingness and ability:

- *Dangerous*: This archetype included individuals who had high levels of arrangement and willingness but low levels of ability, which ultimately created a high risk that the new venture would fail.
- *Professionals*: This archetype included individuals with high levels of arrangements, willingness, and ability cognitions, which made them to be more likely than any of the other archetypes to be successful in their new venture activities due to their higher relative levels of expertise and experience.
- *Arrangers*: This archetype included individuals with low levels of both of the "doing" cognitions—willingness and ability— which meant that while they are likely to possess a protectable niche they would not be actively seeking other opportunities.
- *Conservatives*: This archetype included individuals have relatively higher levels of arrangements and ability cognitions, but lower willingness cognitions. Individuals in this category tended to be extremely careful about pursuing opportunities even though they had access to the necessary resources and

---

[109] Glaser, R. 1984. "Education and Thinking." *American Psychologist* 39, pp. 93–104.

[110] Mitchell, R., B. Smith, K. Seawright, and E. Morse. 2000. "Cross-Cultural Cognitions and the Venture Creation Decision." *Academy of Management Journal* 43, no. 5, 974–93.

[111] Stevenson, H., M. Roberts, and H. Grousbeck. 1994. *New Business Ventures and the Entrepreneur*. Homewood, IL: Irwin.

the skills that are necessary to form a new venture to exploit an opportunity.

Using the framework discussed above, Mitchell et al. used their survey group to test several hypotheses. They found, for example, that it was universally true (i.e., true across all the countries in the survey) that "entry" and "doing" differed between "professional" entrepreneurs and nonentrepreneurs. There was only mixed support for differences between the other entrepreneurial archetypes and nonentrepreneurs. In addition, they found that entrepreneurs could be differentiated into archetypes described in all of the countries in the survey, which they argued was evidence that entrepreneurs share a number of common cognitive constructs—an "entrepreneurial way of thinking"—regardless of the country in which they are operating.[112] However, evidence of cultural influence on entrepreneurial cognitions was also found in the form of country-based differences in the script content of the arrangements, willingness, and ability cognitions of entrepreneurs and differences among countries with respect to the proportion of individuals populating a given entrepreneurial archetype. For example, entrepreneurs in the United States were observed to have higher seeking focus and commitment tolerance cognitions than entrepreneurs in Mexico, the United Kingdom, Germany, or France, and greater resource access cognitions than entrepreneurs in Mexico, Italy, Germany, and France. However, there were also some similarities such as situational knowledge, venture diagnostic ability, and opportunity recognition, which indicates an important similarity in entrepreneurial cognitions.

The general conclusion seems to be that the search for universality is of limited utility and attempts to develop universal theories of business formation should be abandoned in favor of focusing on more robust

---

[112] Meyer, D., W. Gartner, and S. Venkataraman. 2000. "The Research Domain of Entrepreneurship." *Entrepreneurship Division Newsletter* 15, no. 6; Stevenson, H., and J. Jarillo. 1990. "A Paradigm of Entrepreneurship: Entrepreneurial Management." *Strategic Management Journal* 11, pp. 17–27; and Venkataraman, S. 1997. "The Distinctive Domain of Entrepreneurship Research." In *Advances in Entrepreneurship, Firm Emergence and Growth*, ed. J. Katz, 119–38. 3 vols. Greenwich, CT: JAI Press.

models that acknowledge and accept culture-based differences among entrepreneurs, their organizations, and the processes they follow to create new businesses.[113] If this is true, researchers have a wide array of questions that need to be addressed including identifying and measuring just how cultural values influence entrepreneurial activity and the institutions that support entrepreneurship, a topic discussed in more detail below. Another challenge is isolating and understanding the influence of cultural factors in the face of evidence that the level of entrepreneurship is also significantly related to other factors such as economic development and growth, the quality of the legal and regulatory environment, access to financing and other resources, and the prevalence of informality.[114]

Institutional Environment and Entrepreneurship

Several scholars have argued that the rate of new venture formation and growth is directly influenced by the institutional environment, both formal and informal, in which the venture is operating.[115] New ventures, being both new and small, must struggle to gain legitimacy and survive in their external environment and one way to do that is to conform to the norms and practices that have been prescribed and sanctioned by the institutional environment. In many ways, the institutional environment

---

[113] Gartner, W. 1985. "A Conceptual Framework for Describing the Phenomenon of New Venture Creation." *Academy of Management Review* 10, no. 4, pp, 696–706; and Gibb, A., and J. Richie. 1982. "Understanding the Process of Starting Small Business." *European Small Business Journal* 1, no. 1, pp. 26–45.
[114] Klapper, L., R. Amit, and M. Guillén. February 2008. *Entrepreneurship and Firm Formation across Countries*. Washington, DC: The World Bank Group.
[115] Eunni, R. March 2010. "Institutional Environments for Entrepreneurship in Emerging Economies: Brazil vs. Mexico." *World Journal of Management* 2, no. 1, pp. 1–18 (citing Hwang, H., and W. Powell. 2005. "Institutions and Entrepreneurship." In *Handbook of Entrepreneurship Research*, eds. Z. Acs and D. Audretsch, 179–210. Norwell, MA: Kluwer; Gnyawali, D., and D. Fogel. 1994. "Environments for Entrepreneurship Development: Key Dimensions and Research Implications." *Entrepreneurship Theory and Practice* 18, no. 4, pp. 43–62; and Aldrich, H. 1990. "Using an Ecological Perspective to Study Organizational Founding Rates." *Entrepreneurship Theory and Practice* 14, no. 3, pp. 7–24).

limits the range of strategic options that are available to new ventures in a society[116] and thus plays an important role in both the creation and destruction of entrepreneurial activities in that society.[117] It is, therefore, not surprising that one area of comparative research with respect to international entrepreneurship is comparing the institutional environment of different societies for to their favorability for entrepreneurship. The need for this type of research is particularly compelling for emerging economies as they struggle to identify and implement policies that can promote economic development including policies to encourage entrepreneurs to form new ventures that hopefully create new jobs and contribute to an increase in overall economic welfare.[118] In fact, several researchers have asserted that the rate and trajectory of entrepreneurial activities in emerging countries is significantly influenced by the institutional environment in those countries.[119]

---

[116] Ahlstrom, D., and G. Bruton. 2002. "An Institutional Perspective on the Role of Culture in Shaping Strategic Actions by Technology-focused Entrepreneurial Firms in China." *Entrepreneurship Theory and Practice* 26, no. 4, pp. 53–70; and Roy, W. 1997. *Socializing Capital: The Rise of the Large Industrial Corporation in America.* Princeton, NJ: Princeton University Press.

[117] Aldrich, H., and G. Wiedenmayer. 1993. "From Traits to Rates: An Ecological Perspective on Organizational Foundings." In *Advances in Entrepreneurship, Firm Emergence, and Growth*, eds. J. Katz and A. Brockhaus, 145–95. Greenwich, CT: JAI Press.

[118] Wennekers, A., and A. Thurik. 1999. "Linking Entrepreneurship and Economic Growth." *Small Business Economics* 13, no. 1, pp. 27–55; and Baumol, W. 2002. *The Free Market Innovation Machine: Analyzing the Growth Miracle of Capitalism.* Princeton, NJ: Princeton University Press (both observing that new venture creation leads to the creation of new jobs and economic welfare).

[119] Peng, M., and P. Heath. 1996. "The Growth of the Firm in Planned Economies in Transformation: Institutions, Organizations and Strategic Choice." *Academy of Management Review* 21, no. 2, pp. 492–528; Ahlstrom, D., and G. Bruton. 2002. "An Institutional Perspective on the Role of Culture in Shaping Strategic Actions by Technology-Focused Entrepreneurial Firms in China." *Entrepreneurship Theory and Practice* 26, no. 4, pp. 53–70; Smallbone, D., and F. Welter. 2001. "The Distinctiveness of Entrepreneurship in Transition Economies." *Small Business Economics* 16, no. 4, pp. 249–62; and Smallbone, D., and F. Welter. 2006. "Conceptualizing Entrepreneurship in a Transition Context." *International Journal of Entrepreneurship and Small Business* 3, no. 2, pp. 190–206.

While North defined the "institutional framework" of a society as "the fundamental political, social, and legal ground rules, which establish the basis for production and distribution,"[120] Scott laid the foundation for meaningful comparison by suggesting that the formal and informal institutions that influence business can be categorized as follows: regulatory institutions, which include the formal system of laws and regulations that have been adopted and enforced in a given community, society, or country; normative institutions, which include the commercial standards and conventions that have been established and recognized through professional and trade associations in a given community, society, or country; and cognitive institutions, which encompass the culture-specific beliefs regarding socially appropriate behavior, which are acquired by persons as they undergo the socialization process in the community, society, or country.[121] These categories served as the basis for the creation of a survey instrument by Busenitz et al., which has often been used as a means

---

[120] North, D. 1990. *Institutions, Institutional Change, and Economic Performance.* New York, NY: Norton. In a later work, North commented that institutions "form the incentive structure of a society, and the political and economic institutions, in consequence, are the underlying determinants of economic performance" and then defined institutions as "the humanly devised constraints that structure human interaction . . . [t]hey are made up of formal constraints (such as rules, laws, constitutions), informal constraints (such as norms of behavior, conventions, self-imposed codes of conduct), and their enforcement characteristics." North, D. 1994. "Economic Performance through Time." *American Economic Review* 84, no. 3, pp. 359–68, 360.

[121] Scott, W. 1995. *Institutions and Organizations.* Thousand Oaks, CA: Sage. Scott's classification model has been adopted by a number of other researchers. See, for example, Ahlstrom, D., and G. Bruton. 2002. "An Institutional Perspective on the Role of Culture in Shaping Strategic Actions by Technology-Focused Entrepreneurial Firms in China." *Entrepreneurship Theory and Practice* 26, no. 4, pp. 53–70; Kostova, T. 1997. "Country Institutional Profiles: Concept and Measurement." *Academy of Management Best Paper Proceedings*, no. 1, pp. 180–89; Parkhe, A. 2003. "Institutional Environments, Institutional Change and International Alliances." *Journal of International Management* 9, no. 3, pp. 305–16; and Bruton, G., V. Fried, and S. Manigart. 2005. "Institutional Influences on the Worldwide Expansion of Venture Capital." *Entrepreneurship Theory and Practice* 29, no. 6, pp. 737–60.

for measuring a country's institutional profile.[122] The survey items for the various categories, sometimes referred to as "dimensions," included the following:

- *Regulatory*: The level of government assistance and special support to individuals looking to start their own business; the degree to which the government sets aside contracts for new and small businesses; the level of government sponsorship of organizations that assist in the development of new businesses; and the degree to which the government assists entrepreneurs who have failed in earlier business to start new businesses.

- *Cognitive*: The knowledge and skills possess by people in the country pertaining to establishing and operating a new business as indicated by the degree to which individuals know how to legally protect a new business; the degree to which entrepreneurs know how to cope with high levels of risk and manage those risks; and the availability of information regarding markets for products and services to be offered by new businesses.

- *Normative*: The degree to which entrepreneurship is an admired career path within the society; the degree to which innovative and creative thinking is valued and viewed as a route to success within the society; and the degree to which entrepreneurs are admired in the society.[123]

---

[122] Busenitz, L., C. Gomez, and J. Spencer. 2000. "Country Institutional Profiles: Unlocking Entrepreneurial Phenomena." *Academy of Management Journal* 43, no. 5, pp. 994–1003.

[123] It should be noted, however, that when discussing the normative dimension a comparison of the institutional environment for entrepreneurship in Mexico and Brazil, Eunni included the role of industry and trade associations, formalization of recordkeeping and accounting requirements, the sophistication of local banking and insurance industries, support for new business incubation, and the availability of funding for the promotion of innovation. Eunni, R. March 2010. "Institutional Environments for Entrepreneurship in Emerging Economies: Brazil vs. Mexico." *World Journal of Management* 2, no. 1, pp. 1–18.

Eunni used the survey instrument to study and compare the institutional environment for entrepreneurship in two emerging economies: Mexico and Brazil.[124] Eunni first concluded that the Busenitz et al. survey methodology, which was originally designed for industrialized economies, would also be valid for emerging economies in Latin America. Eunni went on to observe that the results of the surveys in the two countries included evidence of significant differences between them with respect to both the regulatory and cognitive dimensions, with Mexico performing much better on both of those dimensions than Brazil. When discussing the regulatory dimension, Eunni noted the importance of measuring the time and difficulty associated with starting a business, employing workers, and registering property. With regard to the cognitive dimension, relevant factors might include religious beliefs and the influence of parents and other family members. Mexico also scored higher than Brazil with respect to its overall institutional profile; however, it was quite telling to see that while there were differences between the two countries neither of them were especially favorable to new venture creation.[125] Eunni recommended that the number of countries included in the test to be sampled be increased in future and validate the survey instrument and cautioned that, of course, institutional environments can be expected to evolve as time goes by and that it is therefore necessary to conduct follow-up surveys as policy initiatives are implemented.

---

[124] Id. (citing Hwang, H., and W. Powell. 2005. "Institutions and Entrepreneurship." In *Handbook of Entrepreneurship Research*, eds. Z. Acs and D. Audretsch, 179–210. Norwell, MA: Kluwer; Gnyawali, D., and D. Fogel. 1994. "Environments for Entrepreneurship Development: Key Dimensions and Research Implications." *Entrepreneurship Theory and Practice* 18, no. 4, pp. 43–62; and Aldrich, H. 1990. "Using an Ecological Perspective to Study Organizational Founding Rates." *Entrepreneurship Theory and Practice* 14, no. 3, pp. 7–24).

[125] Eunni reported that for both countries the means of their scores were below "4" on the 7-point Likert scale and observed that the findings were consistent with how the countries fared in other studies such as the World Economic Forum's Global Competitiveness Report (in 2008 Mexico ranked 60th and Brazil 64th among 134 surveyed countries on indicators of economic competitiveness) and the World Bank's "Ease of Doing Business" rankings (in 2008 Mexico ranked 56th and Brazil ranked 125th among 181 surveyed countries). Id.

The Global Entrepreneurship Monitor (GEM) is a partnership between the London Business School and Babson College that administers a comprehensive research program to produce annual assessments of national levels of entrepreneurial activity. The project was first launched in 1999, when it covered just 10 countries, and has since grown to cover as many as 85 countries in subsequent years and is recognized as the largest ongoing study of entrepreneurial dynamics in the world. The main objectives of the GEM program are measurement of differences in the level of entrepreneurial activity between countries, uncovering the factors that lead to appropriate levels of entrepreneurship and making suggestions for policies that may lead to enhancement of national levels of entrepreneurial activity.[126]

The GEM is based on a conceptual model of the institutional environment and its effect on entrepreneurship. The model recognizes the importance of the social, cultural, and political context in which entrepreneurial activities occur and assumes that these contextual factors influence three sets of conditions: basic requirements, which include institutions, infrastructure, macroeconomic stability, health, and primary education; "efficiency enhancers," which include higher education, goods and labor market efficiency, financial market sophistication, technological readiness, and market size; and the following entrepreneurial framework conditions (EFCs), which represent elements of the institutional environment for entrepreneurship in a particular country:

- *Finance*: The availability of financial resources—equity and debt—for small and medium enterprises (SMEs) (including grants and subsidies);
- *Government policies*: The extent to which taxes or regulations are either size-neutral or encourage SMEs;
- *Government programs*: The presence and quality of direct programs to assist new and growing firms at all levels of government (national, regional, municipal);

---

[126] For further discussion of the GEM, see "Research in Entrepreneurship" in "Entrepreneurship: A Library of Resources for Sustainable Entrepreneurs." Prepared and distributed by the Sustainable Entrepreneurship Project (www.seproject.org).

- *Entrepreneurial education and training*: The extent to which training in creating or managing SMEs is incorporated within the education and training system at all levels (primary, secondary, and postschool);
- *R&D transfer*: The extent to which national research and development will lead to new commercial opportunities and is available to SMEs;
- *Commercial and professional infrastructure*: The presence of property rights and commercial, accounting, and other legal services and institutions that support or promote SMEs;
- *Entry regulation*: Contains two components including "market dynamics," which is the level of change in markets from year to year, and "market openness," which is the extent to which new firms are free to enter existing markets;
- *Physical infrastructure and services*: Ease of access to physical resources—communication, utilities, transportation, land, or space—at a price that does not discriminate against SMEs; and
- *Cultural and social norms*: The extent to which social and cultural norms encourage or allow actions leading to new business methods or activities that can potentially increase personal wealth and income.

The study of the relationship of the institutional environment, regardless of how it is defined and measured, and entrepreneurship is part of the larger field of new institutional economics (NIE), which was pioneered by scholars, such as Coase, North, and Williamson,[127] who were interested in making sure that there was a recognition that "institutions matter" and that the structure and performance of institutions has a substantial influence on economic behavior. Work in NIE has included property rights analysis, transaction cost economics, public choice theory,

---

[127] See, for example, Coase, R. 1937. "The Nature of the Firm." *Economica*, 4, no. 4, pp. 386–405; Williamson, O. 1998. "The Institutions of Governance." *American Economic Review* 88, no. 2, pp. 75–79; North, D. 1994. "Economic Performance through Time." *American Economic Review* 84, no. 3, pp. 359–68.

and comparative economic systems.[128] While there appears to be growing acceptance that institutions must be considered when developing and testing economic theories, particularly with respect to growth and development, the processes remain fairly new[129] and it has been observed that "the causality of the various links and channels of influence between the institutional set-up and development outcome is still not well or fully understood."[130] It has also been acknowledged that the effectiveness of formal institutions and institutional change depends on other factors. For example, Milo noted that "[f]ormal rules must be securely nested in hospitable informal norms for them to function well, since it is the latter that legitimizes the former."[131] In addition, several scholars have cautioned that economic institutions must have the support of the appropriate political institutions in order to be effective.[132] In fact, enlightened political leadership can make even ineffective economic institutions workable and Milo advised that "[t]here are times when it is preferable to work within the context of imperfect existing institutions, rather than use up political capital on long-term institutional reforms."[133]

---

[128] Milo, M. 2007. *Integrated Financial Supervision: An Institutional Perspective for the Philippines*, 18. Tokyo: Asian Development Bank Institute, ADBI Discussion Paper 81.

[129] Aron, J. 2000. "Growth and Institutions: A Review of the Evidence." *The World Rank Research Observer* 15, no. 1, pp. 99–135.

[130] Milo, M. 2007. *Integrated Financial Supervision: An Institutional Perspective for the Philippines*, 19. Tokyo: Asian Development Bank Institute, ADBI Discussion Paper 81, (citing Jütting, J. 2003. *Institutions and Development: A Critical Review*. Paris: OECD Development Centre, Work Paper No. 210).

[131] Id.

[132] See, for example, Chu, K. 2003. "Collective Values, Behavioural Norms and Rules: Building Institutions for Economic Growth and Poverty Reduction." In *Perspectives on Growth and Poverty*, eds. R. van der Hoeven and A. Shorrocks. Tokyo: United Nations University Press; Fukuyama, F. January 19–21, 2006. "Development and the Limits of Institutional Design." Paper Presented at the Seventh Annual Global Development Network Conference, St. Petersburg; and North, D. 1994. "Economic Performance through Time." *American Economic Review* 84, no. 3, pp. 359–68.

[133] Milo, M. 2007. *Integrated Financial Supervision: An Institutional Perspective for the Philippines*, 19. Tokyo: Asian Development Bank Institute, ADBI Discussion Paper 81.

While much time, effort, and capital has been invested in institutional reform in both developed and developing countries, the results have not always been what had been expected.[134] It seems clear that creating institutions is not sufficient and that growth and economic development only follows when the institutions are "efficient" and "encourage individuals to engage in productive activities by providing appropriate incentives and establish a stable structure of human interactions, which reduce uncertainty." Scholars have identified and defined two types of "efficiency" with respect to institutions. The first is "substantive efficiency," which includes rules that promote allocative efficiency, and the second is "procedural efficiency," which include rules designed to either reduce the cost or increase the accuracy of participating in and using the system of rules that form the institutions.[135] Milo has suggested that to achieve the institutional efficiency necessary for achieving development countries must have institutions "that promote exchange by lowering transaction costs and promoting trust . . . and [institutions] that induce the state to protect rather than expropriate private property."[136] Institutions that are likely to have the desired effect of improving the efficiency and integrity of economic transactions include "contracts and contract enforcement mechanisms, commercial norms and rules, and habits and beliefs favoring shared values and the accumulation of human capital" and institutions that can be expected to contribute to the creation and protection of private property rights include "[c]onstitutions, electoral rules, laws governing speech and education, and legal and civic norms."[137]

---

[134] For discussion of the role of institutions in establishing a platform for entrepreneurship that can lead to economic growth and development, see "Entrepreneurship in Developing Countries." Prepared and distributed by the Sustainable Entrepreneurship Project (www.seproject.org).

[135] Milo, M. 2007. *Integrated Financial Supervision: An Institutional Perspective for the Philippines*, 19. Tokyo: Asian Development Bank Institute, ADBI Discussion Paper 81 (citing Posner, R. 1998. "Creating a Legal Framework for Economic Development." *The World Bank Research Observer*. Washington DC: The World Bank).

[136] Id.

[137] Id. at p. 20 (citing Shirley, M. 2005. "Institutions and Development." In *Handbook of New Institutional Economics*, eds. C. Menard and M. Shirley, Dordrecht, Netherlands: Kluwer Academic Publishers).

Innovation Clusters and Entrepreneurial Ecosystems

Many believe that the first serious reference to geographic concentrations of interconnected companies—clusters—appeared in the work of the Cambridge economist Alfred Marshall, who described "industrial districts" that arose from an observed tendency of specialized companies to cluster together to form geographic concentrations of expertise and economic activity.[138] Marshall viewed these tendencies positively and, in fact, wrote in 1890 about how "...great are the advantages which people following the same skilled trade get from near neighboring to one another..."[139] Other economists built on Marshall's initial theory by suggesting and adding other "necessary elements" for the creation and maintenance of "innovation clusters" including the importance of a "self-interested economic agents" or "entrepreneurs" willing to take on and attempt to overcome the risks associated with unproven technologies to seek substantial profits. According to Schumpeter, these entrepreneurs drove the process of transferring and transforming emergent technologies into new products, services, and product models and creating new methods for organizing economic activities to establish new industries and markets.[140] Romer suggested that technological progress is driven by researchers searching for new ideas for innovations, which can eventually provide them with monopoly profits.[141]

A century after Marshall's work Porter undertook an extension examination and analysis of business clusters and uncovered evidence of a strong positive relationship between the proximity of specialized companies and extraordinary competitive success.[142] Dearlove provided the following description of how Porter painted the boundaries of clusters:

---

[138] Lazzeretti, L., S. Sedita, and A. Caloffi, 2014. "Founders and Disseminators of Cluster Research." *Journal of Economic Geography* 14, no. 1, p. 21.

[139] Dearlove, D. July 1, 2001. "The Cluster Effect: Can Europe Clone Silicon Valley?" *Strategy+Business* (citing Marshall, A. 1890. *Principles of Economics*).

[140] For extensive discussion of Schumpeter's theories relating to "entrepreneurship," see Schumpeter, J. 1949. *Theory of Economic Development*.

[141] See Romer, D. 2011. "Endogenous Growth." In *Advanced Macroeconomics*, 4th ed. 101.

[142] Porter explained his research and theories in a number of articles including Porter, M. 1998. "Clusters and the New Economics of Competition." *Harvard*

Professor Porter suggests that clusters encompass an array of linked industries and other entities important to competition, including suppliers of specialized inputs and providers of specialized infrastructure. Clusters also extend downstream to channels and customers and laterally to manufacturers of complementary products, and to companies in industries with common skills, technologies, or inputs. Clusters often include governmental and other institutions, such as universities, standard-setting agencies, and think tanks, as well as providers of specialized training, education, information, research, and technical support.[143]

Porter famously observed that the importance of clustering contrasts dramatically with the idea that the emerging global economy is breaking down barriers and making location less important as a condition for becoming a "global player" and referred to what he called the "paradox of location": "Paradoxically, the enduring competitive advantages in a global economy lie increasingly in local things—knowledge, relationships, and motivation that distant rivals cannot match."[144]

In recent years it has become increasingly popular to refer to innovation clusters as "entrepreneurial ecosystems," a concept that Mason and Brown discussed in 2013 as part of the broader question of what types of policy initiatives should be taken to promote the creation and maturation of high-growth firms (HGFs).[145] Mason and Brown cited the

Business Review 76, no. 6, pp. 77–90; and Porter, M. 2000. "Location, Competition, and Economic Development: Local Clusters in a Global Economy." *Economic Development Quarterly* 14, no. 1, pp. 15–34, 16.

[143] Dearlove, D. July 1, 2001. "The Cluster Effect: Can Europe Clone Silicon Valley?" *Strategy+Business*.

[144] Id. (citing Porter, M. 2000. "Location, Competition, and Economic Development: Local Clusters in a Global Economy." *Economic Development Quarterly* 14, no. 1, p. 16).

[145] Mason, C., and R. Brown. November 7, 2013. "Entrepreneurial Ecosystems and Growth Oriented Entrepreneurship." International Workshop on Entrepreneurial Ecosystems and Growth Oriented Entrepreneurship Organized by OECD LEED Programme and Dutch Ministry of Economic Affairs Workshop; Background Paper (Final Version: January 2014).

works of several researchers that supported the premise that HGFs have a significant impact on economic development. For example, the OECD and Brown et al. have reported that HGFs drive productivity growth, create new employment, increase innovation, and promote business internationalization.[146] Henrekson and Johansson, after conducting a meta-analysis of prior empirical studies, concluded that "a few rapidly growing firms generate a disproportionately large share of all net new jobs compared with non-high growth firms. This is a clear-cut result… [T]his is particularly pronounced in recessions when Gazelles continue to grow."[147] Others have suggested that HGFs have important spill-over effects that are beneficial to the growth of other firms in the same locality and industrial cluster.[148]

Mason and Brown noted that the recognition of the disproportionate value of HGFs to economic development has led policymakers to consider adopting support programs for high-growth entrepreneurship that are more "systems-based" and which rely mainly on "relational" forms

---

[146] Organisation for Economic Co-operation and Development. 2013. *An International Benchmarking Analysis of Public Programmes for High-growth Firms.* OECD LEED programme, Paris; and Brown, R., C. Mason, and S. Mawson. 2014. *Increasing the Vital 6%: Designing Effective Public Policy to Support High Growth Firms.* London: National Endowment for Science Technology & Arts (NESTA).

[147] Henrekson, M., and D. Johansson. 2010. "Gazelles as Job Creators: A Survey and Interpretation of the Evidence." *Small Business Economics* 35, no. 2, pp. 227–44.

[148] Mason, G., K. Bishop, and C. Robinson. 2009. *Business Growth and Innovation: The Wider Impact of Rapidly Growing Firms in UK City-Regions.* London: NESTA [http:// niesr.ac.uk/pdf/ 190509_94959.pdf]; Du, J., Y. Gong, and Y. Temouri. 2013. *High Growth Firms and Productivity: Evidence from the UK.* London, NESTA. [http://nesta.org.uk/publications/working_papers/assets/features/high_growth_ firms_and_productivity]; Feldman, M., J. Francis, and J. Bercovitz, 2005. "Creating a Cluster While Building a Firm: Entrepreneurs and the Formation of Industrial Clusters." *Regional Studies* 39, pp. 129–41; and Brown, R. 2011. "The Determinants of High Growth Entrepreneurship in the Scottish Food and Drink Cluster." In *The Handbook of Research on Entrepreneurship in Agriculture and Rural Development*, eds. G. Alsos, S. Carter, E. Ljunggren, and F. Welter. Cheltenham: Edward Elgar.

of support including building connections and networks among entre-preneurs, prioritizing development of "blockbuster entrepreneurs" with significant economic potential and institutional alignment of priorities. A number of researchers have referred to the overall framework for pro-viding this type of support as an "entrepreneurial ecosystem,"[149] which Mason and Brown defined, based on their own synthesis of definitions throughout the relevant literature, as

> a set of interconnected entrepreneurial actors (both potential and existing), entrepreneurial organisations (e.g., firms, venture cap-italists, business angels, banks), institutions (universities, public sector agencies, financial bodies) and entrepreneurial processes (e.g., the business birth rate, numbers of high growth firms, levels of "blockbuster entrepreneurship," number of serial entrepreneurs, degree of sell-out mentality within firms and levels of entrepre-neurial ambition) which formally and informally coalesce to connect, mediate and govern the performance within the local entrepreneurial environment.[150]

While Mason and Brown added that entrepreneurial ecosystems were geographically bounded, they noted that cities did not have to be a partic-ular size to qualify and pointed to Austin, Texas, and Boulder, Colorado in the United States and Cambridge in England as examples of smaller cities that had been successful at developing what they referred to as "thriving entrepreneurial ecosystems." Mason and Brown also explained

---

[149] Zacharakis, A., D. Shepard, and J. Coombs. 2003. "The Development of Venture-Capital-backed Internet Companies: An Ecosystem Perspective." *Journal of Business Venturing* 18, p. 217; Napier, G., and C. Hansen. 2011. *Ecosystems for Young Scaleable Firms* (FORA Group,); and Feld, B. 2012. *Startup Communities: Building an Entrepreneurial Ecosystem in Your City*. Hoboken, NJ: Wiley.

[150] Mason, C., and R. Brown. November 7, 2013. "Entrepreneurial Ecosystems and Growth Oriented Entrepreneurship." International Workshop on Entre-preneurial Ecosystems and Growth Oriented Entrepreneurship Organized by OECD LEED Programme and Dutch Ministry of Economic Affairs Workshop; Background Paper, 5 (Final Version: January 2014).

that a system could emerge around one industry or evolve and expand to cover several industries.[151]

For researchers like Isenberg, an entrepreneurial ecosystem is a "strategy for economic development" that depends on several key factors or domains: a conducive culture, enabling policies and leadership, availability of appropriate finance, quality human capital, venture friendly markets for products, and a range of institutional supports.[152] For their part, Mason and Brown argued that the distinguishing features of entrepreneurial ecosystems include

> a core of large established businesses, including some that have been entrepreneur-led (entrepreneurial blockbusters); entrepreneurial recycling—whereby successful cashed out entrepreneurs reinvest their time, money, and expertise in supporting new entrepreneurial activity; and an information-rich environment in which this information is both accessible and shared.[153]

Mason and Brown also believed that in order for entrepreneurial ecosystems to thrive there must be a group of "dealmakers" who are involved in a fiduciary capacity in several entrepreneurial ventures, ready availability of startup and growth capital, and a supportive community of large firms, universities, and service providers.[154] Others have suggested that an effective entrepreneurial ecosystem needs accessible domestic markets, including access to small and large companies and governments as customers; human capital, including managerial and technical talent and

---

[151] Id. at pp. 5–6.

[152] Isenberg, D. 2011. *The Entrepreneurship Ecosystem Strategy as a New Paradigm for Economy Policy: Principles for Cultivating Entrepreneurship*, 4. Babson Park, MA: Babson Entrepreneurship Ecosystem Project, Babson College.

[153] Mason, C., and R. Brown. November 7, 2013. "Entrepreneurial Ecosystems and Growth Oriented Entrepreneurship." International Workshop on Entrepreneurial Ecosystems and Growth Oriented Entrepreneurship Organized by OECD LEED Programme and Dutch Ministry of Economic Affairs Workshop; Background Paper, 1 (Final Version: January 2014).

[154] Id.

experience in launching and building knowledge-intensive firms; funding and finance; support systems, including mentors/advisors, professional services, incubators/accelerators and a network of entrepreneurial peers; regulatory framework and infrastructure; education and training; major universities as catalysts; and cultural support.[155]

On a practical level, entrepreneurial ecosystems should be able to provide entrepreneurs with the resources and tools they need to launch their emerging companies, including networks that can be used to tap into the human resources necessary to build a founding team and recruit knowledge workers who can create and develop new products and services; professional investors (e.g., venture capitalists) and/or corporate partners with the capital necessary to support the product development activities of the founders and the expansion of the company to the point required for effective promotion and distribution of the product or service; professional and business advisors, including attorneys, accountants, bankers, insurance brokers, and consultants; regulatory framework that facilitates creation of business entities and establishment of governance systems and allows entrepreneurs to create and protect an intellectual property rights portfolio; and strategic partners that can collaborate with the new firm as suppliers, customers, manufacturers, distributors, and research and development partners.[156]

As for the specific steps that should be taken to launch and stimulate entrepreneurial ecosystems, Mason and Brown argued that policymakers would need to focus on several dimensions including direct support of entrepreneurial actors through accelerators and incubators; development of entrepreneurial organizations and resource providers such as business angels, venture capital, banks, service providers, universities; creation of

---

[155] World Economic Forum. September 2013, *Entrepreneurial Ecosystems around the Globe and Company Growth Dynamics: Report Summary for the Annual Meeting of the New Champions 2013.*

[156] For a further discussion of the specific issues and challenges associated with launching an emerging company, as well as a description of the characteristics of such a firm, see the Part on "Launching a New Business" in "Entrepreneurship: A Library of Resources for Sustainable Entrepreneurs." prepared and distributed by the Sustainable Entrepreneurship Project (www.seproject.org).

connectors within the ecosystem through public–private partnerships and alliances and peer-to-peer learning; and development and nurturing of an entrepreneurial environment or culture within the ecosystem through entrepreneurship education, role models, peer-to-peer networking, and entrepreneurial recycling.[157] Mason and Brown noted while there was a role for governments to play in developing entrepreneurial ecosystems, they should limit their involvement to facilitation and leave the details to the private sector, experienced local entrepreneurs, and/or leading local companies. Key to success would be the ability to create a local culture that was favorable to startup activity and which promoted and accepted entrepreneurial risk-taking. Experienced entrepreneurs could do their part by training, coaching, and mentoring their prospective peers and local companies could contribute by allowing and encouraging spinoff of promising ideas into new firms. In many cases it will be necessary to provide training to both local entrepreneurs and investors on the financing process until such time as the ecosystem has a community of experienced angel and venture capital investors.

Institutional Environment and Entrepreneurship in Developing Countries

There has been growing interest among researchers focusing on economic and social development in developing countries to understand the relationship between the institutional framework that exists in a country and the level and type of entrepreneurship practiced in that country. For example, when discussing the important and fundamental role that institutions play with respect to economic development, Acemoglu began by referring to the evidence from economic analysis that has confirmed that differences between countries with respect to prosperity and per capita income are strongly related to differences in the traditional

---

[157] Mason, C., and R. Brown. November 7, 2013. "Entrepreneurial Ecosystems and Growth Oriented Entrepreneurship." International Workshop on Entrepreneurial Ecosystems and Growth Oriented Entrepreneurship Organized by OECD LEED Programme and Dutch Ministry of Economic Affairs Workshop; Summary Report.

factors of production: human capital, physical capital, and technology.[158] He went on to argue that these findings raised a fundamental question for researchers: why is it that some countries have less human capital, physical capital, and technology than other countries and/or make worse use of these factors than other countries (i.e., failure to identify and/ or exploit entrepreneurial opportunities effectively)? Certainly some of the differences can be attributed to geographical differences or cultural factors; however, Acemoglu observed that "[i]nstitutions have emerged as a potential fundamental cause."[159] In the same vein, Chu argued that countries that have achieved relative affluence in relation to others have done so in large part because they were able to establish and maintain "efficient" institutions while countries that have remained undeveloped have suffered from the lack of efficient institutions.[160] Milo described and analyzed several different institutional indicators and concluded that there was a positive relationship between economic performance and institutional quality among member countries of the ASEAN and noted, in particular, that the strong relative economic performance of countries such as Malaysia, Singapore, and Thailand was consistent with their high scores on measures of institutional quality.[161]

Other scholars, while often using different definitions of "institutions," have reached similar conclusions: "institutions explain economically and statistically significant differences in per capita incomes across

---

[158] Acemoglu, D. "Challenges for Social Sciences: Institutions and Economic Development." http://aeaweb.org/econwhitepapers/white_papers/Daron_Acemoglu.pdf

[159] Id.

[160] Chu, K. 2003. "Collective Values, Behavioural Norms and Rules: Building Institutions for Economic Growth and Poverty Reduction." In *Perspectives on Growth and Poverty*, eds. R. van der Hoeven and A. Shorrocks. Tokyo: United Nations University Press.

[161] Milo, M. 2007. *Integrated Financial Supervision: An Institutional Perspective for the Philippines*, 23–29. Tokyo: Asian Development Bank Institute, ADBI Discussion Paper 81.

countries."[162] Olson tackled the question of why there continued to be widely differing standards of living around the world if, in fact, markets everywhere were working efficiently.[163] He first investigated whether the variations among countries might be attributable to different resource endowments (i.e., poorer countries have problems with economic growth and social development because "they lack land and natural resources, physical and human capital, or access to the latest technology"[164]). He systematically dismissed this proposition noting, for example, that there was evidence showing that knowledge was and is equally available to all countries at a reasonable cost, population density does not explain economic performance, capital flows are driven by the quality of institutions, and there was no basis for assuming that citizens of richer countries were innately "smarter" than citizens of poorer countries. Olson thus concluded that

> the large differences in per capita income across countries cannot be explained by differences in access to the world's stock of productive knowledge or to its capital markets, by differences in the quality of marketable human capital or personal culture.[165]

---

[162] Id. at p. 20 (citing Eicher, T., and A. Leukert. August 24–28, 2006. "Institutions and Economic Performance: Endogeneity and Parameter Heterogeneity." Paper Presented at the European Economic Association and Econometric Society Parallel Meetings, 2. Vienna).

[163] Olson, M. 2008. "Big Bills Left on the Sidewalk: Why Some Nations Are Rich, and Others Poor." In *Making Poor Nations Rich: Entrepreneurship and the Process of Economic Development*, ed. B. Powell, 25–53. Stanford, CA: Stanford Economics and Finance.

[164] Powell, B. 2008. "Introduction." In *Making Poor Nations Rich: Entrepreneurship and the Process of Economic Development*, 1–22, 3. ed. B. Powell, Stanford, CA: Stanford Economics and Finance.

[165] Olson, M. 2008. "Big Bills Left on the Sidewalk: Why Some Nations Are Rich, and Others Poor." In *Making Poor Nations Rich: Entrepreneurship and the Process of Economic Development*, 25–53, 44. ed. B. Powell. Stanford, CA: Stanford Economics and Finance.

Assuming this to be true, "[t]he only plausible explanation left is that differing performances are caused by differences in the quality of countries' institutions and policies."[166] Olson predicted that poorer countries that elect to adopt better economic policies and institutions would enjoy higher rates of growth in per capita incomes in relation to richer countries because they were so far short of their potential prior to the adoption of the new policies and there was such a huge gap to close between actual and potential income in those countries.[167]

Holcombe took a different approach by arguing that differences in the economic performance of countries could be explained by the "entrepreneurial opportunities" that are available in those countries and that decentralized free economies are the ones that do the best job of generating more opportunities that can be seized for their profitability and which also continuously generate new opportunities that ultimately will create an "endogenous engine of economic growth."[168] He placed so much importance on the availability of entrepreneurial opportunities that he argued that often-used techniques for launching economic development such as encouraging investment in industrial activities and research and development, calling for increased savings, and funding education would not, in and of themselves, be successful unless and until fundamental market reforms, including the creation and support of appropriate institutions, were made to facilitate creation of entrepreneurial opportunities. As an example, Holcombe pointed out that when developing countries have educated their citizens they often migrate to other countries due

---

[166] Id. Olson's article also includes citations to other studies that he and other conducted that provide "direct evidence of the linkage between better economic policies and institutions and better economic performance." Id. at p. 47.

[167] Id. at pp. 45–46. Olson noted during the 1970s the fastest growing countries in the world (apart from the oil-exporting countries) were poorer countries that grew at rates that far exceeded the growth achieved by the U.S. economy during that period. Id. A similar spree of spectacular growth rates, relative to industrialized countries, has been achieved in countries such as China and India in recent years.

[168] Holcombe, R. 2008. "Entrepreneurship and Economic Growth." In *Making Poor Nations Rich: Entrepreneurship and the Process of Economic Development*, 54–78. Stanford, CA: Stanford Economics and Finance.

to lack of entrepreneurial opportunities in their homelands and pointed out that this sort of "brain drain" will continue until governments in those countries create and support institutions that are conductive to entrepreneurship.[169]

It should be noted that there are some who have questioned the relationship between institutional development and entrepreneurship in developing countries. Lingelbach et al., whose studies of "what makes entrepreneurs in developing countries different" are described elsewhere in this chapter, argued that the data collected from studies of new- and growth-oriented firms in developing countries suggested

> several important, but counterintuitive findings: freer, more competitive, poor countries are not correlated in a statistically significant way with higher levels of opportunity entrepreneurs; recent economic growth in a poor country is not correlated in a statistically significant way with higher levels of opportunity entrepreneurship; and protection of property rights and levels of corruption don't seem to matter either.[170]

In spite of these assessments of the data, the general consensus appears to be that institutions do matter; however, as they await institutional improvements small but growing numbers of entrepreneurs in developing countries are developing and implementing strategies to create successful businesses in spite of higher risks and uncertainties, difficulties in accessing financial and human capital, and the absence of mentors and role models.

Setting the appropriate policies for promoting entrepreneurship in developing countries is not an easy task and policymakers have often failed mightily in their efforts and seen huge amounts of resources effectively wasted. Accepting the importance of institutions, notice

---

[169] Id. at p. 71.

[170] Lingelbach, D., L. De La Vina, and P. Asel. March 2005. *What's Distinctive about Growth-Oriented Entrepreneurship in Developing Countries?* 3. San Antonio, TX: UTSA College of Business Center for Global Entrepreneurship Working Paper No. 1.

should be taken of the advice of Milo, who suggested that to achieve the institutional efficiency necessary for achieving development countries must have institutions "that promote exchange by lowering transaction costs and promoting trust . . . and [institutions] that induce the state to protect rather than expropriate private property."[171] Institutions that are likely to have the desired effect of improving the efficiency and integrity of economic transactions include "contracts and contract enforcement mechanisms, commercial norms and rules, and habits and beliefs favoring shared values and the accumulation of human capital" and institutions that can be expected to contribute to the creation and protection of private property rights include "[c]onstitutions, electoral rules, laws governing speech and education, and legal and civic norms."[172]

---

[171] Milo, M. 2007. *Integrated Financial Supervision: An Institutional Perspective for the Philippines*, 19. Tokyo: Asian Development Bank Institute, ADBI Discussion Paper 81.

[172] Id. at p. 20 (citing Shirley, M. 2005. "Institutions and Development." In *Handbook of New Institutional Economics*, eds. C. Menard and M. Shirley. Dordrecht, Netherlands: Kluwer Academic Publishers).

About the Author

Dr Alan S. Gutterman is the Founding Director of the Sustainable Entrepreneurship Project (www.seproject.org). In addition, Alan's prolific output of practical guidance and tools for legal and financial professionals, managers, entrepreneurs, and investors has made him one of the best-selling individual authors in the global legal publishing marketplace. His cornerstone work, *Business Transactions Solution*, is an online-only product available and featured on Thomson Reuter's Westlaw, the world's largest legal content platform, which includes almost 200 book-length modules covering the entire lifecycle of a business. Alan has also authored or edited over 40 books on sustainable entrepreneurship, management, business law and transactions, international law business and technology management for a number of publishers including Thomson Reuters, Kluwer, Aspatore, Oxford, Quorum, ABA Press, Aspen, Sweet & Maxwell, Euromoney, CCH, and BNA. Alan has over three decades of experience as a partner and senior counsel with internationally recognized law firms counselling small and large business enterprises in the areas of general corporate and securities matters, venture capital, mergers and acquisitions, international law and transactions, strategic business alliances, technology transfers, and intellectual property, and has also held senior management positions with several technology-based businesses including service as the chief legal officer of a leading international distributor of IT products headquartered in Silicon Valley and as the chief operating officer of an emerging broadband media company. He has been an adjunct faculty member at several colleges and universities, including Boalt Hall, Golden Gate University, Hastings College of Law, Santa Clara University, and the University of San Francisco, teaching classes on a diverse range of topics including corporate finance, venture capital, corporate law, Japanese business law, and law and economic development, He received his AB, MBA, and JD from the University of California at Berkeley, a DBA from Golden

Gate University, and a PhD from the University of Cambridge. For more information about Alan, his publications, or the Sustainable Entrepreneurship Project, please contact him directly at alangutterman@gmail.com, and follow him on LinkedIn (https://linkedin.com/in/alangutterman/).

Index

OTHER TITLES IN THE ENTREPRENEURSHIP AND SMALL BUSINESS MANAGEMENT COLLECTION

Scott Shane, Case Western University, Editor

- *Open Innovation Essentials for Small and Medium Enterprises: A Guide to Help Entrepreneurs in Adopting the Open Innovation Paradigm in Their Business* by Luca Escoffier, Adriano La Vopa, Phyllis Speser, and Daniel Satinsky
- *The Technological Entrepreneur's Playbook* by Ian Chaston
- *Licensing Myths & Mastery: Why Most Ideas Don't Work and What to Do About It* by William S. Seidel
- *Arts and Entrepreneurship* by J. Mark Munoz and Julie Shields
- *The Human Being's Guide to Business Growth: A Simple Process for Unleashing the Power of Your People for Growth* by Gregory Scott Chambers
- *Understanding the Family Business: Exploring the Differences Between Family and Nonfamily Businesses, Second Edition* by Keanon J. Alderson

Announcing the Business Expert Press Digital Library

Concise e-books business students need for classroom and research

This book can also be purchased in an e-book collection by your library as

- a one-time purchase,
- that is owned forever,
- allows for simultaneous readers,
- has no restrictions on printing, and
- can be downloaded as PDFs from within the library community.

Our digital library collections are a great solution to beat the rising cost of textbooks. E-books can be loaded into their course management systems or onto students' e-book readers.
The **Business Expert Press** digital libraries are very affordable, with no obligation to buy in future years. For more information, please visit **www.businessexpertpress.com/librarians**. To set up a trial in the United States, please email **sales@businessexpertpress.com**.